战地钟声

For Whom the Bell Tolls

名著镜头

第二辑

——英汉双语经典阅读

Lens Masterpiece Classical English-Chinese bilingual reading

天津科学技术出版社

图书在版编目(CIP)数据

名著镜头：英汉双语经典阅读. 第2辑 / 李四清主编.
天津：天津科学技术出版社，2009.2
ISBN 978-7-5308-4210-2

Ⅰ. 名… Ⅱ. 李… Ⅲ. ①英语—汉语—对照读物②长篇小说—作品集—世界—缩写本 Ⅳ. H319.4：I

中国版本图书馆 CIP 数据核字(2008)第155869号

责任编辑：侯 萍 傅雪莹
责任印制：王 莹

天津科学技术出版社出版
出版人：胡振泰
天津市西康路35号 邮编300051
电话：(022)23332394(编辑室) (022)23332393(发行部)
网址：www.tjkjcbs.com.cn
新华书店经销
北京世纪雨田印刷有限公司印刷

开本 787×1092 1/24 印张38 字数1 000 000
2009年5月第1版第1次印刷
定价：(共四册)88.00元

编译者名单

主　编　　李四清

副主编　　赵冬梅　李正鸿

编译者　　晏尚元（悲惨世界）

　　　　　傅　铮（战地钟声）

　　　　　李　彦（西线无战事）

　　　　　李媛霞（王子复仇记）

　　　　　齐晓亮　庞双子（乱世佳人）

简 介

海明威(Ernest Hemingway, 1899-1961)是美国现代著名小说家，世界公认的20世纪优秀作家之一。《战地钟声》(For Whom the Bell Tolls，1940)是以西班牙内战为背景正面描写战争的一部重要长篇小说。主人公罗伯特·乔丹是美国人，为帮助西班牙共和政府作战，被派往法西斯分子占领的后方，在当地游击队的配合下执行炸桥任务，负伤后牺牲。这部作品反映了作者热爱西班牙人民、反对法西斯的立场。由于在文学创作上所取得的巨大成就以及其作品所产生的世界性影响，1954年海明威获得诺贝尔文学奖。

《战地钟声》于1943年被改编为同名电影，并于转年获得了第16届奥斯卡最佳女配角奖和最佳电影、最佳男主角、最佳女主角、最佳男配角、最佳摄影、最佳艺术指导、最佳剪辑以及最佳音乐的八项提名。

小说人物关系谱

Robert Jordan 罗伯特·乔丹——美国爆破专家

María 玛丽亚——罗伯特·乔丹的爱人

Pablo 巴勃罗——游击队队长

Pilar 比拉尔——巴勃罗的妻子

Anselmo 安塞尔莫——年长的巴勃罗游击队队员

Rafael 拉斐尔——吉普赛人，巴勃罗游击队队员

Agustín 奥古斯——巴勃罗游击队队员

Fernando 费尔南多——巴勃罗游击队队员

Andres 安德烈斯——巴勃罗游击队队员，埃拉迪奥的兄弟

Eladio 埃拉迪奥——巴勃罗游击队队员，安德烈斯的兄弟

Primitivo 普里米蒂伏——巴勃罗游击队队员

El Sordo 艾苏道——另一支游击队队长

Joaquin 华金——艾苏道游击队队员

Golz 戈尔兹将军——共和军总司令

Kashkin 卡希金——俄罗斯爆破手

Captain Mora 莫拉上尉——法西斯政府军队指挥官

Lieutenant Berrendo 贝仑多中尉——法西斯政府军队军官

On April 14th, 1931, Spanish monarchy was overthrown and the Republic was established. In the congressional election on February 16th, 1936, the people front composed of the Communist Party, the Socialist Party, and the Left Wing of the Republican Party, as an overwhelming majority, established the united government. With the open military support of Germany and Italy, General Franco rebelled on July 18th and Spanish Fascists soon occupied the northwest and the southwest in Spain. The international progressive force positively supported the Spanish Republic under the leadership of the Communist Parties of many countries. The International Brigades consisting of volunteers from many countries was established in France and its members participated in the Spanish Civil War in October.

The story occurred in May, 1937 in the mountain area of Madrid northwest. Fascist rebels occupied the mouth of the mountain, but several guerilla units were still taking activities. It told the story of Robert Jordan, a young American in the International Brigades attached to an antifascist guerilla unit in the mountains during the Spanish Civil War. As an expert in the use of explosives, he was given an assignment to blow up a bridge to accompany a simultaneous attack on the important city of Segovia.

西班牙于1931年4月14日推翻君主制，成立共和国。1936年2月16日的国会选举中，以共产党、社会党、共和党“左派”等为中坚力量的人民阵线，成立联合政府。在德国和意大利的公开武装支持下，弗朗哥将军于7月18日发动叛乱，西班牙法西斯组织很快占领了西班牙西北部及西南部。国际进步力量在各国共产党的领导下积极支援西班牙共和政府，在法国成立由许多国家的志愿者组成的国际纵队，于10月在西班牙参战。

本故事发生在1937年5月，地点是马德里西北部的山区。法西斯叛军占领山口，但在深山中有几个游击小组在开展敌后活动。一个年轻的国际纵队队员，美国人罗伯特·乔丹与西班牙内战期间在山区活动的反法西斯游击队取得了联系，作为爆破专家，他的任务是炸桥以配合收复重镇塞哥维亚的进攻。

战地钟声 *For Whom the Bell Tolls*

罗伯特·乔丹和一名俄罗斯志愿者卡希金执行炸火车的任务。火车稳稳地开来，他们远远地看到了火车，望到了火车喷出的蒸汽，接着听到汽笛声。火车突——突——突，稳稳地开来了，越开越近。在爆炸的那一刹那，火车头的前轮腾空飞了起来，整块地面似乎全被炸飞了，一团黑烟，一声轰响，火车头在一片升腾的灰尘和枕木中间飞得老高，然后侧翻着倒在地上，像头受了伤的巨大野兽，炸飞的泥巴溅落在他们身上，这时，锅炉一声爆炸，迸发出一片白色蒸汽。

炸火车的任务完成了。他们在黑夜里撤退，遇到了法西斯巡逻队，在奔跑中，卡希金背脊的上部挨了一枪，其实没打中骨头，只伤了肩胛。他跑了很长一段路，但由于负了伤他再也跑不动了。他不愿意留下来当俘虏，请求罗伯特开枪打死他。罗伯特就听从了卡希金的话，把他打死了。

Robert Jordan and Kashkin, a Russian volunteer, carried out the task to blow up the train. The train was coming steadily. They saw it far away. They saw steam from it and then later came the noise of the whistle. Then it came chu-chu-chu steadily larger and larger and then, at the moment of the explosion, the front wheels of the engine rose up and all of the earth seemed to rise in a great cloud of blackness and a roar and the engine rose high in the cloud of dirt and of the Wooden ties rising in the air and then it fell onto its side like a great wounded animal and there was an explosion of white steam before the clods of the other explosion had ceased to fall on them.

The train was successful. It was returning from a train. Returning in the dark they encountered a fascist patrol and as they ran Kashkin was shot high in the back but without hitting any bone except the shoulder blade. He traveled quite a long way, but with the wound was unable to travel more. He was unwilling to be left behind and begged Robert to shoot him. So Robert did.

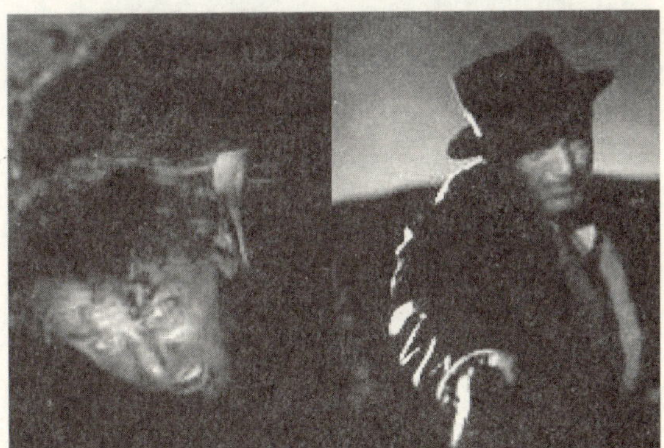

After the explosion of the train, Robert Jordan met General Golz of Government Army for his new mission.

"To blow the bridge is nothing," Golz had said, the candlelight on his scarred, shaved head, pointing with a pencil on the big map. "You understand?"

"Yes, I understand."

"Absolutely nothing. Merely to blow the bridge is a failure."

"Yes, Comrade General."

"To blow the bridge at a stated hour based on the time set for the attack is how it should be done. You see that naturally. That is your right and how it should be done."

"So when is the bridge to be blown?" Robert Jordan had asked.

"After the attack starts. As soon as the attack has started and not before. So that no reinforcements will come up over that road." He pointed with his pencil. "I must know that nothing will come up over that road."

"And when is the attack?"

"I will tell you. But you are to use the date and hour only as an indication of a probability. You must be ready for that time. You will blow the bridge after the attack has started. You see?" he indicated with the pencil.

完成了炸火车的任务后，罗伯特·乔丹见到了政府军戈尔兹将军，有新的任务分派给他。“炸桥本身没什么了不起，”戈尔兹说着，烛光照在他有伤疤的光头上，他用铅笔在一张大地图上指着，“你懂吗？”

“是，我懂。”

“完全不是那么一回事。仅仅炸掉桥只能算是一种失败。”

“是，将军同志。”

“应该做到的是根据发动进攻的时间，在指定的时刻炸桥。你当然明白这一点。这就是你的权利，这就是你的任务。”

“那么什么时候炸桥呢？”罗伯特·乔丹问。

“在进攻开始之后。进攻一开始就炸桥，不能提前。这样，敌人的增援部队就不能从那条路上来。”他用铅笔指着。“我必须肯定那条路上来不了援兵。”

“什么时候进攻？”

“我会告诉你的。但是你只能把日期和时间当做一种可能性的参考。你必须在进攻前准备就绪。进攻开始后你就炸桥。明白吗？”他用铅笔指着说。

"That is the only road on which they can bring up reinforcements. That is the only road on which they can get up tanks, or artillery, or even move a truck toward the pass which I attack. I must know that bridge is gone. Not before, so it can be repaired if the attack is postponed. No. It must go when the attack starts and I must know it is gone. There are only two sentries. The man who will go with you has just come from there. He is a very reliable man, they say. You will see. He has people in the mountains. Get as many men as you need. Use as few as possible, but use enough. I do not have to tell you these things."

"And how do I determine that the attack has started?"

"It is to be made with a full division. There will be an aerial bombardment as preparation. You are not deaf, are you? It can be successful with that bridge eliminated. We can take Segovia. I show you how it goes. You see? It is not the top of the pass where we attack. We hold that. It is much beyond."

"他们增援兵力只能从那条路经过。他们只能从那条路把坦克、大炮以及卡车开到我发动进攻的山口。我必须确定桥被炸掉。不能提前，不然的话如果进攻推迟，他们就会把桥修好。不行。进攻开始的时候，就必须炸掉那座桥，我必须有充分把握。那里只有两个岗哨。跟你一起去的那人刚从那里来。据说他非常可靠。你就会明白的。他在山里有人。你需要多少人，就要多少。尽可能少用人，但要够用。我不必对你多说这些事情了。"

"我怎样才能断定进攻已经开始了呢？"

"整整一师兵力将会发动进攻。先有飞机轰炸作为准备。你耳朵不聋吧，是不是？把桥毁掉了，这一战是可能打胜的。我们会拿下塞哥维亚。我来指给你看这是怎么回事。明白吗？我们的目标可不是进攻山口的顶端。我们要坚守它。我们的目标在远远的那边。"

战地钟声 *For Whom the Bell Tolls*

Anselmo, the old man who General mentioned, took Robert Jordan into the mountains. Now he was lying flat on the brown, pine-needled floor of the forest, his chin on his folded arms, and high overhead the wind blew in the tops of the pine trees. The mountainside sloped gently where he lay; but below it was steep and he could see the dark of the oiled road winding through the pass.

The late afternoon sun that still came over the brown shoulder of the mountain showed the bridge dark against the steep emptiness of the gorge. It was a steel bridge of a single span and there was a sentry box at each end. It was wide enough for two motorcars to pass and it spanned, in solid-flung metal grace, a deep gorge at the bottom of which, far below, a brook leaped in white water through rocks and boulders down to the main stream of the pass.

The sun was in Robert Jordan's eyes and the bridge showed only in outline. Then the sun lessened and was gone and looking up through the trees at the brown, rounded height that it had gone behind, he saw, now, that he no longer looked into the glare, that the mountain slope was a delicate new green and that there were patches of old snow under the crest.

将军提到的那个老人安塞尔莫把罗伯特·乔丹带到了山里。现在他正匍匐在树林里落满一层褐色松针的地上，手臂交叉支撑着下颚；在高空中，风从松树顶上呼啸而过。他所处的山坡是个缓坡，再往下却很陡峭，他看到了黑黢黢的柏油路蜿蜒穿过山口。

夕阳依然越过褐色的山肩照射过来，那座桥在峻峭的峡谷中间的辽阔空间的映衬下，显得黑黝黝的。那是一座单孔铁桥，两端各有一个岗亭。桥面很宽，两辆汽车可以并行通过。坚固的铁桥线条优美，横跨幽谷，桥下深深的谷底，白浪翻腾，溪水顺着岩石和大块圆石流过，奔向山口的主流。

阳光正照着罗伯特·乔丹的眼睛，那座桥只现出一个剪影。随着太阳落到圆滚滚的褐色山头后面，阳光逐渐减弱消失，他透过树林眺望这个山头，不再直视着刺眼的阳光，发现山坡竟然是一片葱翠的新绿，山峰下还有一摊摊积雪。

Robert Jordan saw there was a stream alongside the road and far down the pass and a mill beside the stream and the falling water of the dam, white in the summer sunlight. He studied the country, took his glasses from the pocket of his faded, khaki flannel shirt, wiped the lenses with a handkerchief, screwed the eyepieces around until the boards of the mill showed suddenly clearly and he saw the wooden bench beside the door; the huge pile of sawdust that rose behind the open shed where the circular saw was, and a stretch of the flume that brought the logs down from the mountainside on the other bank of the stream. The stream showed clear and smooth-looking in the glasses and, below the curl of the falling water, the spray from the dam was blowing in the wind.

"Where is the next post?" Robert Jordan asked.

"Below the bridge. It is at the road-mender's hut at kilometer five from the top of the pass." Anselmo answered quickly.

"How many men are here?" He pointed at the mill.

"Perhaps four and a corporal."

"And below?"

"More. I will find out."

"And at the bridge?"

"Always two. One at each end."

罗伯特·乔丹看到沿柏油路有条小河，有家锯木厂在山口远处的小河边，拦水坝的泄水在夏天的阳光下泛着白光。他一边研究着地形，一边从褪色的黄褐色法兰绒衬衫口袋里掏出望远镜，用手帕擦拭镜片，转动目镜，直到锯木厂的板壁突然显得清晰。他看到门边的一条长板凳，安放圆锯的敞棚后面堆起的一大堆木屑；他还看到从小河对岸山坡上运木材的滑槽的一段。小河在望远镜里显得清澈而平静，打着漩涡从拦河坝倾泻而下，坝底的水花在风中飞溅。

"另一个哨所在哪里？"罗伯特·乔丹问。

"在桥下方。在养路工的小屋边，离山口5千米。"安塞尔莫迅速地答道。

"这里有多少士兵？"他指指锯木厂。

"也许有四个，外加一个班长。"

"下面呢？"

"更多些。我能探听明白。"

"那么桥头呢？"

"总是两个。一边一个。"

Robert Jordan continued his observation. In the sentry box that faced toward them up the road, the sentry was sitting holding his rifle, the bayonet fixed, between his knees. He was smoking a cigarette and he wore a knitted cap and blanket style cape. At fifty yards, one could not see anything about his face. Even though there was now no sun to make a glint, Robert Jordan put up his field glasses, shading the lenses carefully with his cupped hands, and there was the rail of the bridge as clear as though you could reach out and touch it and there was the face of the sentry so clear he could see the sunken cheeks, the ash on the cigarette and the greasy shine of the bayonet. It was a peasant's face, the cheeks hollow under the high cheekbones, the beard stubbled, the eyes shaded by the heavy brows, big hands holding the rifle, heavy boots showing beneath the folds of the blanket cape. The sentry rubbed his cigarette out on the plank wall of the box, then took a leather tobacco pouch from his pocket, opened the paper of the dead cigarette and emptied the remnant of used tobacco into the pouch. The sentry stood up, leaned his rifle against the wall of the box and stretched, then picked up his rifle, slung it over his shoulder and walked out onto the bridge.

战地钟声 *For Whom the Bell Tolls*

罗伯特·乔丹继续观察。公路这头面对着他们的岗亭里，坐着一个哨兵，他的膝间夹着一支上了刺刀的步枪。他在抽烟，头上戴着顶绒线帽，身上穿着件毯子式的披风。相距50码，没法看清他脸上的五官。即使没有太阳的反光，罗伯特·乔丹举起望远镜，两手捏成空拳，小心地拿着镜片。桥上的栏杆也显得非常清晰，仿佛触手可及，而那哨兵的脸也清晰可见，甚至他凹陷的腮帮、香烟上的烟灰和刺刀上闪亮着的油迹都历历在目。那是一张农民的脸，高颧骨下腮帮深陷，满脸胡子茬，浓眉毛遮住了眼睛，一双大手握着步枪，毯子式的披风下面露出了笨重的长筒靴。哨兵在岗亭的板壁上熄灭了烟卷，然后从口袋里掏出一只皮制的烟荷包，剥开熄灭了的烟蒂的烟纸，把剩下的烟丝倒进荷包。哨兵站起来，把步枪靠在岗亭的墙上，伸了个懒腰，然后提起步枪，挎在肩上，走上了桥。

"Must we kill him?" Anselmo asked. "Will we be punished by God?"

"Clearly I miss Him, having been brought up in religion. But now a man must be responsible to himself. Then it is yourself who will forgive you for killing." Robert Jordan answered.

"I believe so," Anselmo said. "Since you put it clearly in that way I believe that must be it. But with or without God, I think it is a sin to kill. To take the life of another is to me very grave. I will do it whenever necessary but I am not of the race of Pablo."

"To win a war we must kill our enemies. That has always been true."

"Clearly. In war we must kill. But I have very rare ideas," Anselmo said. "I would not kill even a Bishop. I would not kill a proprietor of any kind. I would make them work each day as we have worked in the fields and as we work in the mountains with the timber all of the rest of their lives. So they would see what man is born to. That they should sleep where we sleep. That they should eat as we eat. But above all that they should work. Thus they would learn." He watched Robert fixing his eyes on the bridge.

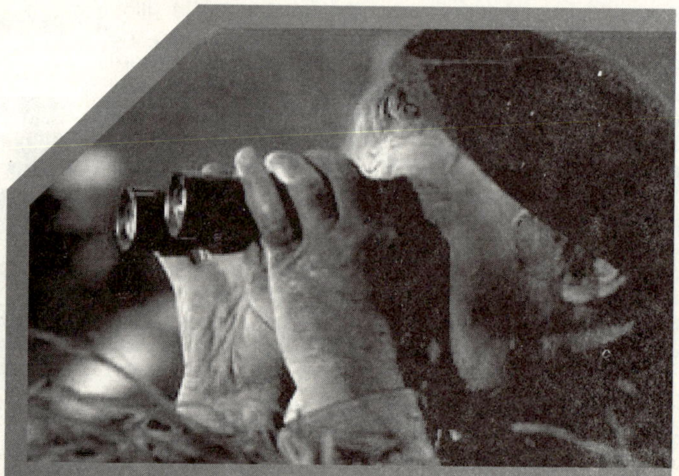

战地钟声 *For Whom the Bell Tolls*

“一定要杀掉他吗？”安塞尔莫问。“我们会不会受到上帝惩罚？”

“我是在宗教环境中长大的，当然怀念上帝。不过现在得由自己负责了。那么你杀了人，就自我宽恕。”罗伯特·乔丹答道。

“我就相信，”安塞尔莫说。“既然你实话实说，我看一定有理。不过，不管有没有上帝，我还是认为杀人就是罪过。我觉得取人性命可不是儿戏。我不得已才杀人，不过我可不是巴勃罗那号人。”

“要打胜仗，我们就必须杀死敌人。这是历来的真理。”

“那当然。打仗就得杀人。不过我有些古怪想法，”安塞尔莫说。“我连一位主教也不想杀。我也不想杀哪个地主。我要叫他们后半生像我们一样，天天在地里干活，在山里砍树。这样他们才会明白，人生在世该干什么。让他们睡我们睡的地方。让他们吃我们吃的东西。不过，最要紧的是让他们劳动。这样他们就会得到教训了。”他看到罗伯特目不转睛地盯着这座桥。

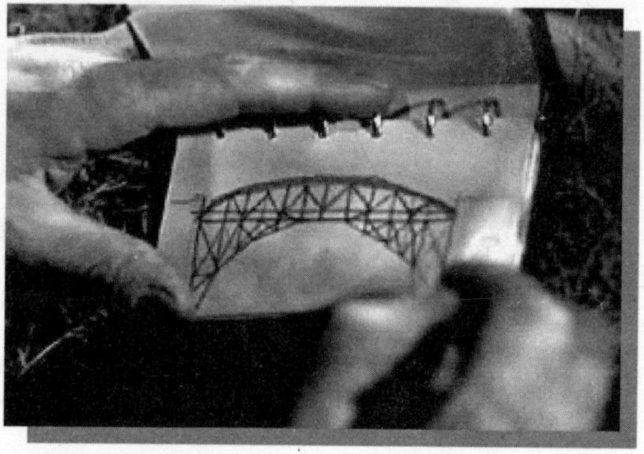

Then Robert Jordan was watching the bridge in the sudden short trueness of the little light that would be left, and studying its construction. The problem of its demolition was not difficult. As he watched he took out a notebook from his breast pocket and made several quick line sketches. As he made the drawings he did not figure the charges. He would do that later. Now he was noting the points where the explosive should be placed in order to cut the support of the span and drop a section of it into the gorge. It could be done unhurriedly, scientifically and correctly with a half dozen charges laid and braced to explode simultaneously; or it could be done roughly with two big ones. They would need to be very big ones, on opposite sides and should go at the same time. He sketched quickly and happily; glad at last to have the problem under his hand; glad at last actually to be engaged upon it. Then he shut his notebook, pushed the pencil into its leather holder in the edge of the flap, put the notebook in his pocket and buttoned the pocket. They began to climb the mountain for the deep mountain area.

接着罗伯特·乔丹在短暂的余晖中注视着突然显得真切的桥梁，观察着它的结构。要炸掉这座桥不算难。他一边望着，一边从胸口衣袋里掏出个笔记本，迅速勾勒了几张草图。他在本子上画图时没有同时计算出炸药的用量。他准备以后再计算。他现在注意的是安放炸药的位置，以便炸断桥面的支撑，让桥的一部分掉到峡谷中去。安放六个炸药包，同时引爆，就能从容不迫、井井有条而精确无误地成功把桥炸掉；或者，用两个大炸药包也能勉强完成，但那就需要非常大的炸药包，放在两侧同时引爆。他快速而兴奋地勾勒着草图；他高兴的是终于开始做这件事了，终于真的动手干起来了。接着他合上笔记本，把铅笔插进本子封皮里边的皮套，把笔记本放进衣袋，扣好衣袋的扣子。他们开始爬山，往山区深处进发。

Robert Jordan, who was tall and thin, with sun-streaked fair hair, and a wind-and sun-burned face, who wore the sun-faded flannel shirt, a pair of peasant's trousers and rope-soled shoes, leaned over, put his arm through one of the leather pack straps and swung the heavy pack filled with dynamite up onto his shoulders.

Bending under the weight of the packs, sweating, he and Anselmo climbed steadily in the pine forest that covered the mountainside. There was no trail that Robert Jordan could see, but they were working up and around the face of the mountain and now they crossed a small stream and Anselmo went steadily on ahead up the edge of the rocky stream bed. The climbing now was steeper and more difficult, until finally the stream seemed to drop down over the edge of a smooth granite ledge that rose above them and the old man waited at the foot of the ledge for the young man to come up to him.

"Wait here now for me. I go ahead to warn them. You do not want to be shot at carrying that stuff."

"Not even in a joke," Robert Jordan said. "Is it far?"

"It is very close."

罗伯特·乔丹是个瘦高个儿，长着闪亮的金发和一张饱经风吹日晒的脸，穿着一件晒得褪了色的法兰绒衬衫，一条农民穿的裤子和一双绳底鞋。他弯下腰去，一条胳臂伸进背包皮带圈里，把装满炸药的沉重背包甩上肩头。

他和安塞尔莫被背包压得弯下了腰，身上淌着汗，在山坡上的松林里一步步向上爬。罗伯特·乔丹发现林中并没有路径，但是他们继续向上攀爬，绕到前山，跨过了一条小溪，安塞尔莫踩着山石河床的边缘稳健地走在前面。山路更陡峭了，爬山更艰难了，到后来，溪水似乎是从他们头顶上一个平滑的花岗石悬崖边上直泻下来，老人在悬崖下停了下来，等着年轻人赶上来。

"在这里等着我。我先去通知他们。你带了这东西总不希望人家朝你开枪吧。"

"哪怕开开玩笑也不希望，"罗伯特·乔丹问，"还远吗？"

"不远了。"

Robert Jordan sat by the packs and watched the old man climb the ledge. It was not hard to climb and from the way he found hand-holds without searching for them the young man could see that he had climbed it many times before. Yet whoever was above had been very careful not to leave any trail.

This Anselmo had been a good guide and he could travel wonderfully in the mountains. Robert Jordan trusted the man, Anselmo, so far, in everything except judgment. He did not worry about Anselmo and the problem of the bridge was no more difficult than many other problems. He knew how to blow any sort of bridge that you could name and he had blown them of all sizes and constructions. There was enough explosive and all equipment in the two packs to blow this bridge properly even if it were twice as big as Anselmo reported it, as he remembered it when he had walked over it on his way to La Granja on a walking trip in 1933, and as Golz had read him the description of it night before last in the house outside of the Escorial.

罗伯特·乔丹坐在背包旁边，注视着老人攀登悬崖。这悬崖不难攀登，他还发现，从老人不用摸索就找到攀手的地方的利落样子来看，这地方他已经爬过好多次了。然而，凡是爬到上面的人都一向小心翼翼地不留下任何痕迹。

这个安塞尔莫一直是个好向导，他走山路的本事真是了不起。到目前为止，除了判断力以外，罗伯特·乔丹事事都信得过这个安塞尔莫。他不愁安塞尔莫，而炸桥的事也不见得比许多其他的事更棘手。他会炸各式各样的桥，只要你说得出来的。他炸过各种大小和结构的桥。即使这座桥比安塞尔莫所说的大两倍，这两只背包里的炸药和引爆装置也足够把它全炸掉，因为他记得 1933 年徒步旅行到拉格兰哈去的时候曾走过这座桥，而且戈尔兹前晚在埃斯科里亚尔城外一幢房子里曾给他念过关于这座桥的资料。

战地钟声 *For Whom the Bell Tolls*

Pushing himself up on his hands, Robert Jordan turned his head and saw the old man coming down the ledge. With him was another man, also in a black peasant's smock and the dark gray trousers that were almost a uniform in that province, wearing rope-soled shoes and with a carbine slung over his back. The two of them came scrambling down the rock like goats. They came up to him and Robert Jordan got to his feet.

"Hello, comrade," he said to the man with the carbine and smiled.

"Hello," the other said, grudgingly. Robert Jordan looked at the man's heavy, beard-stubbled face. It was almost round and his head was round and set close on his shoulders. His eyes were small and set too wide apart and his ears were small and set close to his head. He was a heavy man about five feet ten inches tall and his hands and feet were large. His nose had been broken and his mouth was cut at one corner and the line of the scar across the upper lip and lower jaw showed through the growth of beard over his face.

The old man nodded his head at this man and smiled.

罗伯特·乔丹双手撑起身体，转过头来，看见老人正从悬崖上爬下来。和他一起的还有一个人，也穿着几乎成为这地区制服的农民穿的黑色罩衣和深灰色的裤子，脚上一双绳底鞋，还背着一支卡宾枪。两人像山羊般灵活地从悬崖上爬下来。他们走上前来，罗伯特·乔丹站起身。

"你好，同志，"他对背卡宾枪的人说，并且微微一笑。

"你好，"对方应付了一声。罗伯特·乔丹望着这个人满是胡子茬的大脸。这张脸盘差不多是滚圆的，脑袋也是圆滚滚的，脖子短粗。这人眼睛很小而且两眼间距较大，一对小耳朵紧贴在脑袋上。他身子粗壮，身高 5 英尺 10 英寸左右，长着大手大脚，鼻子磕破过，一边嘴角被刀砍过，满脸的胡子中露出了一道横过上唇和下颌的刀疤。

老人对这个人点点头，笑了笑。

"He is the boss here," Anselmo grinned, then flexed his arms as though to make the muscles stand out and looked at the man with the carbine in a half-mocking admiration. "A very strong man."

"I can see it," Robert Jordan said and smiled again. He did not like the look of this man and inside himself he was not smiling at all.

"What have you to justify your identity?" asked the man with the carbine.

Robert Jordan unpinned a safety pin that ran through his pocket flap and took a folded paper out of the left breast pocket of his flannel shirt and handed it to the man.

He opened it, looked at it doubtfully and turned it in his hands. So he cannot read, Robert Jordan noted.

"Look at the seal," he said.

The old man pointed to the seal and the man with the carbine studied it, turning it in his fingers.

"What seal is that?"

"Have you never seen it?"

"No."

"There are two," said Robert Jordan. "One is SIM, the service of the military intelligence. The other is the General Staff."

"Yes, I have seen that seal before. But here no one commands but me," the other said sullenly.

战地钟声 *For Whom the Bell Tolls*

“他是这里的头儿，”安塞尔莫露齿笑着说，然后屈起双臂，仿佛要显露肌肉似的。他以一种带有半嘲弄的钦佩神情望着这个背卡宾枪的人。“一条壮汉。”

“我看得出，”罗伯特·乔丹说，又笑了笑。他不喜欢这个人的神情，心里没有一丁点儿笑意。

“什么能证明你的身份？”背卡宾枪的人问。

罗伯特·乔丹解开了别住衣袋盖的安全别针，从法兰绒衬衣的左胸袋里掏出一张折好的纸，交给这个人。

这个人摊开证件，怀疑地看看，在手里翻弄着。罗伯特·乔丹看出原来他不识字。

“看这公章，”他说。

老人指指印鉴，背卡宾枪的人把证件在手指间翻来翻去地端详着。

“什么公章？”

“你以前没见过吗？”

“没见过。”

“有两个公章，”罗伯特·乔丹说。“一个是 SIM，即军事情报部。另一个是总参谋部的。”

“对，我以前见过那个公章。不过在这里要我说了才算数，”对方阴郁地说。

"What have you in the packs?"

"Dynamite," the old man said proudly. "Last night we crossed the lines in the dark and all day we have carried this dynamite over the mountain."

"I can use dynamite," said the man with the carbine. He handed back the paper to Robert Jordan and looked him over. "Yes. I have use for dynamite. How much have you brought me?"

"I have brought you no dynamite," Robert Jordan said to him evenly. "The dynamite is for another purpose. What is your name?"

"What is that to you?"

"He is Pablo," said the old man. The man with the carbine looked at them both sullenly.

"What are you going to do with the dynamite?"

"Blow up a bridge."

"What bridge?"

"That is my business."

"If it is in this territory, it is my business. You cannot blow bridges close to where you live. You must live in one place and operate in another. I know my business. One who is alive, now, after a year, knows his business."

"This is my business," Robert Jordan said. "We can discuss it together."

“你包里装的什么？”

“炸药，”老人神气地说。“昨晚我们摸黑越过了火线，今天一整天，背着炸药赶山路。”

“我用得着炸药，”背卡宾枪的人说。他把证件还给罗伯特·乔丹，上下打量着他，“好啊。炸药对我很有用。给我带来了多少？”

“我带来的炸药不是给你的，”罗伯特·乔丹平静地对他说。“炸药别有用途。你叫什么名字？”

“这跟你有什么相干？”

“他叫巴勃罗，”老人说。背卡宾枪的人阴郁地看着他们俩。

“你打算用炸药干什么？”

“炸毁一座桥。”

“什么桥？”

“那是我的事。”

“如果桥在这个地区，那就是我的事。你不能在紧挨你住的地方炸桥。你在一个地方住，就必须到另一个地方去活动。我清楚这儿的事。在这儿能待上一年没死掉的人都了解自己的事。”

“这是我的事，”罗伯特·乔丹说，“我们可以一起商量。”

They had come through the heavy timber to the cup-shaped upper end of the little valley and he saw where the camp must be under the rim-rock that rose ahead of them through the trees and where a man kept guard.

There was a large cave in the rim-rock formation and beside the opening, Rafael, a gypsy, sat with his back against the rock, his legs stretched out on the ground and his carbine leaning against the rock. He was cutting away on a stick with a knife and he stared at them as they came up, and then went on whittling.

"What do you make?" Robert Jordan sat down by the gypsy. The gypsy showed him. It was a figure four trap and he was whittling the crossbar for it.

"For foxes," he said.

"He catches rabbits," Anselmo said. "He is a gypsy. So if he catches rabbits he says it is foxes. If he catches a fox he would say it was an elephant."

"And if I catch an elephant?"

"You'd say it was a tank."

"I'll get a tank. And you can say it is what you please."

"Gypsies talk much and kill little," Anselmo told him.

The gypsy winked at Robert Jordan and went on whittling.

战地钟声 For Whom the Bell Tolls

他们穿过浓密的树林，来到这小山谷的形如茶杯的上端，他看到前面树林里突起的岩石和站岗的人，那下面肯定就是营地。

在突起的岩石层上有一个大山洞，在洞口，吉卜赛人拉斐尔背靠山岩而坐，伸着的两腿搁在地上，一支卡宾枪靠在山石旁。他在用刀子削一根木棍，他们走近时，他盯了他们一眼，然后继续削木棍。

“你在做什么东西?”罗伯特·乔丹在吉卜赛人身边坐下。吉卜赛人拿给他看的是一个4字形的捕猎器，他正在削上面的横挡。

“逮狐狸用的。”他说。

“他喜欢逮兔子，”安塞尔莫说。“他是吉卜赛人，所以逮到兔子说是狐狸，逮到狐狸说是大象。”

“那么逮到大象呢？”

“你会说是坦克。”

“我会俘获一辆坦克。那时候随你说我逮到的是什么吧。”

“吉卜赛人讲得多，可杀人少，”安塞尔莫对他说。

吉卜赛人朝罗伯特·乔丹眨眨眼睛，继续削木棍。

Anselmo came out of the mouth of the cave with a deep stone basin full of red wine and with his fingers through the handles of three cups. "Look," he said. "They have cups and all." Pablo came out behind them. "There is food soon," he said. "Do you have tobacco?"

Robert Jordan went over to the packs and opening one, felt inside an inner pocket and brought out one of the flat boxes of Russian cigarettes he had gotten at Golz's headquarters. He ran his thumbnail around the edge of the box and, opening the lid, handed them to Pablo who took half a dozen. Pablo, holding them in one of his huge hands, picked one up and looked at it against the light. They were long narrow cigarettes with pasteboard cylinders for mouthpieces.

"Much air and little tobacco," he said. "I know these. The other with the rare name had them."

"Kashkin," Robert Jordan said and offered the cigarettes to the gypsy and Anselmo, who each took one.

"Take more," he said and they each took another. He gave them each four more, they making a double nod with the hand holding the cigarettes so that the cigarette dipped its end as a man salutes with a sword, to thank him.

安塞尔莫从洞口走出来，端着一个深的石制盆子，里面盛满红酒，手指勾着三只杯子的杯柄。“看，”他说。“杯子呀什么的，他们全有。”巴勃罗在他们背后出现了。

“吃的马上就来，”他说。“有烟吗？”

罗伯特·乔丹走到背包边，打开了一只，伸手摸到里面的夹层口袋，掏出一盒他在戈尔兹司令部里弄到的扁盒装的俄国烟卷。他用拇指指甲划开了烟盒一边的封口，打开盒盖，递给巴勃罗，巴勃罗拿了6支。他用一只大手握住烟卷，拣了1支，对着光瞧了瞧。烟卷细长，一头有硬纸咬嘴。

“卷得松，烟丝少，”他说。“这烟我知道。那个名字古怪的人也抽这种烟。”

“卡希金，”罗伯特·乔丹说着，把烟盒递给吉卜赛人和安塞尔莫，他们每人拿了1支。

“多拿几支，”他说，于是他们每人又拿了1支。他再给了他们每人4支。他们手拿烟卷，连连点头致谢，因此烟卷的头也随着上下摆动，就像人们持剑行礼一样。

"Look now who brings it," the gypsy told him.

The girl stooped as she came out of the cave mouth carrying the big iron cooking platter and Robert Jordan saw her face turned at an angle and at the same time saw the strange thing about her. She smiled and said, "Hello, Comrade," and Robert Jordan said, "Hello," and was careful not to stare and not to look away. She set down the flat iron platter in front of him and he noticed her handsome brown hands.

Now she looked him full in the face and smiled. Her teeth were white in her brown face and her skin and her eyes were the same golden tawny brown. She had high cheekbones, bright eyes and a straight mouth with full lips. Her hair was the golden brown of a grain field that has been burned dark in the sun but it was cut short all over her head so that it was but little longer than the fur on a beaver pelt. She smiled in Robert Jordan's face and put her brown hand up and ran it over her head, flattening the hair which rose again as her hand passed. She has a beautiful face, Robert Jordan thought. She'd be beautiful if they hadn't cropped her hair.

"瞧，谁拿吃的来了？"吉卜赛人对他说。一个姑娘端着一只大的铁制的食盘，弯腰从洞中钻出来，罗伯特看到她脸的侧面，同时看到她有点异样。她微笑着说，"你好，同志。"罗伯特·乔丹也说"你好"，并且注意尽量避免盯着她看，但也不转头。她把平底铁盘放到他面前，他注意到她有双漂亮的褐色的手。

她这时正望着他的脸，微微一笑。她褐色的脸庞衬着一口白牙齿，她的皮肤和眼睛也是这种金褐色。她有着高颧骨，明亮的眼睛，端正的嘴巴，丰满的双唇。她的头发像金黄色的麦田被阳光晒得加深了颜色，可是给全部剪短了，只比海狸皮的毛稍长一点。她冲着罗伯特·乔丹微笑着，举起褐色的手捋捋头发，手过之处，抚平的头发随即又翘起来。她的脸很美，罗伯特·乔丹想，要是没有人把她的头发剪短，她一定很美。

"That is the way I comb it," she said to Robert Jordan and laughed. "Go ahead and eat. Don't stare at me. They gave me this haircut in Valladolid. It's almost grown out now."

She sat down opposite him and looked at him. He looked back at her and she smiled and folded her hands together over her knees. Her legs slanted long and clean from the open cuffs of the trousers as she sat with her hands across her knees. Every time Robert Jordan looked at her he could feel a thickness in his throat.

"There are no plates," Anselmo said. "Use your own knife." The girl had leaned four forks, tines down, against the sides of the iron dish.

They were all eating out of the platter, not speaking, as is the Spanish custom. It was rabbit cooked with onions and green peppers and there were chick peas in the red wine sauce. It was well cooked, the rabbit meat flaked off the bones, and the sauce was delicious. Robert Jordan drank another cup of wine while he ate. The girl watched him all through the meal.

"我就是这样梳头的，"她笑着对罗伯特·乔丹说。"吃你的吧。别盯着我看。他们是在瓦利阿多里德把我的头发剃成这副样子的。现在算是长出来啦。"

她坐在他对面看着他。他也回头看她，她微微一笑，双手交叉着搁在膝头。她两条腿斜搁着，裤管口露出一截颀长而干净的小腿。罗伯特·乔丹每次朝她看的时候，都感到自己的喉咙梗塞起来。

"没有碟子，"安塞尔莫说。"用你自己的刀吧。"姑娘在铁盘子边上搁了四把叉子，叉尖朝下。

大家都就着大铁食盘里拿东西吃，没人说话，保持着西班牙人的就餐习惯。他们吃的是洋葱青椒烧兔肉，加红酒的调味汁里放着青豆。菜烧得不错，兔肉烂得从骨头上掉下来，调味汁也很鲜美。罗伯特·乔丹吃着，又喝了杯酒。姑娘一直在看他吃饭。

Every one else was watching his food and eating. Robert Jordan wiped up the last of the sauce in front of him with a piece of bread, piled the rabbit bones to one side, wiped the spot where they had been for sauce, then wiped his fork clean with the bread, wiped his knife and put it away and ate the bread. He leaned over and dipped his cup full of wine and the girl still watched him.

Robert Jordan drank half the cup of wine but the thickness still came in his throat when he spoke to the girl.

"How are you called?" he asked. Pablo looked at him quickly when he heard the tone of his voice. Then he got up and walked away.

"Maria. And you?"

"Robert—my Christian name. Have you been long in the mountains?"

"Three months."

"Three months?" He looked at her hair, that was as thick and short and rippling when she passed her hand over it, now in embarrassment, as a grain field in the wind on a hillside. "It was shaved," she said, "They shaved it regularly in the prison at Valladolid."

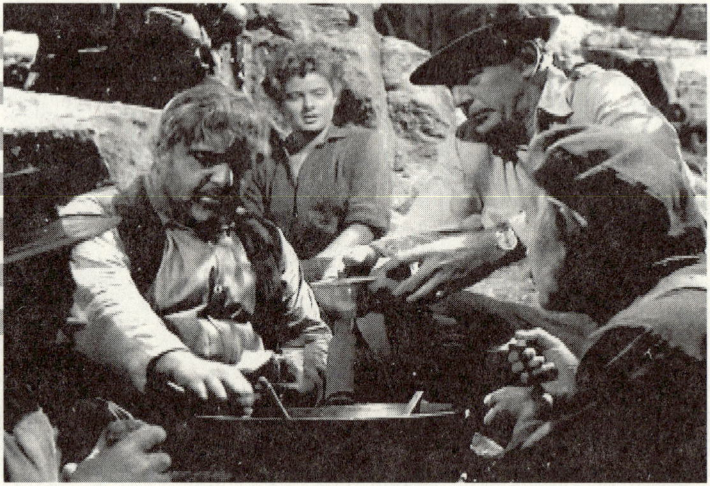

其余的人都看着自己的食物，只顾吃着。罗伯特·乔丹拿一片面包擦干净自己前面盘里剩下的调味汁，把骨头堆在一边，擦净底下的调味汁，然后拿面包擦净他用的叉子，再擦净自己的刀子，把刀收好，再吃掉面包。他凑过去，满满地舀了一杯酒，那姑娘仍然注视着他。

罗伯特·乔丹喝了半杯酒，可是等到和姑娘搭话时，喉咙又梗塞起来了。

“你叫什么名字？”他问。巴勃罗听到他说话的声调，马上对他瞥了一眼，接着站起来走开了。

“玛丽亚。你呢？”

“罗伯特——我的天主教教名。你在山里待了很久吗？”

“三个月。”

“三个月？”他望着她那密而短的头发，她这时局促不安地用手一捋，她的头发就像山坡上的麦田在风中泛起麦浪一样波动着。“头发给剃光了。“她说，“在瓦利阿多里德监狱里，都得按期剃光头。”

"It has taken three months to grow to this. I was on the train. They were taking me to the south. Many of the prisoners were caught after the train was blown up but I was not. I came with these."

"I found her hidden in the rocks," the gypsy said. "It was when we were leaving. Man, but this one was ugly. We took her along but many times I thought we would have to leave her."

"And the other one who was with them at the train?" asked Maria. "The other blond one. The foreigner. Where is he?"

"Dead," Robert Jordan said. "In April."

"In April? The train was in April."

"Yes," Robert Jordan lied. "He died ten days after the train."

"Poor man," she said. "He was very brave. And you do that same business?"

"Yes."

"You have done trains, too?"

"Yes. Three trains."

"Here?"

"In Estremadura," he said. "I was in Estremadura before I came here. We do very much in Estremadura. There are many of us working in Estremadura."

"三个月才长成这样。我那时也在火车上。他们打算把我带到南方去。火车被炸后，很多犯人又被逮住了，但我没有。我跟着这些人来了。"

"我瞅见她躲在岩石间，"吉卜赛人说。"那时我们正在撤退。天啊，那时她可真难看哪。我们带着她走，可有好多次，依我看，我们差一点不得不扔下她。"

"跟他们一起炸火车的那个人呢？"玛丽亚问。"也是个金黄头发的。那个外国人。他在哪儿？"

"死了，"罗伯特·乔丹说。"4月份死的。"

"4月？炸火车是4月份。"

"是的，"罗伯特·乔丹说了谎，"他在炸火车10天之后死的。"

"真可怜，"她说，"他非常勇敢。那你也是干这一行的？"

"是的。"

"你也炸过火车？"

"炸过。三列火车。"

"在这里吗？"

"在埃斯特雷马杜拉，"他说。"我来这里以前在埃斯特雷马杜拉。我们在那里做了不少事。我们有很多人在那里活动。"

"And why do you come to these mountains now?"

"I take the place of the other blond one. Also I know this country from before the movement."

"You know it well?"

"No, not really well. But I learn fast. I have a good map and I have a good guide."

"Anselmo," she nodded. "The old man is very good."

"Thank you," Anselmo said to her and Robert Jordan realized suddenly that he and the girl were not alone and he realized too that it was hard for him to look at her because it made his voice change so. He was violating the second rule of the two rules for getting on well with people that speak Spanish; give the men tobacco and leave the women alone; and he realized, very suddenly, that he did not care. There were so many things that he had not to care about, why should he care about that?

"You have a very beautiful face," he said to Maria. "I wish I would have had the luck to see you before your hair was cut."

"It will grow out," she said, "In six months it will be long enough."

"那你现在为什么到山里来？"

"接替那个金黄头发的人。还因为革命以前我就熟悉这个地区。"

"你很熟悉这里？"

"不，其实不是很熟。不过我很快能熟悉这里。我有一张好地图，还有一位好向导。"

"安塞尔莫？"她点点头，"老头子人很好。"

"谢谢你，"安塞尔莫对她说，于是罗伯特·乔丹突然意识到，在场的不只是他和姑娘两个人，他还意识到，他很难正眼看这个姑娘，这会使他说话时声音变样。他正在违反和西班牙人搞好关系的两条纪律中的第二条：给男人让烟，别碰女人。他突然意识到自己并不在乎了。很多事情他都不在乎了，为什么要计较这一点呢？

"你的脸很美，"他对玛丽亚说。"我要是有幸在你的头发剃掉之前见到你就好了。"

"会长出来的，"她说，"六个月之后就够长了。"

"You should have seen her when we brought her from the train. She was so ugly it would make you sick." The gypsy said.

"Whose woman are you?" Robert Jordan asked, trying not to pull out of it. "Are you Pablo's?"

She looked at him and laughed, then slapped him on the knee.

"Of Pablo? You have seen Pablo?"

"Well, then, of Rafael. I have seen Rafael."

"Of Rafael neither."

"Of no one," the gypsy said. "This is a very strange woman. Is of no one. But she cooks well."

"Really of no one?" Robert Jordan asked her.

"Of no one. No one. Neither in joke nor in seriousness. Nor of you either."

"No?" Robert Jordan said and he could feel the thickness coming in his throat again. "Good. I have no time for any woman. That is true."

"Not fifteen minutes?" the gypsy asked teasingly. "Not a quarter of an hour?" Robert Jordan did not answer. He looked at the girl, Maria, and his throat felt too thick for him to trust himself to speak.

"你该在我们炸了火车把她带来时见见她。她难看得叫人恶心。"吉卜赛人说。

"你是谁的女人?"罗伯特·乔丹问,不想纠缠这件事情了。"是巴勃罗的吗?"

她望着他笑,然后在他膝盖上打了一下。

"巴勃罗的?你见过巴勃罗吗?"

"噢,那么是拉斐尔的喽。我见过拉斐尔。"

"也不是拉斐尔的。"

"她不属于任何人,"吉卜赛人说。"这女人挺奇怪。她不属于任何人。可她饭菜做得不赖。"

"真的不属于任何人吗?"罗伯特·乔丹问她。

"不属于任何人。不管是说笑话,还是说正经的,都是这样。也不是你的。"

"是吗?"罗伯特·乔丹说,他感到喉咙里又梗塞起来了。"好啊。我没时间跟女人打交道,那倒是真的。"

"连 15 分钟也没有?"吉卜赛人戏弄地问。"一刻钟工夫也没有?"罗伯特·乔丹不回答。他望着姑娘玛丽亚,觉得喉咙里梗塞得不敢开口说话了。

Maria looked at him and laughed, then blushed suddenly but kept on looking at him.

"You are blushing," Robert Jordan said to her. "Do you blush much?"

"Never."

"You are blushing now."

"Then I will go into the cave."

"Stay here, Maria."

"No," she said and did not smile at him. "I will go into the cave now." She picked up the iron plate they had eaten from and the four forks. She moved awkwardly as a colt moves, but with that same grace as of a young animal.

"Do you want the cups?" she asked.

Robert Jordan was still looking at her and she blushed again.

"Don't make me do that," she said. "I do not like to do that."

"Leave them," the gypsy said to her. "Here," he dipped into the stone bowl and handed the full cup to Robert Jordan who watched the girl duck her head and go into the cave carrying the heavy iron dish.

"Thank you," Robert Jordan said. His voice was all right again, now that she was gone. "This is the last one. We've had enough of this."

玛丽亚望着他笑，接着突然脸红了，但是仍旧盯住他看。

"你在脸红，"罗伯特·乔丹对她说。"你常脸红吗？"

"从来不。"

"你现在脸红了。"

"我要到山洞里去了。"

"别走，玛丽亚。"

"不，"她说，不对他微笑了。"我现在要到里面去了。"她收拾起他们吃饭的那只铁盘和四把叉子。她走起路来像小马驹一样笨拙，但同时也像小动物一样姿态优美。

"你们还要用杯子吗？"她问。

罗伯特·乔丹仍旧望着她，她又脸红了。

"别惹我脸红，"她说。"我不喜欢这样。"

"别拿走，"吉卜赛人对她说。"来一杯吧，"他在酒缸里舀了满满一杯递给罗伯特·乔丹，而罗伯特正注视着姑娘端着沉重的铁盘低着头钻进山洞。

"谢谢你，"罗伯特·乔丹说。她走了，他的声调又恢复了常态。"最后一杯。我们已经喝得够多了。"

“你们一共有多少人？”罗伯特·乔丹问。

“七个男的，两个女的。”

“两个女的？”

“对。一个是巴勃罗的老婆。”

“她人呢？”

“在山洞里。那姑娘稍许会做些饭菜。我刚才说她做得不赖是为了让她高兴。但她多半是给巴勃罗的老婆搭下手。”

“巴勃罗的女人，她人怎么样？”

“有点儿野蛮，”吉卜赛人露齿笑笑。“实在太野了。如果你以为巴勃罗长得丑，那你应当见见他老婆。不过，那女人很勇敢。要比巴勃罗勇敢一百倍。只是有点野。”

“当初巴勃罗也很勇敢，”安塞尔莫说。“当初巴勃罗是很热诚的。”

“他杀死的人比霍乱害死的人还多，”吉卜赛人说。“革命开始时，巴勃罗杀死的人比伤寒害死的人还多。”

“可是很久以来，他太糟糕了，”安塞尔莫说。“他很懦弱，还非常怕死。”

“可能是因为当初杀的人太多了，”吉卜赛人富有哲理地说。“巴勃罗杀的人比鼠疫害死的人还多。”

“How many are you?” Robert Jordan asked.

“We are seven and there are two women.”

“Two?”

“Yes. The wife of Pablo.”

“And she?”

“In the cave. The girl can cook a little. I said she cooks well to please her. But mostly she helps the wife of Pablo.”

“And how is she, the wife of Pablo?”

“Something barbarous,” the gypsy grinned. “Something very barbarous. If you think Pablo is ugly you should see his woman. But brave. A hundred times braver than Pablo. But something barbarous.”

“Pablo was brave in the beginning,” Anselmo said. “Pablo was something serious in the beginning.”

“He killed more people than the cholera,” the gypsy said. “At the start of the movement, Pablo killed more people than the typhoid fever.”

“But since a long time he is terrible,” Anselmo said. “He is very flaccid. He is very much afraid to die.”

“It is possible that it is because he has killed so many at the beginning,” the gypsy said philosophically. “Pablo killed more than the bubonic plague.”

Robert Jordan sat up now and took a swallow of the wine.

"Let us see the wife of Pablo now," he said.

"I would not disturb her," Rafael said. "She has a strong hatred for me."

"Why?"

"She treats me as a time waster."

"What injustice," Anselmo taunted.

"She is against gypsies."

"What an error," Anselmo said.

"She has gypsy blood," Rafael said. "She knows of what she speaks." He grinned. "But she has a tongue that scalds and that bites like a bull whip. With this tongue she takes the hide from any one. In strips. She is of an unbelievable barbarousness."

"How does she get along with the girl, Maria?" Robert Jordan asked.

"Good. She likes the girl. But let any one come near her seriously—" He shook his head and clucked with his tongue.

"She is very good with the girl," Anselmo said. "She takes good care of her."

"When we picked the girl up at the time of the train she was very strange," Rafael said. "She would not speak and she cried all the time."

这时罗伯特·乔丹坐起来，喝了一大口酒。

"我们现在去见见巴勃罗的老婆吧，"他说。

"我不想去打扰她，"拉斐尔说。"她很讨厌我。"

"为什么？"

"她认为我整天混日子。"

"太不公平啦，"安塞尔莫嘲弄地说。

"她跟吉卜赛人作对。"

"真是大错特错，"安塞尔莫说。

"她有吉卜赛血统，"拉斐尔说。"她说话有谱。"他露齿笑笑。"可她的舌头太伤人，像条牛皮鞭子。她那条舌头能把人的皮都扒下来，撕成一条条的。她真野得不得了。"

"她和那姑娘玛丽亚相处得怎么样？"罗伯特·乔丹问。

"相处得不错。她疼那丫头。让谁当真去接近这丫头……"他摇摇头，舌头啧啧作响。

"她待那姑娘真挺好，"安塞尔莫说。"把她照顾得好好的。"

"我们炸了火车把她带走时，她很奇怪，"拉斐尔说，"她不肯说话，哭个没完。"

"It was the only good thing we have done," said a deep voice. "What are you doing now, you lazy drunken obscene unsayable son of an unnameable unmarried gypsy obscenity? What are you doing?"

Robert Jordan saw a woman of about fifty almost as big as Pablo, almost as wide as she was tall, in black peasant skirt, with heavy wool socks on heavy legs, black rope-soled shoes and a brown face like a model for a granite monument. She had big but nice-looking hands and her thick curly black hair was twisted into a knot on her neck.

"Answer me," she said to the gypsy, ignoring the others.

"I was talking to these comrades. This one comes as a dynamiter."

"I know all that," the wife of Pablo said. "Get out of here and relieve Andrés who is on guard at the top."

"I go," the gypsy said. He turned to Robert Jordan. "I will see you at the hour of eating."

"Not even in a joke," said the woman to him. "Three times you have eaten today according to my count. Go now and send me Andrès."

“我们就做了这样一件好事，”一个深沉的声音响起。“你在干什么，你这个没羞没臊的吉卜赛私生子、懒酒鬼、孬种，你在干什么？”

罗伯特·乔丹见到面前是个五十多岁的女人，个头跟巴勃罗差不多一般高大，肩膀宽得和身高差不多，她穿着农民穿的黑裙子，粗壮的腿上套着厚羊毛袜，脚蹬一双黑色绳底鞋，褐色的脸像座花岗石雕像。她长着一双粗大但好看的手，浓密的黑色鬈发在脑后挽了个发髻。

“回答我！”她对吉卜赛人说，也不理会有别人在场。

“我在跟这些同志说话。这个人是来当爆破手的。”

“我都知道，”巴勃罗的老婆说。“滚，到山顶上去换安德烈斯的班。”

“我走，”吉卜赛人说。他转身对着罗伯特·乔丹说：“吃饭时见。”

“开什么玩笑，”妇人对他说。“照我算来，你今天已经吃过三顿饭啦。快去给我把安德烈斯叫来。”

"Hello," she said to Robert Jordan and put out her hand and smiled. "How are you and how is everything in the Republic?"

"Good," he said and returned her strong handgrip. "Both with me and with the Republic."

"I am happy," she told him. She was looking into his face and smiling and he noticed she had fine gray eyes. "Do you come for us to do another train?"

"No," said Robert Jordan, trusting her instantly. "For a bridge."

"A bridge is nothing," she said. "When do we do another train now that we have horses?"

"Later. This bridge is of great importance."

"Where is it?"

"Quite close."

"All the better," the wife of Pablo said. "Let us blow all the bridges there are here and get out. I am sick of this place. Here is too much concentration of people. No good can come of it. Here is a stagnation that is repugnant."

She sighted Pablo through the trees.

"Drunkard." she called to him. "Rotten drunkard!" She turned back to Robert Jordan cheerfully. "He's taken a leather wine bottle to drink alone in the woods," she said. "He's drinking all the time. This life is ruining him."

"你好,"她对罗伯特·乔丹说,伸出手来并微笑着。"你好,共和国那边一切都好吗?"

"很好,"他说,也紧紧地握了握她的手。"我和共和国都很好。"

"我很高兴,"她对他说。她紧盯着他的脸,笑盈盈的。他注意到她长着一对漂亮的灰眼睛。"你是来找我们再炸一次火车吗?"

"不炸火车,"罗伯特·乔丹说,马上就信赖她了。"是来炸桥的。"

"桥算不上什么。"她说。"现在我们有马匹啦,什么时候再炸火车?"

"以后再说。这座桥很重要。"

"桥在哪里?"

"不远。"

"那更好,"巴勃罗的老婆说。"让我们把这里的桥统统炸掉了再撤走。我厌烦了这个地方。这里人太集中了。这不会有什么好处。这里死气沉沉得叫人讨厌。"

她看到巴勃罗在林子里。

"酒鬼!"她向他喊着。"烂酒鬼!"她愉快地转身对着罗伯特·乔丹。"他带了皮酒袋独自在林子里喝酒,"她说。"他老是喝个没完。这样的生活会把他毁了。"

"And listen to me about another thing. Be very good and careful about the girl. The Maria. She has had a bad time. Do you understand?"

"Yes. Why do you say this?"

"I saw how she was from seeing you when she came into the cave. I saw her watching you before she came out."

"I joked with her a little."

"She was in a very bad state," the woman of Pablo said. "Now she is better, she ought to get out of here."

"Clearly, she can be sent through the lines with Anselmo."

"You and Anselmo can take her when this terminates."

Robert Jordan felt the ache in his throat and his voice thickening. "That might be done," he said.

The wife of Pablo looked at him and shook her head. "Are all men like that?" she said.

"I said nothing. She is beautiful, you know that."

"I do not want her crazy here after you will go. I have had her crazy before and I have enough without that," the woman of Pablo said.

战地钟声 *For Whom the Bell Tolls*

"还有一桩事你听我说。要善待那丫头，要爱护她，那个玛丽亚。她受过很多苦。你懂吗？"

"我懂。你为什么说这话？"

"她见了你之后回到山洞里，我看出了她的心思。我还发现她没有走出山洞时就在打量着你。"

"我跟她说笑了几句。"

"她原来状况很糟，"巴勃罗的老婆说，"现在她好多了，她应该离开这里。"

"那当然，可以安排安塞尔莫把她送过火线去。"

"这次行动结束后，你和安塞尔莫可以把她带走。"

罗伯特·乔丹觉得喉咙作痛，嗓音也走了样。"也许能行吧，"他说。

巴勃罗的老婆望着他摇摇头。"难道男人都是这副样子的吗？"她说。

"刚才我没说什么啊。她长得很美，这你也知道。"

"我不希望你走了以后让她在这里发疯。我见过她疯疯癫癫的模样，不疯疯癫癫，我已经受够了。"巴勃罗的老婆说。

"We will take her after the bridge," Robert Jordan said. "If we are alive after the bridge, we will take her."

"I do not like to hear you speak in that manner. That manner of speaking never brings luck."

"I spoke in that manner only to make a promise," Robert Jordan said.

"Let me see your hand," the woman said. Robert Jordan put his hand out and the woman opened it, held it in her own big hand, rubbed her thumb over it and looked at it, carefully, and then dropped it.

"What did you see in it?" Robert Jordan asked her. "I don't believe in it. You won't scare me."

"Nothing," she told him. "I saw nothing in it."

"Yes you did. I am only curious. I do not believe in such things."

"I try to speak frankly."

"Then tell me what you saw in the hand."

"No," she said and shook her head. "I saw nothing. Go now to your bridge. I will look after your equipment."

"Cover it and that no one should touch it. It is better there than in the cave."

"It shall be covered and no one shall touch it," the woman of Pablo said. "Go now to your bridge." So he and Anselmo went to watch the bridge closely.

“炸桥后我们一定带她走,”罗伯特·乔丹说。“只要我们炸桥后还活着,一定带她走。”

“我不喜欢听你用这种口气说话。这种口气决不会带来好运。”

“我用这种口气只是为了向你保证,”罗伯特·乔丹说。

“让我看看你的手掌,”那妇人说。罗伯特·乔丹伸出一只手,妇人把它摊平,放在她自己的大手上,用大拇指摸了摸他的手掌,仔细端详了一番才放下他的手。

“你在我手上看出了什么?”罗伯特·乔丹问她。“我不相信手相这一套。你唬不了我。”

“没什么,”她对他说。“我什么也看不出来。”

“不,你看出来了。我只是好奇罢了。我不信这个。”

“我说话喜欢坦率。”

“那就告诉我你在我手上看出了什么。”

“不,”她说着,摇摇头。“我什么也没有看出,快到桥那边去吧。我会照看你的东西。”

“把背包遮盖起来,谁也别让碰。搁在那儿要比放在山洞里好。”

“会遮盖好的,没有人碰,”巴勃罗的老婆说,“快到桥那边去吧。”他和安塞尔莫去近距离察看那座桥。

Having observed the bridge, they came down to the mouth of the cave, where a light shone out from the edge of a blanket that hung over the opening. Robert Jordan stood up to follow Anselmo, then reconsidered and, lifting the canvas off the two packs, picked them up, one in each hand, and started with them, just able to carry them, for the mouth of the cave. He laid one pack down and lifted the blanket aside, then with his head stooped and with a pack in each hand, carrying by the leather shoulder straps, he went into the cave.

It was warm and smoky in the cave. There was a table along one wall with a tallow candle stuck in a bottle on it and at the table were Pablo, three men Robert did not know, and the gypsy, Rafael. The candle made shadows on the wall behind the men and Anselmo stood where he had come in to the right of the table.

The wife of Pablo was standing over the charcoal fire on the open fire hearth in the corner of the cave. The girl knelt by her stirring in an iron pot. She lifted the wooden spoon out and looked at Robert Jordan as he stood there in the doorway and he saw, in the glow from the fire the woman was blowing with a bellows, the girl's face, her arm and the drops running down from the spoon and dropping into the iron pot.

他们观测完桥，下山来到山洞口，一道光线从挂在洞口的毯子边缘透出来。罗伯特·乔丹站起身正要跟安塞尔莫进去，他考虑一下，揭去那两个背包上的帆布，一手提着一个，走到洞口。他放下一个背包，撩开洞口的毯子，低下头，抓住皮背带，两手各提一个背包，走进山洞。

洞内暖暖烘烘的，烟雾缭绕。沿洞壁摆放着一张桌子，桌上有一个插着一支牛脂烛的瓶子，巴勃罗、三个罗伯特不认识的人和吉卜赛人拉斐尔围在桌边。烛光在洞壁上映出了他们的影子，安塞尔莫站在桌子右边他刚进来的地方。

巴勃罗的老婆站在山洞角落生炭火的炉灶边。姑娘跪在她身旁，在一只铁锅里搅拌着。见罗伯特·乔丹站到洞口，她就提起木汤匙，望着他。他借着炉灶火的光看到妇人在拉风箱，姑娘的脸庞和她的一只胳膊，汤汁顺着汤匙滴下来，滴入铁锅。

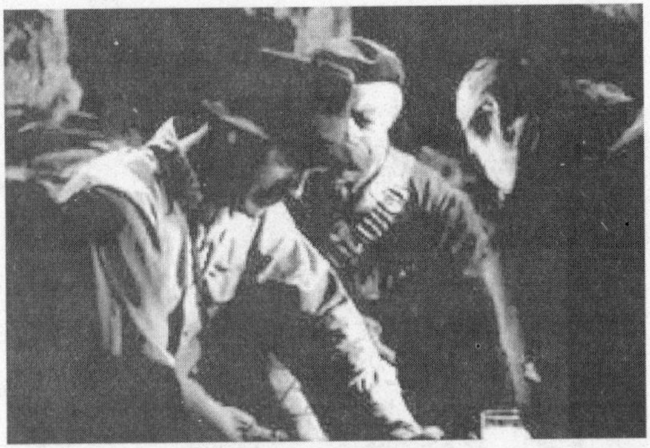

"Well, did you see the bridge?" the gypsy asked.

"Yes," Robert Jordan said. "It is something easy to do. Would you like me to show you?"

"Yes, man. With much interest."

Robert Jordan took out the notebook from his shirt pocket and showed them the sketches.

"Look how it seems," the flat-faced man, who was named Primitivo, said. "It is the bridge itself."

Robert Jordan with the point of the pencil explained how the bridge should be blown and the reason for the placing of the charges.

"What simplicity," the scarred-faced brother, who was called Andrès keeping guard in the daytime, said. "And how do you explode them?"

Robert Jordan explained that too and, as he showed them, he felt the girl's arm resting on his shoulder as she looked. The woman of Pablo was watching too. Only Pablo took no interest, sitting by himself with a cup of wine that he replenished by dipping into the big bowl.

"Have you done much of this?" the girl asked Robert Jordan softly.

"Yes."

"And can we see the doing of it?"

"Yes. Why not?" Robert Jordan said.

战地钟声 *For Whom the Bell Tolls*

"呃，你看那座桥去了？"吉卜赛人问。

"看过了，"罗伯特·乔丹说。"这件事挺容易。要我讲给你们听听吗？"

"好的，伙计。我很有兴趣。"

罗伯特·乔丹从衬衫袋里掏出笔记本，给他们看草图。

"瞧这桥的样子，"那个叫普里米蒂伏的扁脸汉子说。"这桥画得真好。"

罗伯特·乔丹用铅笔尖指着，讲解炸桥的方法，像那样安放炸药包的原因。

"简单极了，"两兄弟中脸上有刀疤的那个说，他叫安德烈斯，白天一直在站岗。"那你怎样引爆炸药包呢？"

罗伯特·乔丹又作了解释。他给他们讲解着，发觉姑娘在旁边望着，手臂搁在他肩上。巴勃罗的老婆也在看着。只有巴勃罗不感兴趣，拿杯子在大缸里又舀满了酒，独自坐在一旁喝酒。

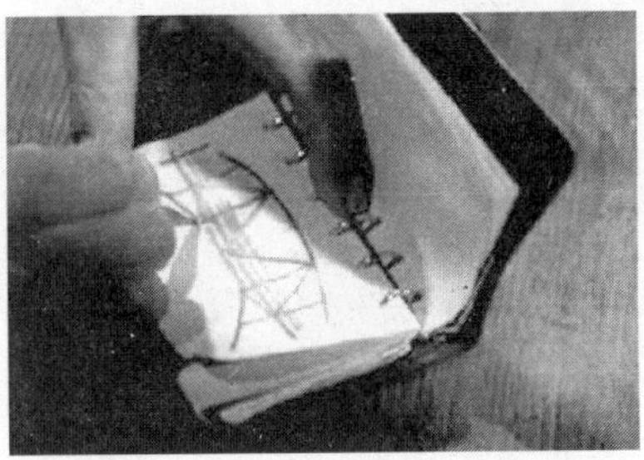

"你干过很多这种事吗？"姑娘悄声问罗伯特·乔丹。

"是的。"

"我们可以去看炸桥吗？"

"当然。干吗不？"罗伯特·乔丹说。

"I do not go for the bridge," Pablo said, looking down at the table. "Neither me nor my people."

Robert Jordan said nothing. He looked at Anselmo and raised the cup. "Then we shall do it alone, old one," he said and smiled.

"Without this coward," Anselmo said.

"What did you say?" Pablo spoke to the old man.

"Nothing for you. I did not speak to you," Anselmo told him.

Robert Jordan now looked past the table to where the wife of Pablo was standing by the fire. She had said nothing yet, nor given any sign. But now she said something he could not hear to the girl and the girl rose from the cooking fire, slipped along the wall, opened the blanket that hung over the mouth of the cave and went out. I think it is going to come now, Robert Jordan thought. I believe this is it. I did not want it to be this way but this seems to be the way it is.

"Then we will do the bridge without your aid," Robert Jordan said to Pablo.

"No," Pablo said, and Robert Jordan watched his face sweat. "You will blow no bridge here."

"No?"

"You will blow no bridge," Pablo said heavily.

“我可不赞成炸桥，”巴勃罗说，低头望着桌子。“我也好，我手下也好，都不赞成。”

罗伯特·乔丹什么也没说。他望着安塞尔莫，举起了杯子。“那样我们只好单干啦，老伙计，”他微笑着说道。

“不用这个胆小鬼，”安塞尔莫说。

“你说什么？”巴勃罗对老人说。

“与你无关。我不跟你说话，”安塞尔莫对他说。

罗伯特·乔丹这时隔着桌子望望站在炉灶边的巴勃罗的老婆。她还没开口表态，也不动声色。但她对姑娘说了些他听不清的话，姑娘就从炉灶边站起身，沿洞壁悄悄走过去，揭开挂在洞口的毯子出去了。罗伯特·乔丹想，“我看现在要摊牌了。我相信就在眼前了。我不希望发生这种情况，可是实际情况看来就是如此。”

“那我们就不靠你的帮助来炸桥，”罗伯特·乔丹对巴勃罗说。

“不行，”巴勃罗说；罗伯特·乔丹注视到他的脸在出汗。“你不能在这里炸桥。”

“不能？”

“你不能炸桥，”巴勃罗沉重地说。

"And you?" Robert Jordan spoke to the wife of Pablo who was standing, still and huge, by the fire. She turned toward them and said, "I am for the bridge." Her face was lit by the fire and it was flushed and it shone warm and dark and handsome now in the firelight as it was meant to be.

"What do you say?" Pablo said to her and Robert Jordan saw the betrayed look on his face and the sweat on his forehead as he turned his head.

"I am for the bridge and against you," the wife of Pablo said. "Nothing more."

"I am also for the bridge," Primitivo with the flat face and the broken nose said.

"To me the bridge means nothing," one of the brothers said. "I am for the wife of Pablo."

"Equally," said the other brother.

"Equally," the gypsy said.

Robert saw the wife of Pablo standing there and watched her blush proudly and soundly and healthily as the allegiances were given.

"I am for the Republic," the woman of Pablo said happily. "And the Republic is the bridge. Afterwards we will have time for other projects."

战地钟声 *For Whom the Bell Tolls*

“那你呢？”罗伯特·乔丹冲巴勃罗的老婆说，她站在炉灶边，显得镇静而高大。她转身对着大家说，“我同意炸桥。”她的脸被炉火照亮了，红扑扑的，显得热情、黝黑而漂亮，流露出她的本色。

“你说什么？”巴勃罗对她说。罗伯特·乔丹看到他转过头来，脸上显出了被人出卖的神色，前额上在冒汗。

“我赞成炸桥，不赞成你。”巴勃罗的老婆说，“没别的话啦。”

“我也赞成炸桥，”长着扁脸和断鼻梁的普里米蒂伏说。

“对我来说，那座桥不算什么，”两兄弟中的一个说。“我拥护的是巴勃罗大娘。”

“一样，”另一个说。

“一样，”吉卜赛人说。

罗伯特注视着巴勃罗的老婆在众人表态时激动得脸上显露出了骄傲、坚强的神情和健康的红润肤色。

“我拥护共和国，”巴勃罗的老婆兴奋地说。“炸这座桥就等于拥护共和国。我们以后有的是时间干别的。”

"And you," Pablo said bitterly. "With your head of a seed bull and your heart of a whore. You think there will be an afterwards from this bridge? You have an idea of that which will pass?"

"That which must pass," the woman of Pablo said. "That which must pass, will pass."

"And it means nothing to you to be hunted then like a beast after this thing from which we derive no profit? Nor to die in it?"

"Nothing," the woman of Pablo said. "And do not try to frighten me, coward."

"Coward," Pablo said bitterly. "You treat a man as coward because he has a tactical sense. Because he can see the results of an idiocy in advance. It is not cowardly to know what is foolish."

"Neither is it foolish to know what is cowardly," said Anselmo, unable to resist making the phrase.

"Shut up! I am for the good and the safety of all."

"Safety," the wife of Pablo said. "There is no such thing as safety. There are so many seeking safety here now that they make a great danger. In seeking safety now you lose all."

“你呀，”巴勃罗刻薄地说。“你这个猪脑袋，见识短的东西。你以为炸了桥还会有以后？你考虑过以后会发生什么事吗？”

“会发生该发生的事，”巴勃罗的老婆说。“该发生的事总会发生的。”

“炸这座桥我们捞不到任何好处，炸桥后我们会像野兽一样被搜捕，你觉得无所谓？炸桥时死掉也无所谓？”

“无所谓，”巴勃罗的老婆说。“你别吓唬我，胆小鬼。”

“胆小鬼，”巴勃罗愤愤地说。“你把有战术头脑的人叫做胆小鬼，因为他能事先看到干蠢事要倒霉。懂得什么叫蠢事的才不是胆小鬼哩。”

“懂得什么叫胆小鬼的也不见得愚蠢嘛，”安塞尔莫忍不住插了一句。

“闭嘴！我关心的是大家的好处和安全。”

“安全，”巴勃罗的老婆说。“安全这回事根本不存在。到这里来寻求安全的人太多了，以致引起了很大的危险。为了寻求安全，你就会失去一切的。”

"What illusions I put in you and how they have turned out! From one year of war you have become lazy, a drunkard and a coward."

"In that way you have no right to speak," Pablo said. "And less even before the people and a stranger."

"In that way will I speak," the wife of Pablo went on. "Have you not heard? Do you still believe that you command here?"

"Yes," Pablo said. "Here I command."

"Not in joke," the woman said. "Here I command! Haven't you heard it? Here no one commands but me. You can stay if you wish and eat of the food and drink of the wine, but not too bloody much, and share in the work if you wish. But here I command."

"I should shoot you and the foreigner both," Pablo said sullenly.

"Try it," the woman said. "And see what happens."

Robert Jordan held the cup in one hand and his other hand rested, frankly now, on the pistol.

She went on, "Listen to me, drunkard. You understand who commands here?"

"I command."

"No. Listen. Take the wax from your hairy ears. Listen well. I command."

"All right. You command," Pablo said.

"Pay no attention to what that drunkard says," she said to Robert.

"Maria, enter now and serve the supper."

They prepared to eat.

"我把指望全放在你身上，现在落得这样的下场！打了一年仗，你就变成了个懒鬼、酒鬼、胆小鬼。"

"你不应当这样说，"巴勃罗说。"尤其是当着大家的面，当着陌生人的面。"

"我就是要这样说，"巴勃罗的老婆接着说。"你听到没有？你还以为这里是你指挥？"

"对，"巴勃罗说。"这里我指挥。"

"开什么玩笑，"那妇人说，"这里我指挥！难道你没有听到吗？这里除了我没人能指挥。你要愿意，就待着，吃你的饭，喝你的酒，可不准拼命死喝。你要愿意，也有一份干的。可这里我指挥。"

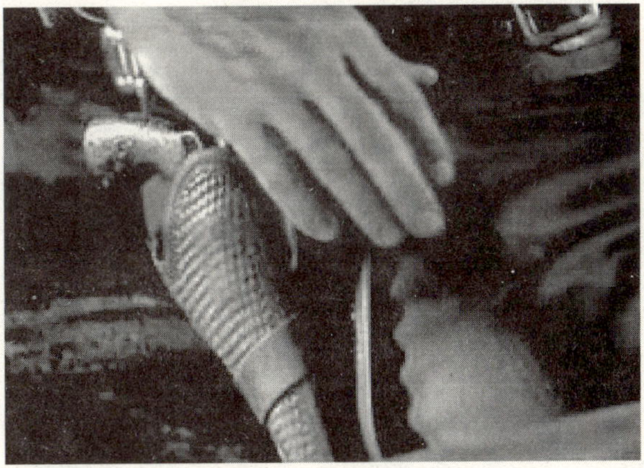

"我把你和这外国人一起毙了，"巴勃罗阴沉地说。

"试试看，"那妇人说。"看看会怎么样。"

罗伯特·乔丹一手握住杯子，一手毫不掩饰地放在手枪上。

她接着说，"听我说，酒鬼。你明白这里是谁指挥吗？"

"我指挥。"

"不对。听着。把你那毛耳朵里的耳屎掏干净。听仔细。我指挥。"

"好吧。你指挥，"巴勃罗说。

"别介意酒鬼说的话，"她对罗伯特说。

"玛丽亚，进来端饭吧。"

他们准备吃饭。

Outside the cave, Robert prepared to sleep in his robe and Maria warned him to be alert. She put her hand on his arm and looked in his face. He looked at her brown face and at the eyes that, since he had seen them, had never been as young as the rest of her face but that now were suddenly hungry and young and wanting.

"Now I know why I have felt as I have," Maria said. "Now it is clear."

Robert Jordan reached over; he ran his hand over the top of her head. He had been wanting to do that all day and now he did it, he could feel his throat swelling. She moved her head under his hand and smiled up at him and he felt the thick but silky roughness of the cropped head rippling between his fingers. Then his hand was on her neck and then he dropped it.

"Do it again," she said. "I wanted you to do that all day."

"Later," Robert Jordan said and his voice was thick.

在山洞外，罗伯特铺好睡袋准备睡觉。玛丽亚来警告他多注意安全。她把手放在他胳膊上，凝视着他的脸。他望着她褐色的脸，望着她的眼睛；自从他见到她以来，总觉得她的眼睛不及她脸上的其他五官那么年轻，而现在，顷刻之间，这双眼睛却焕发青春，并带着渴求和欲望。

"我现在才明白，为什么我一直有那样的心情，"玛丽亚说。"现在清楚了。"

罗伯特·乔丹伸手去抚摸她的头顶。整天来，他一直想抚摸它，现在抚摸着，只觉得自己的喉咙堵塞得难受。她的头顺着他的抚摸而挪动着，她抬头向他微笑；他感到她浓密而柔顺的短发给捋平了又在他指缝中翘起来。接着，他把手放在她脖子上，然后垂下去。

"再摸一下，"她说，"我整天都盼望着你这样做。"

"以后吧。"罗伯特·乔丹说，嗓音沙哑。

Robert Jordan watched the gypsy walk over to a tree and then come toward him. Robert hid Maria in his robe.

"Robert," the gypsy said softly.

"Yes, Rafael," he said.

"Why did you not kill Pablo?" the gypsy said very softly.

"Why kill him?"

"You have to kill him sooner or later. Why did you not approve of the moment?"

"That you all should kill him."

"That is your business. Three or four times we waited for you to kill him. Pablo has no friends." the gypsy said quietly.

"I had the idea," Robert Jordan said. "But I left it."

"I go down there," the gypsy said angrily.

"To do what?"

"At least to prevent him from leaving."

They came down to the meadow and heard Pablo speaking to the bay horse, but Robert did not hear him because now, convinced that Pablo was only down checking on his horses, and having decided that it was not a practical move to kill him at this time, Robert stood up and walked back to sleep. The first day when Robert Jordan came to the mountain area seemed to pass peacefully.

罗伯特·乔丹看见吉卜赛人走到一棵树边，然后向他这边走来。罗伯特迅速把玛丽亚藏到睡袋里。

"罗伯特，"吉卜赛人轻声说。

"嗯，拉斐尔，"他说。

"你为什么不杀了巴勃罗？"吉卜赛人悄悄地说。

"为什么要杀他？"

"你迟早得杀了他。当时有机可乘，你为什么不赞成？"

"我以为你们大家会杀他的。"

"那是该你干的事。有三四次我们等你动手干掉他。巴勃罗没有朋友。"吉卜赛人冷静地说。

"我起过这念头，"罗伯特·乔丹说，"不过我打消了。"

"我到下面去，"吉卜赛人愤愤地说。

"去干什么？"

"至少防止他溜掉呗。"

他们来到草地，听到了巴勃罗跟栗色马匹谈心，但罗伯特没听清他说的话，他深信巴勃罗是下来检查他的马匹，认为在这时杀他并不太合适，罗伯特站起身来回去睡觉了。罗伯特·乔丹来到山区的第一天似乎平静地过去了。

Robert Jordan felt with his hand the light frost that lay on the robe and then settled into it again. It was the worn, spotted green balloon silk outer covering of the five-year-old down robe. Good, he said to himself, feeling the familiar caress of the flannel lining as he spread his legs wide, then drew them together and then turned on his side so that his head would be away from the direction where he knew the sun would come.

He slept again until the sound of airplane motors woke him.

Lying on his back, he saw them, a fascist patrol of three Italy-made Fiats, tiny, bright, and fast-moving across the mountain sky, headed in the direction from which Anselmo and he had come yesterday. The three passed and then came nine more, flying much higher in the minute, pointed formations of threes, threes and threes.

Pablo and the gypsy were standing at the cave mouth, in the shadow, watching the sky and as Robert Jordan lay still, the sky now full of the high hammering roar of motors, there was a new droning roar and three more planes came over at less than a thousand feet above the clearing. These three were Germany-made twin-motor bombers.

战地钟声 *For Whom the Bell Tolls*

罗伯特·乔丹用手摸摸睡袋外面的薄霜，就又缩回到睡袋里。这只有斑点的绿色旧鸭绒睡袋的面子是用热气球的绸布做的，已经用了五年。他自言自语地说“好呀！”他伸开两腿，身子挨着睡袋的法兰绒衬里，感到熟悉舒适，然后他并起双腿，侧过身子，不让脑袋面对着他知道太阳将要升起的方向。

飞机的引擎声把他吵醒前，他又睡着了。

他平躺着，看到了飞机，三架意大利产的菲亚特巡逻机组成的法西斯巡逻小队，三个闪亮的小点，急速越过山巅上空，向着安塞尔莫和他昨天来的方向飞去。三架飞机过去后又来了九架，飞的高得多，一丁点大，组成三角形的三三编队。

巴勃罗和吉卜赛人站在山洞口的背阴处仰望天空；罗伯特·乔丹安静地躺着，这时，天空中充满了引擎的轰鸣声，接着传来了另一阵隆隆吼声，在林中空地上空不到 1000 英尺的地方又飞来了三架德国产的双引擎轰炸机。

Robert Jordan slipped along the rocks to the mouth of the cave where one of the brothers, the gypsy, Anselmo and Agustín stood in the mouth looking out.

"Have there been planes like this before?" he asked.

"Never," said Pablo. "Get in. They will see you."

The sun had not yet hit the mouth of the cave. It was just now shining on the meadow by the stream and Robert Jordan knew they could not be seen in the dark, early morning shadow of the trees and the solid shade the rocks made, but he went in the cave in order not to make them nervous.

"They are many," the woman said.

"And there will be more," Robert Jordan said.

"How do you know?" Pablo asked suspiciously.

"Those, just now, will have pursuit planes with them."

Just then they heard them, the higher, whining drone, and as they passed at about five thousand feet, Robert Jordan observed with his binoculars and counted fifteen Fiats in echelon of echelons like a wild-goose flight of the V-shaped threes.

罗伯特·乔丹沿着山崖闪身走到洞口，站在那里观望的有两兄弟中的一个、吉卜赛人、安塞尔莫和奥古斯丁。

“以前来过这么多的飞机吗？”他问。

“从来没有过，”巴勃罗说。“进来吧。他们会看到你的。”

阳光刚刚照到溪边的草地上，还没有照射到山洞口，罗伯特·乔丹知道，在晨曦朦胧的树阴和山岩浓浓的阴影中藏身是不会被发现的，不过为了让他们放心，他还是走进了山洞。

“太多了，”那妇人说。

“还会有更多的飞机，”罗伯特·乔丹说。

“你怎么知道？”巴勃罗疑神疑鬼地问。

“刚才这些飞机得有驱逐机伴随。”

说着，他们就听到了飞得更高的飞机的呜咽般的嗡鸣声，它们在 5000 英尺左右的高空飞过，罗伯特·乔丹用望远镜一边观察，一边数数，共有十五架菲亚特飞机，每三架排成 V 字形，一队队地构成梯阵，像一群大雁。

It is bad, Robert Jordan thought. This is really bad. Here is a concentration of planes which means something very bad. I must listen for them to unload. But no, they cannot have brought up the troops yet for the attack. Certainly not before tonight or tomorrow night, certainly not yet. Certainly they will not be moving anything at this hour.

"I want you to go to watch the road. Make a note of everything that passes both up and down the road," Robert Jordan said to Anselmo.

"I do not write."

"There is no need to," Robert Jordan took out two leaves from his notebook and with his knife cut an inch from the end of his pencil. "Take this and make a mark for tanks thus," he drew a slanted tank, "and then a mark for each one and when there are four, cross the four strokes for the fifth."

"In this way we count also."

"Take the gypsy with you that he will know from what point you will be watching so you may be relieved. Pick a place that is safe, not too close and from where you can see well and comfortably. Stay until you are relieved."

"I understand."

糟了，罗伯特·乔丹想，真是太糟糕了。飞机集中飞到这里来，说明形势很糟糕。我得注意听它们扔炸弹的声音。可是不对，他们现在还不可能把部队调来准备进攻。当然，今晚或明晚之前是不可能的，目前是绝对不可能的。他们这时候是绝对不会采取任何行动的。

"我要你去守望公路。把路上来往的车辆人马都记下来，"罗伯特·乔丹对安塞尔莫说。

"我不会写字。"

"不需要写字，"罗伯特·乔丹从笔记本上撕下两张纸，用刀把自己的铅笔的一端截下 1 英寸。"把这个带着，用这个记号代表坦克，"他画了一辆倾斜的坦克。"每见一辆坦克就画一道，画了四道后，看见第五辆就在四条线上横着画一道。"

"我们也会用这办法记数。"

"带吉卜赛人一起去，让他知道你要守望的地点，以便派人去换你的班。选择一个安全而不太靠近公路的地方，可以既看清楚又舒服。要待到换你的时候。"

"我明白。"

"Good. And that when you come back, I should know everything that moved upon the road. One paper is for movement up. One is for movement down the road."

"Listen," Robert Jordan said and felt in his pocket for the cigarettes. "I wish you to go with Anselmo to a place from which he will observe the road. There you will leave him, noting the place in order that you may guide me to it or guide whoever will relieve him later. You will then go to a place where you can observe the saw mill and note if there are any changes in the post there."

"What changes?"

"How many men are there now?"

"Eight. The last I knew."

"See how many are there now. See at what intervals the guard is relieved at that bridge."

"Intervals?"

"How many hours the guard stays on and at what time a change is made."

"I have no watch."

"Take mine." He unstrapped it.

"What a watch," Rafael said admiringly. "Look at what complications. It's a watch to end watches."

"I want you to check on the guard at the big bridge and the post on the road below in the same manner as the post and the guard at the saw mill and the small bridge."

Then Robert turned to Fernando.

"好的。还有,回来后要让我知道公路上的一切调动情况。一张纸上记去的活动,一张纸上记来的活动。"

"听着,"罗伯特·乔丹一边说,一边在衣袋里掏烟卷。"我要你跟安塞尔莫一起去一个地方,好让他观察公路。你就在那里和他分开,记住那个地点,以便过后可以领我或别的人到那儿去换班。然后你找一个可以观察锯木厂的地方,注意那边的哨所发生的任何变化。"

"什么变化?"

"那里现在有多少人?"

"8个。这是我最近了解的情况。"

"去看看现在有多少人。看看那边桥头的哨兵间隔多久换一次岗。"

"间隔?"

"哨兵值一班要几小时,什么时候换岗。"

"我没有手表。"

"把我的手表拿去用。"他解下手表。

"多棒的表啊,"拉斐尔羡慕地说。"你看它多复杂。这样一块手表能把其他的表全比下去。"

"我要你监视大桥边的哨兵和公路下段的哨所,就像监视锯木厂边的哨所和小桥边的哨兵那样。"

然后,罗伯特转向了费尔南多。

Fernando went to La Granja yesterday and came back to the cave that morning.

"What movement was there on the road last night?" Robert Jordan asked Fernando. The girl Maria was close to him but he did not look at her.

"You," the woman said. "Fernando. You were in La Granja last night. What movement was there?"

"Nothing," a short, open-faced man of about thirty-five with a cast in one eye answered. "A few camions as usual. Some cars. No movement of troops while I was there."

"You go into La Granja every night?" Robert Jordan asked him.

"I or another," Fernando said. "Some one goes."

"They go for the news. For tobacco. For small things." the woman said.

"What was the news?"

"The officers speak in the cafés in Segovia and Avila and the waiters note it. The rumors come running. Since some time they speak of an offensive by the Republic in these parts. There was some talk that the Republicans would try to blow up the bridges, if there was to be an offensive. But the bridges are guarded."

"Thank you for all the news." said Robert Jordan.

费尔南多昨天去了拉格兰哈，今天早上才回到山洞里。

“昨晚公路上有什么动静？”罗伯特·乔丹问费尔南多。姑娘玛丽亚就挨在他身边，但他没有看她。

“你，”妇人说。“费尔南多。你昨晚在拉格兰哈。那边有什么动静？”

“没什么动静，”回答的是个三十五岁左右的矮个子，表情坦率，一只眼睛有点斜视。“还是老样子，有几辆军用卡车，几辆汽车。我在那里的时候，没有部队调动。”

“你每天晚上都到拉格兰哈去吗？”罗伯特·乔丹问他。

“不是我去，就是别人去，”费尔南多说。“总得有人去。”

“他们是去探听消息。去买烟草。买些零星东西。”妇人说。

“有什么消息吗？”

“军官们在塞哥维亚和阿维拉的咖啡馆里都在讲，侍者们听见了谈话。谣言就传开来了。很久以来，他们谣传共和国在这些地区要发动一次进攻。有些人还说，如果发动进攻，共和国的人打算炸桥。不过每座桥都有人把守。”

“谢谢你报告了这些情况。”罗伯特·乔丹说。

Robert Jordan arranged everything well and Pilar, the woman of Pablo, took him and Maria to talk about the bridge with El Sordo, a leader of anther guerilla. As they came up, still deep in the shadow of the pines, after dropping down from the high meadow into the wooden valley and climbing up it on a trail that paralleled the stream and then left it to gain, steeply, the top of a rimrock formation, a man with a carbine stepped out from behind a tree and he was Joaquin, a member of El Sordo's guerilla.

"Halt," he said. Then, "Hello, Pilar. Who is this with you?"

"An English," Pilar said. Because American people also spoke English, Pilar always mistook Robert for an Englishman. "And what an obscenity of steepness it is to arrive here."

"Hello, Comrade," the guard said to Robert Jordan and put out his hand.

"Hello," said Robert Jordan.

Now they were in sight of El Sordo's camp in the last of the pines, where there was a rounded gulch-head shaped like an upturned basin. All these limestone upper basins must be full of caves, he thought. There are two caves there ahead. The scrub pines growing in the rock hide them well. This is as good or a better place than Pablo's.

罗伯特·乔丹安排完这些事情后，巴勃罗的老婆比拉尔带着他和玛丽亚去找另一支游击队的队长艾苏道谈炸桥的事。他们从高山坡上的草地笔直朝下走进树木葱茏的山谷，再爬上一条和小溪平行的山路，随即在松树的浓阴里登上一座陡峭的悬崖顶，这时，只见一个手握卡宾枪的男人从一棵树后闪了出来，他是艾苏道的游击队队员华金。

“站住，”他说。接着他又说，“是你，比拉尔。跟你一起的是谁？”

“一个英国人，”比拉尔说。因为美国人也说英语，所以比拉尔误认为罗伯特是英国人。“到这里来的路实在是太陡了。”

“你好，同志，”哨兵对罗伯特·乔丹说，伸出手来。

“你好，”罗伯特·乔丹说。

这时他们能望到松林尽头，也就是艾苏道的营地了，那是一个圆形峡谷的尽头，像只朝天的脸盆。他想，这些石灰岩的盆形高地一定到处是岩洞。前面就有两个岩洞，长在岩石上的矮松树把这两个岩洞隐蔽得很好。这地方和巴勃罗那里差不多，甚至比他那里还要隐蔽。

The man to whom Pilar spoke was short and heavy, brown faced, with broad cheekbones; gray haired, with wide-set yellow brown eyes, a thin-bridged, hooked nose like an Indian's, a long upper lip and a wide, thin mouth. He was clean shaven and he walked toward them from the mouth of the cave, moving with the bow-legged walk that went with his cattle herdsman's breeches and boots. The day was warm but he had on a sheep's-wool-lined short leather jacket buttoned up to the neck. He put out a big brown hand to Pilar. "Hello, woman," he said.

"Hello," he said to Robert Jordan and shook his hand and looked him keenly in the face. Robert Jordan saw his eyes were yellow as a cat's and flat as reptile's eyes are. "Beautiful girl," he said to Maria and patted her shoulder.

"Eaten?" he asked Pilar. She shook her head.

"Eat," he said and looked at Robert Jordan. "Drink?" he asked, making a motion with his hand decanting his thumb downward.

"Yes, thanks."

"Good," El Sordo said. "Whiskey?"

"You have whiskey?"

El Sordo nodded. "English?" he asked. "Not Russian?"

"American."

比拉尔招呼的是个矮墩墩的汉子，棕色脸盘，高颧骨，灰头发，两只黄褐色眼睛间的距离较大，长着一个像印第安人那样的窄鼻梁的鹰钩鼻，一张宽阔的嘴，上嘴唇又长又薄。他的胡子刮得光光的。他迈着罗圈腿，这和他穿的牧牛人的马裤和马靴是相称的，从洞口向他们迎来。天气很暖和，但他穿了件有羊毛衬里的短款皮外套，纽扣直系到脖子。他向比拉尔伸出一只褐色的大手。“你好，太太，”他说。

他向罗伯特·乔丹也打了招呼，还和他握握手，定睛望着他的脸。罗伯特·乔丹看到他的眼睛像猫眼睛那样黄，像爬虫的眼睛那样呆滞。“漂亮姑娘，”他招呼玛丽亚，轻轻拍拍她的肩膀。

“吃了吗？”他问比拉尔。她摇摇头。

“来吃吧，”他说，对罗伯特·乔丹望着。“喝酒？”他问，一边伸出大拇指，做了个朝下斟酒的手势。

“喝，谢谢。”

“好，”艾苏道说。“威士忌？”

“你有威士忌？”

艾苏道点点头。“英国人？”他问，“不是俄国人？”

“美国人。”

El Sordo went into the cave and came out with a pinch bottle of Scotch whiskey and three glasses. The bottle was under one arm, and three glasses were in the hand of that arm, a finger in each glass, and his other hand was around the neck of an earthenware jar of water. He put the glasses and the bottle down on the log and set the jug on the ground.

"No ice," he said to Robert Jordan and handed him the bottle.

"I don't want any," Pilar said and covered her glass with her hand.

"Ice last night on ground," El Sordo said and grinned. "All melt. Ice up there," El Sordo said and pointed to the snow that showed on the bare crest of the mountains. "Too far."

Robert Jordan started to pour into El Sordo's glass but the deaf man shook his head and made a motion for the other to pour for himself.

"Where do you get the whiskey?" Robert Jordan shouted.

"Make it," El Sordo said and watched Robert Jordan's hand check on its way to his mouth with the glass.

"No," El Sordo said and patted his shoulder. "A joke. Comes from La Granja."

艾苏道走进山洞，拿了一瓶苏格兰威士忌和三只玻璃杯出来。他一边的胳肢窝下挟着酒瓶，就用那只手的三个指头勾住三只杯子，另一只手握住一把陶制水壶的颈口。他把杯子和酒瓶放在一段木头上，水壶放在地上。

"没有冰，"他对罗伯特·乔丹说着，把酒瓶递给他。

"我不想喝，"比拉尔说着用手捂住杯口。

"昨晚地上有冰，"艾苏道咧嘴笑着说。"都化了。上面有冰，"他说着，指着光秃秃的山顶上露出来的积雪。"太远了。"

罗伯特·乔丹动手替艾苏道斟酒，可是艾苏道摇摇头，做了个手势，让他往自己的杯子里倒。

"你在哪儿搞到的威士忌？"罗伯特·乔丹大声说。

"酿的，"艾苏道说，看见罗伯特·乔丹刚要把杯子送到嘴边，却停住了。

"不，"艾苏道拍拍他的肩膀说。"开玩笑。从拉格兰哈弄来的。"

El Sordo took a sip of the whiskey. "You want of me?"

"How many men have you?"

"Five."

"To cut the telephone, attack the post at the house of the road menders, take it, and fall back on the bridge."

"It is easy."

"And afterwards for the retreat?" Robert Jordan asked. "We are seven men, two women and five horses. How many do you have?" he shouted into El Sordo's ear.

"Five men and five horses," he said.

"Fourteen people and ten horses," Pilar said. "Without accounting for transport."

El Sordo said nothing.

"Is there no way of getting horses?" Robert Jordan said into El Sordo's best ear.

"In war a year," El Sordo said. "Have five." He showed five fingers. "Now you want four for tomorrow."

"Yes," said Robert Jordan. "Knowing you are leaving. Having no need to be careful as you have been in this neighborhood. Not having to be cautious here now. Couldn't you cut out and steal four head of horses?"

"Maybe," El Sordo said. "Maybe none. Maybe more."

艾苏道咂了一口威士忌。"你要我干什么？"

"你有多少人？"

"五个。"

"割断电话线，攻击并占领养路工小屋边的哨所，再回过头来向桥靠拢。"

"好办。"

"然后掩护撤退？"罗伯特·乔丹问。"我们是七个男的，两个女的，五匹马。你们有多少?"他对着艾苏道的耳朵大声说。

"五个男人，五匹马。"他说。

"十四个人，十匹马，"比拉尔说。"还没有算驮东西的牲口呢。"

艾苏道没说什么。

"没法弄到马吗？"罗伯特·乔丹对着艾苏道那只不太聋的耳朵说。

"打了一年仗，"艾苏道说，"才搞到了五匹马。"他伸出五个指头。"现在你明天要用四匹。"

"不错，"罗伯特·乔丹说。"你要知道，快撤退了。不必像原先那样小心翼翼地在这一带活动。在这里现在不必提心吊胆了。难道你不能豁出去偷四匹马吗？"

"也许，"艾苏道说。"也许一匹也搞不到，也许可以搞到更多。"

"You see," El Sordo said. "In that there is no problem. But to leave afterward and get out of this country in daylight presents a grave problem."

"Clearly,"said Robert Jordan. "I have thought of it. It is daylight for me also."

"But you are one," El Sordo said. "We are various."

"There is the possibility of returning to the camps and leaving from there at dark," Pilar said, putting the glass to her lips and then lowering it.

"That is very dangerous, too," El Sordo explained. "That is perhaps even more dangerous."

"I can see how it would be," Robert Jordan said.

"To do the bridge in the night would be easy," El Sordo said. "Since you make the condition that it must be done at daylight, it brings grave consequences."

"I know it."

"Couldn't you do it at night?"

"I would be shot for it."

"It is very possible we will all be shot for it if you do it in the daytime."

"But I see your viewpoint. Can't you work out a retreat for daylight?"

"Certainly," El Sordo said. "You speak of going to Gredos as though it were a military maneuver to be accomplished. To arrive at Gredos would be a miracle."

"你知道,"艾苏道说,"这方面没有问题。不过,炸桥后在大白天撤离这一带,倒是个严重的问题。"

"当然,"罗伯特·乔丹说。"我也考虑到了。对我也一样是大白天。"

"可你是一个人,艾苏道说。"我们是好几个。

"也许可以先回营地,天黑再撤走,"比拉尔说,把杯子举到唇边,接着又放下。

"那也很危险,"艾苏道说。"也许更危险。"

"这我能想象得到,"罗伯特·乔丹说。

"晚上炸桥可能容易,"艾苏道说。"可你提的条件是必须在大白天干,这就带来了严重的后果。"

"我知道这个。"

"你就不能在晚上干吗?"

"为此我会被枪决。"

"你在白天干,很可能我们大家都会送命。"

"我明白你的意思。你不能制订出白天撤退的方案吗?"

"当然能,"艾苏道说。"你说什么到格雷多斯去,好像是去完成一次军事演习似的。要是能到了格雷多斯就成了奇迹啦。"

战地钟声 For Whom the Bell Tolls

Joaquin had a chat with them and told them his miserable family story. "They were of the left as many others in Valladolid. When the fascists purified the town they shot first the father. He had voted Socialist. Then they shot the mother. She had voted the same. It was the first time she had ever voted. After that they shot the husband of one of the sisters. He was a member of the syndicate of tramway drivers. Clearly he could not drive a tram without belonging to the syndicate. But he was without politics. I knew him well. He was even a little hit shameless. I do not think he was even a good comrade. Then the husband of the other girl, the other sister, who was also in the trams, had gone to the hills as I had. They thought she knew where he was. But she did not. So they shot her because she would not tell them where he was."

"What barbarians," said Pilar.

As the boy stood there, Maria reached up, put her arms around his neck and kissed him. Joaquín turned his head away because he was crying.

华金和他们说闲话，说着说着就提到了他悲惨的身世。"我家里人跟瓦利阿多里德许多人一样，都是"左派"。法西斯分子血洗我家乡的时候，先枪杀了我爹。他投过社会党的票。然后杀了我妈。她也投过社会党的票。她一辈子还是第一次投票。后来，他们杀了我一个姐夫。他是电车司机辛迪加的会员。显然，他不参加辛迪加就不让开电车。不过，他不懂政治。我很了解他。他甚至有点不知廉耻。我看他也算不上一个好同志。后来，我另一个姐夫，也是在电车上干活的，像我一样跑到山里去了。他们以为我姐姐知道他的去向。其实她不知道。他们就把她枪杀了，理由是我姐姐不肯告诉他们我姐夫在哪里。"

"杀人不眨眼的畜生，"比拉尔说。

小伙子站在那里，玛丽亚踮起脚尖，双臂搂住他的脖子，亲吻了他一下。华金哭了，他把头转向一边。

"That is as a brother," Maria said to him. "I kiss you as a brother."

The boy shook his head, crying without making any noise.

"I am your sister," Maria said. "And I love you and you have a family. We are all your family."

"Including the English," boomed Pilar. "Isn't it true, English?"

"Yes," Robert Jordan said to the boy, "We are all your family, Joaquín."

"He's your brother," Pilar said. "Hey, English?"

Robert Jordan put his arm around the boy's shoulder. "We are all brothers," he said. The boy shook his head.

"I am ashamed to have spoken," he said. "To speak of such things makes it more difficult for all. I am ashamed of molesting you."

Pilar stood with her hands on her hips looking at the boy mockingly now.

"When I kiss you," she said to him, "it will not be as any sister. This trick of kissing as a sister."

"It is not necessary to joke," the boy said. "I told you I am all right, I am sorry that I spoke."

“我把你当做弟弟,”玛丽亚对他说。“我把你当做弟弟一样亲吻。”小伙子摇摇头,不出声地哭泣着。

“我是你姐姐,”玛丽亚说。“我爱你,你有家啦。我们都是一家人。”

“包括这个英国人,”比拉尔声音洪亮地说。“不是吗,英国人?”

“对,”罗伯特·乔丹对小伙子说,“我们都是一家人,华金。”

“他是你兄弟,”比拉尔说。“是吗,英国人?”

罗伯特·乔丹搂着小伙子的肩膀。“我们都是兄弟,”他说。小伙子摇摇头。

“我真不该讲出来,”他说。“讲起这种事,叫大家更难受。我真不该叫你们心里难受。”

这时,比拉尔双手放在髋部,戏谑地望着那小伙子。

“我吻你的时候,”她对他说,“可不会像你姐姐那样。像姐姐亲吻弟弟的那套把戏我可不会。”

“不必开玩笑啦,”小伙子说。“我跟你们说我没事了,对不起我说了刚才的话。”

They left El Sordo's after eating and started down the trail. El Sordo had walked with them as far as the lower post.

As they had left him, Pilar had said to him, "Well, El Sordo?"

"Well, nothing, woman," the deaf man said. "It is all right. But I am thinking."

"Me, too," Pilar had said and now as they walked down the trail, the walking easy and pleasant down the steep trail through the pines that they had toiled up, Pilar said nothing. Neither Robert Jordan nor Maria spoke and the three of them traveled along fast until the trail rose steeply out of the wooded valley to come up through the timber, leave it, and come out into the high meadow.

It was hot in the late May afternoon and halfway up this last steep grade the woman stopped. Robert Jordan, stopping and looking back, saw the sweat beading on her forehead. He thought her brown face looked pallid and the skin sallow and that there were dark areas under her eyes.

吃完饭他们离开艾苏道的营地，开始顺着小路下山。艾苏道一直把他们送到半山腰的哨岗。

他们向他告别的时候，比拉尔对他说："怎么样，艾苏道？"

"噢，没什么，太太，"这个耳聋的汉子说。"还行。不过我正在考虑。"

"我也在考虑，"比拉尔说。他们现在穿过松树林，顺着山路轻松愉快地往下走去。他们刚才就是从这条陡峭的山路上费劲地爬上来的。比拉尔这时一句话也不说。罗伯特·乔丹和玛丽亚也不开口，他们仨走得飞快，穿过树木丛生的山谷后，山路又变得陡峭了，朝上穿过一片树林，直通到高坡草地。

5月下旬的下午，天气很热，走到最后一段陡峭的山路中途，妇人停下了脚步。罗伯特·乔丹停下来回头一看，只见她前额上渗出一颗颗汗珠。他发现她棕褐色的脸上失去了血色，皮肤灰黄，眼睛下面有黑眼圈。

"Let us rest a minute," he said. "We go too fast."

"No," she said. "Let us go on."

"Rest, Pilar," Maria said. "You look badly."

"Shut up," the woman said. "Nobody asked for your advice."

She started on up the trail but at the top she was breathing heavily and her face was wet with perspiration and there was no doubt about her pallor now.

"Sit down, Pilar," Maria said. "Please, please sit down."

"All right," said Pilar and the three of them sat down under a pine tree and looked across the mountain meadow to where the tops of the peaks seemed to jut out from the roll of the high country with snow shining bright on them now in the early afternoon sun.

"What rotten stuff is the snow and how beautiful it looks," Pilar said. "What an illusion is the snow." She turned to Maria. "I am sorry I was rude to you, beautiful girl. I don't know what has held me today. I have an evil temper."

"I never mind what you say when you are angry," Maria told her. "And you are angry often."

"No, it is worse than anger," Pilar said, looking across at the peaks.

"咱们歇一会儿吧,"他说。"走得太快了。"

"不,"她说。"继续走吧。"

"歇一下吧,比拉尔,"玛丽亚说。"你的脸色不好看。"

"住嘴,"妇人说。"没有人问你的意见。"

她拔腿顺着山路向上爬,但是到了顶端,她大口喘着粗气,满脸是汗,脸色明显地发白。

"坐下吧,比拉尔,"玛丽亚说。"求求你,求求你坐下吧。"

"好吧,"比拉尔说,于是他们仨在一棵松树下坐下了,眺望着高坡草地对面那些矗立在层层山峦之上的高峰,刚到下午,峰顶的积雪在阳光下明亮地闪耀着。

"雪这东西真讨厌,可看起来多美呀,"比拉尔说。"雪呀真叫人捉摸不透。"她转身对玛丽亚。"我刚才对你很粗暴,对不起,漂亮姑娘。我不知道今天怎么搞的。脾气糟透了。"

"你生气时讲的话我从不往心里去,"玛丽亚对她说,"再说,你常常生气。"

"不,比生气更糟,"比拉尔说,眺望着对面的山峰。

"You are not well," Maria said.

"Neither is it that," the woman said. "Come here, beautiful girl, and put your head in my lap."

Maria moved close to her, put her arms out and folded them as one does who goes to sleep without a pillow and lay with her head on her arms. She turned her face up at Pilar and smiled at her but the big woman looked on across the meadow at the mountains. She stroked the girl's head without looking down at her and ran a blunt finger across the girl's forehead and then around the line of her ear and down the line where the hair grew on her neck.

"You can have her in a little while, English," she said. Robert Jordan was sitting behind her.

"Do not talk like that." Maria said.

"Yes, he can have you," Pilar said and looked at neither of them. "I have never wanted you. But I am jealous."

"Pilar," Maria said. "Do not talk thus."

"He can have you," Pilar said and ran her finger around the lobe of the girl's ear. "But I am very jealous."

"你身体不舒服了。"玛丽亚说。

"也不是这样的。"妇人说,"过来,漂亮姑娘,把脑袋搁在我腿上。"

玛丽亚靠近她,伸出双臂,交叠起来,像人们不用枕头睡觉那样,脑袋枕着双臂躺下。她转过脸来,仰望着比拉尔,对她微笑,但这大个子妇人凝望着草地对面的群山,她并没有低头看着姑娘,而是抚摸着姑娘的头,一只短而粗的手指从姑娘前额上划过去,然后沿着耳朵边向下一直摸到她脖子上的头发根。

"过一会儿,她就是你的人了,英国人,"她说。罗伯特·乔丹坐在她背后。

"别这样说。"玛丽亚说。

"就说,你就是他的人,"比拉尔说,并没有看他们俩。"我从来不想要你。不过我感到妒忌。"

"比拉尔,"玛丽亚说,"别这样说。"

"你就是他的人,"比拉尔说,指头沿着姑娘的耳垂边摸着,"不过我非常妒忌。"

"There is always something like that," the woman said. "There is always something like something that there should not be. But with me there is not. Truly there is not. I want your happiness and nothing more."

Maria said nothing but lay there, trying to make her head rest lightly.

"Listen, beautiful girl," said Pilar and ran her finger now absently but tracingly over the contours of her cheeks. "I love you and he can have you, I am no lesbian but a woman made for men. That is true. But now it gives me pleasure to say thus, in the daytime, that I care for you."

"I love you, too."

"Do not talk nonsense. You do not know even of what I speak."

"I know."

"That you know. You are for the English. That is seen and as it should be. That I would have. Anything else I would not have. I do not make perversions. I only tell you something true. Few people will ever talk to you truly and no women. I am jealous and say it and it is there. And I say it."

"那种情形总是有的,"妇人说。"那种情形照理说不应该有,但终究难免会有。不过,我倒没有这种心情。真的没有。我什么都不要,只想要你幸福。"

玛丽亚没说什么,只是躺在那里,尽量使自己的头轻轻地放在她腿上。

"听着,漂亮姑娘,"比拉尔一边说,一边心不在焉地用指头抚摸她的脸庞。"我爱你,可你是他的人,我不是同性恋,而是个为男人而生的女人。这是真话。但是,我现在大白天里把这种话说出来,是为你好,我心里也很舒畅。"

"我也爱你。"

"别胡说八道。你根本不明白我是什么意思,"比拉尔说。

"我懂。"

"你懂什么!你是为这个英国人而生的。这一看就知道,也该这样。我就是希望这样。不这样,我就不高兴。我不搞不正常的行为。我只不过把真心话告诉你。对你说真心话的人不多,女人根本没有。我感到嫉妒,就说了出来,就是这样。我说了。"

"Do not say it," Maria said. "Do not say it, Pilar."

"Do not say it?" the woman said, still not looking at either of them. "I will say it until it no longer pleases me to say it. And," she looked down at the girl now, "that time has come already. I do not say it more, you understand?"

"Pilar," Maria said. "Do not talk thus."

"You are a very pleasant little rabbit," Pilar said. "And lift your head now because this silliness is over."

"It was not silly," said Maria. "And my head is well where it is."

"No. Lift it," Pilar told her and put her big hands under the girl's head and raised it. "And you, English?" she said, still holding the girl's head as she looked across at the mountains. "What cat has eaten your tongue?"

"No cat," Robert Jordan said.

"What animal then?"

"No animal," Robert Jordan told her.

"You swallowed it yourself, eh?"

"I guess so," Robert Jordan said.

"And did you like the taste?" Pilar turned now and grinned at him.

"Not much."

"别说了，"玛丽亚说，"别说了，比拉尔。"

"不说了？"妇人说，还是不看他们俩。"我要一直说，直到不想说为止。还有，"这时，她低头望着姑娘，"好时光已经到啦。我不多说了，你懂吗？"

"比拉尔，"玛丽亚说，"别这样说。"

"你是只挺讨人喜欢的小兔子，"比拉尔说，"现在你把头抬起来，蠢话已经说完啦。"

"不蠢，"玛丽亚说，"再说，我的头搁在这里很好。"

"不。抬起头来，"比拉尔对她说，把自己的大手放在姑娘脑后，托起她的头。"你怎么不开口，英国人？"她说，仍然托着姑娘的头，眺望对面的群山。"难道你的舌头给猫叼走啦？"

"不是猫，"罗伯特·乔丹说。

"那么是什么野兽？"

"不是野兽，"罗伯特·乔丹对她说。

"那你自己把它吞掉了，呃？"

"我看是吧，"罗伯特·乔丹说。

"那你觉得好吃吗？"现在比拉尔转身对他露齿笑着。

"不太好。"

战地钟声 *For Whom the Bell Tolls*

"What a day it is and how I am contented not to be in pine trees. You cannot imagine how one can tire of pine trees. Aren't you tired of the pines, beautiful girl?"

"I like them," the girl said.

"What can you like about them?"

"I like the odor and the feel of the needles under foot. I like the wind in the high trees and the creaking they make against each other."

"You like anything," Pilar said. "You are a gift to any man if you could cook a little better. But the pine tree makes a forest of boredom. You have never known a forest of beech, nor of oak, nor of chestnut. Those are forests. In such forests each tree differs and there is character and beauty. A forest of pine trees is boredom. What do you say, English?"

"I like the pines, too."

"Two of you. So do I like the pines, but we have been too long in these pines. Also I am tired of the mountains. In mountains there are only two directions. Down and up and down leads only to the road and the towns of the Fascists."

"今天天气真好，离开了松林心里真痛快。你哪里会想到松树会叫人觉得很厌烦。你不讨厌松树吗，漂亮姑娘？"

"我喜欢松树，"姑娘说。

"松树有什么可喜欢的？"

"我喜欢松树的香味和脚踩在松针上的感觉。我喜欢高大的树林间的风声和树枝擦碰的响声。"

"你什么都喜欢，"比拉尔说。"如果你能把饭菜烧得稍微好一点，哪个男人娶了你都是好福气。可是松树林子叫人腻烦得要死。你从没见过山毛榉林、橡树林或栗树林，那才叫树林子呢。在那种林子里每棵树都不一样，有特色，好看。松树叫人讨厌。你说呢，英国人？"

"我也喜欢松树。"

"你们俩挺一致。其实我也喜欢松树，只不过我们在松树林里待得太久了。我还讨厌这些山。山里只有两个方向。下山，上山，而且下山只有一条路，通到法西斯分子占领的城镇。"

"Do you ever go to Segovia?" Robert Jordan asked.

"With this face? This is a face that is known. How would you like to be ugly, beautiful one?" she said to Maria.

"You are not ugly."

"I'm not ugly. I was born ugly. All my life I have been ugly. You, English, who know nothing about women. Do you know how an ugly woman feels? Do you know what it is to be ugly all your life and inside to feel that you are beautiful? It is very rare. Look at the water wagtail," she said and pointed to the gray ball of a bird that was bobbing up and down on a stone up the stream. "Those are no good for anything. Neither to sing nor to eat. Only to jerk their tails up and down. Give me a cigarette, English," she said and took it; Robert Jordan lit it for her.

"Life is very curious," she said, and blew smoke from her nostrils. "I would have made a good man, but I am all woman and all ugly. Yet many men have loved me and I have loved many men. It is curious. Listen, English, this is interesting. Look at me, as ugly as I am. Look closely, English."

"你到过塞哥维亚？"罗伯特·乔丹问道。

"带了这张脸去？这张脸出了名。你愿意长得丑吗，漂亮姑娘？"她对玛丽亚说。

"你不丑。"

"我不丑！我生下来就丑。我一辈子都丑。你这个英国人一点也不懂女人。你可知道丑女人的心情？你知道一辈子都丑的人心里却以为长得美丽是怎么回事吗？是很古怪的。瞧那只鹡鸰，"她说，指着一只在溪水上游一块石头上蹦蹦跳跳的圆滚滚的灰色鸟。"这种鸟一点用处也没有。叫得不好听，肉又不能吃。只会上下摆动尾巴。给我来支烟抽，英国人。"她说着接过烟来，罗伯特·乔丹为她点着了。

"生活真奇怪，"她说着从鼻孔里喷出烟来。"我要是男人准是条好汉，可惜我是个十足的女人，丑得要命。可是有不少男人爱过我，我也爱过不少男人。真古怪。听着，英国人，这是怪有趣的。瞧我这丑样子。仔细看看，英国人。"

"At times many things tire me," Pilar said angrily. "You understand? And one of them is to have forty-eight years. You hear me? Forty-eight years and an ugly face."

"You are not ugly," Robert Jordan said.

"Not ugly? Don't lie to me. Or," she laughed the deep laugh. "Has it begun to work with you? No. That is a joke. No. Look at the ugliness. Yet one has a feeling within one that blinds a man while he loves you. You, with that feeling, blind him, and blind yourself. Then one day, for no reason, he sees you ugly as you really are and he is not blind any more and then you see yourself as ugly as he sees you and you lose your man and your feeling. Do you understand, beautiful girl?"

"No," said Maria. "Because you are not ugly."

"Try to use your head and not your heart, and listen," Pilar said. "I am telling you things of much interest. Does it not interest you, English?"

"Yes. But we should go."

"有时候，很多事情让我厌倦，"比拉尔气愤地说。"你懂吗？其中一个原因是年纪到了四十八。你听到我的话了吗？四十八岁，一张丑脸。"

"你不丑，"罗伯特·乔丹说。

"不丑？别对我说谎。难道说，"她低沉地大笑一声，"你也开始动心了？不，这是说说笑话。不，瞧这副丑相。可是，男人对你有了感情，就分不出来你是美还是丑了。然后，你心里也怀有了这种感情，你自己也分不出美丑了。有一天，没有任何原因，他看出了你本来的丑样，而且他能分辨美丑了，于是你像他一样，也看出了自己的丑样，你就丢了你的男人和你的感情。你懂吗，漂亮姑娘？"

"不懂，"玛丽亚说，"因为你不丑。"

"要用你的头脑，可别用你的心。听着，"比拉尔说，"我跟你们讲的这些事是很有趣的。你觉得有趣吗，英国人？"

"有趣。可是我们得上路啦。"

Pilar went on, addressing herself to Robert Jordan now as though she were speaking to a classroom; almost as though she were lecturing. "After a while, when you are as ugly as I am, as ugly as women can be, then, as I say, after a while the feeling, the idiotic feeling that you are beautiful, grows slowly in one again. It grows like a cabbage. And then, when the feeling is grown, another man sees you and thinks you are beautiful and it is all to do over. Now I think I am past it, but it still might come. You are lucky, beautiful girl, that you are not ugly."

"But I am ugly," Maria insisted.

"Ask him," said Pilar.

"If Robert says we should go, I think we should go," Maria said.

"Listen to you," Pilar said. "I have as much at stake in this as your Robert and I say that we are well off resting here and that there is much time. Furthermore, I like to talk. It is the only civilized thing we have. How otherwise can we divert ourselves? Does what I say not hold interest for you, English?"

"You speak very well."

比拉尔对罗伯特·乔丹继续说下去，仿佛在对着整个班级讲话，像是在讲课。“过不了多久，等你变得跟我一样丑，变得要多丑有多丑的时候，我看，要不了多久，这种感情，这种自以为漂亮的白痴般的感情又会在心里慢慢滋长，像棵卷心菜般长起来了。那时候，等到这种感情滋长起来了，另一个男人看中了你，认为你长得很漂亮，于是又是老一套。我现在觉得自己不会再动情了，不过，说不定以后还会。你很幸运，漂亮姑娘，你长得不丑。”

“我可丑呢，”玛丽亚坚持说。

“问他吧，”比拉尔说。

“罗伯特说我们该走了，我看是该走了。”玛丽亚说。

“听你说的，”比拉尔说，“我在这件事上冒的风险跟你的罗伯特冒的风险一样大，可我说咱们在这儿歇息挺舒服，时间有的是。还有，我喜欢聊天。这是我们仅有的一点文明行为。除此之外，还有什么别的可散散心?你对我说的不感兴趣，英国人? ”

“你说得很好。”

"I am not much like myself today," Pilar said. "Very little like myself. Your bridge has given me a headache, English."

"We can tell it the Headache Bridge," Robert Jordan said. "But I will drop it in that gorge like a broken bird cage."

"Good," said Pilar. "Keep on talking like that."

"I'll drop it as you break a banana from which you have removed the skin."

"I could eat a banana now," said Pilar. "Go on, English. Keep on talking largely."

"There is no need," Robert Jordan said. "Let us get to camp."

"Your duty," Pilar said. "It will come quickly enough. I said that I would leave the two of you."

"No. I have much to do," Robert Jordan said.

Pilar said, "But I am also very delicate. I will leave the two of you. And the talk of jealousness is nonsense. I was angry at Joaquín because I saw from his look how ugly I am. I am only jealous that you are nineteen. It is not a jealousy which lasts. You will not be nineteen always. Now I go."

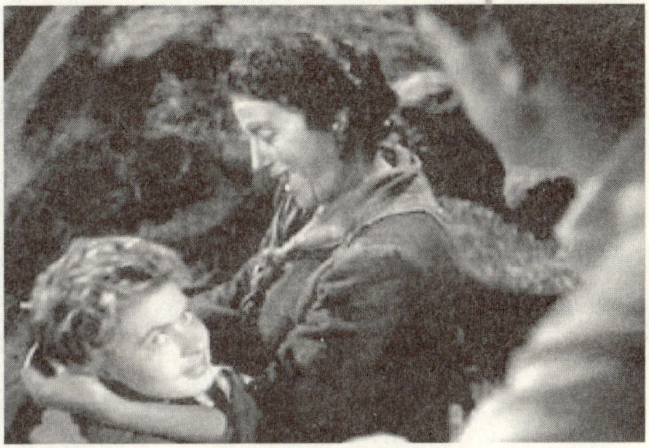

"今天我不大像我平常的样子，"比拉尔说，"简直一点儿不像我自己了。英国人，你的桥叫我头痛。"

"我们就叫它'头痛桥'吧，"罗伯特·乔丹说，"可是我会让它像只破鸟笼似的掉入峡谷。"

"好，"比拉尔说。"该一直这样说话。"

"我要让它坠落，就像折断一只剥了皮的香蕉似的。"

"但愿现在能吃到香蕉，"比拉尔说。"说下去，英国人。尽管说大话吧。"

"不必啦，"罗伯特·乔丹说，"我们回营地吧。"

"你的任务，"比拉尔说，"就在眼前。我说过要让你们俩一起待一会儿。"

"不，我有不少事要做。"罗伯特·乔丹说。

比拉尔说，"可我也很体贴人呢。我要让你们俩在一起了。妒忌的话是胡扯。我从华金神色上看出来我是多么丑，这让我恼恨他。叫我妒忌的是你才十九岁。但是妒忌并不会持续很久。因为你不会永远都是十九岁。现在我得走了。"

She stood up and with a hand on one hip looked at Robert Jordan. Maria sat on the ground under the tree, looking at Pilar.

"Let us all go to camp together," Robert Jordan said. "It is better and there is much to do."

Pilar nodded with her head toward Maria, who sat there, her head turned away from them, saying nothing.

Pilar smiled and shrugged her shoulders almost imperceptibly and said, "You know the way?"

"I know it," Maria said, not raising her head.

"Then I am going. We'll have something hearty for you to eat, English." Pilar said. She started to walk off into the heather of the meadow toward the stream that led down through it toward the camp.

"Wait," Robert Jordan called to her. "It is better that we should all go together."

Maria sat there and said nothing.

Pilar did not turn. "Go together?" she said. "I will see you at the camp."

Robert Jordan stood there.

"Is she all right?" he asked Maria. "She looked ill before."

"Let her go," Maria said, her head still down.

"I think I should go with her."

"Let her go," said Maria. "Let her go!"

比拉尔站起来,一只手放在髋部上,望着罗伯特·乔丹。玛丽亚坐在树下的地上,看着比拉尔。

“我们大家一起回营地吧,”罗伯特·乔丹说。“这样好些,有不少事情要做呢。”

比拉尔朝玛丽亚点点头,玛丽亚坐在那里没说什么,头转向别处。

比拉尔笑了笑,几乎使人毫无觉察地耸耸肩,说,“你们认得路吗?”

“我认得,”玛丽亚低着头说。

“我走了。我们要给你多准备些好吃的,英国人。”比拉尔说。她拔腿走进草地里石楠树丛,朝着通往营地的小河走去。

“等等,”罗伯特·乔丹喊她,“我们还是一起走好。”

玛丽亚坐在那里不说话。

比拉尔没转身。“一起走?”她说,“我们营地见。”

罗伯特·乔丹站在那里。

“她没事吗?”他问玛丽亚。“看来她刚才病了。”

“让她走,”玛丽亚说,仍然低着头。

“我看我应该跟她一起走。”

“让她走,”玛丽亚说。“让她走!”

"Don't you want to be alone with me?" Maria asked.

"Of course."

"I want to be with you, Robert." She smiled to him. "It's a wonderful day. What are you worrying about?"

"About you."

"Me? Why? Because I'm so happy."

"I wish you weren't here, Maria. I mean it. I'm thinking about what's going to happen to you after the bridge."

"Can't I go with you? El Sordo can steal enough horses for us. I know we can't escape without them, but he'll get us horses. I know it."

"You've got to understand, Maria. I'm in this war to the finish. I can't have anything serious in my life. A man doing what I'm doing never knows what's going to happen."

"Whatever happens to you will happen to me."

"Haven't you any people in the Republic?"

"No. My parents passed away. My father was the mayor of the village and an honorable man. My mother was an honorable woman and a good Catholic and they shot her with my father because of the politics of my father who was a Republican."

“难道你不想和我在一起吗？”玛丽亚问。

“当然愿意。”

“我想和你在一起，罗伯特。”她朝他笑笑，“今天天气多好。你在担心什么？”

“担心你。”

“我？为什么？因为我高兴。”

“我希望你不在这儿，玛丽亚。我是认真的。我在想炸桥后你怎么办？”

“我不能和你一起撤退吗?艾苏道能够偷足够的马匹。我知道没有马我们无法撤退，但他会给我们弄到马的。我知道。”

“你得明白，玛丽亚，我要参加战斗直到结束。我不能动真感情，像我这样干这一行的人不会知道会发生什么事。”

“在你身上发生的事也会在我身上发生的。”

“你在共和国没有其他的亲人吗？”

“是的。我父母去世了。我父亲是当地的村长，是个受人尊重的人。我母亲也是个受人尊重的人，是个虔诚的天主教徒，因为我父亲拥护共和国的政治观点，他们把我母亲和父亲一起枪杀了。”

Maria continued, "I saw both of them shot and my father said, 'Long life Republic', when they shot him standing against the wall of the slaughterhouse of our village. My mother standing against the same wall said, 'Long life my husband who was the Mayor of this village,' and I hoped they would shoot me too and I was going to say 'Long life Republic and my parents', but instead there was no shooting but instead the doing of the things. After the shooting at the slaughterhouse they took us, those relatives who had seen it but were not shot, back from the slaughterhouse up the steep hill into the main square of the town. Nearly all were weeping but some were numb with what they had seen and the tears had dried in them. I myself could not cry. I did not notice anything that passed for I could only see my father and my mother at the moment of the shooting and my mother saying, 'Long life my husband who was Mayor of this village,' and this was in my head like a scream that would not die but kept on and on. For my mother was not a Republican and she would not say, 'Long life Republic' but only long life my father who lay there, on his face, by her feet."

战地钟声 *For Whom the Bell Tolls*

玛丽亚继续说："我眼看着他们俩被枪杀，当时，父亲站在村子里屠宰场墙边，在被枪杀前说'共和国万岁'。我母亲也靠着那堵墙站着，她说'我丈夫，本村村长万岁'。我希望他们也把我杀了，我打算说'共和国万岁，父母万岁'，可他们没开枪，而是干出伤天害理的事来。在屠宰场上枪毙人之后，他们把我们这些看到枪毙而没有被枪杀的人从屠宰场带到一座陡峭的山上，来到镇上的大广场。几乎所有的人都在哭，除了有些看得发呆的人，他们眼泪已经干了。我也哭不出来。枪杀的时候我没注意其他情况，只看着临刑时的父母亲，而母亲说的'我丈夫，本村村长万岁'这句话在我头脑里像是一声尖叫，不断回响着，再不会消失。我母亲不是共和分子，没有说'共和国万岁'，而只是高喊我父亲万岁，他那时栽倒在她脚边，脸朝下躺着。"

"But what she had said, she had said very loud, like a shriek and then they shot and she fell and I tried to leave the line to go to her but we were all tied. The shooting was done by the civil guard and they were still there waiting to shoot more when the Falangists herded us away and up the hill leaving the civil guard leaning on their rifles and leaving all the bodies there against the wall. We were tied by the wrists in a long line of girls and women and they herded us up by the hill and through the streets to the square and in the square they stopped in front of the barbershop which was across the square from the city hall. Then the two men looked at us and one said, 'That is the daughter of the Mayor,' and the other said, 'Commence with her.' Then they cut the rope that was on each of my wrists, one saying to others of them, 'Tie up the line,' and these two took me by the arms and into the barbershop and lifted me up and put me in the barber's chair and held me there."

Robert covered Maria's mouth and stopped her, because she was too grievous to hold herself.

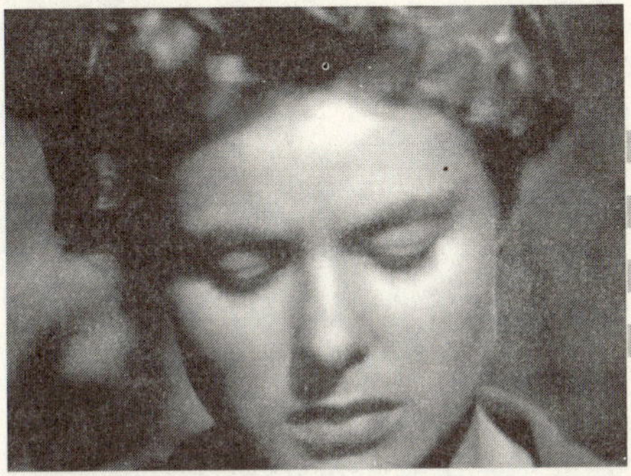

“可是她说话的声音很大，大得像尖叫，他们就开枪，她倒下了。我想离开队伍扑到她身边去，可是我们都被缚在一起。开枪的是民防军，他们还在那儿等着要枪毙更多的人，这时，长枪党党徒们把我们像赶牲口般轰上山去，把民防军留在后面，支着步枪，还撇下了墙脚下的那些尸体。我们这些姑娘和妇女的手腕被绑着，连成一长串，他们把我们赶上了山，穿过街道来到广场上。到了广场上，他们在镇公所对面的理发店门口停下了。那时有两个人瞧瞧我们，一个说，‘她是村长的女儿’，另一个说，‘拿她开头’，他们割断了我手腕上的绳子，有一个人对其他人说，‘把其他人用绳子捆好’。这两个人就抓住了我的胳膊，把我拖进理发店，把我提起来按在理发椅上不让动。”

玛丽亚已伤心得不能自持，罗伯特用手捂住了她的嘴，不让她再继续说下去。

"I love you, Maria," Robert Jordan said. "And no one has done anything to you. You, they cannot touch. No one has touched you, little rabbit."

"You believe that?"

"I know it."

"And you can love me?"

Now he was holding her face. "I can love you more."

"I will try to kiss you very well."

"Kiss me a little."

"I do not know how."

"Just kiss me."

She kissed him on the cheek.

"No."

"Where do the noses go? I always wondered where the noses would go."

"Look, turn your head," and then their mouths were tight together and she lay close pressed against him and her mouth opened a little gradually and then, suddenly, holding her against him, he was happier than he had ever been, lightly, lovingly, exultingly, innerly happy and unthinking and untired and unworried and only feeling a great delight.

She held herself tight to him and her lips looked for his and then found them and were against them and he felt her, fresh, new and smooth and young and lovely with the warm, scalding coolness. It was unbelievable to hold her tight too. After that, they began to climb down the hill to the camp.

"我爱你，玛丽亚，"罗伯特·乔丹说，"谁也没能把你怎么样。他们碰不了你。谁也没有碰过你，小兔子。"

"你相信是那样吗？"

"我相信。"

"那么你会爱我吗？"

这时他捧着她的脸，"我会更爱你。"

"我要好好吻你。"

"吻我一下吧。"

"我不会。"

"吻我就是了。"

她吻他的脸颊。

"不。"

"我们的鼻子怎么办？我老是想知道鼻子该往哪里搁。"

"瞧，把头偏一点，"他们俩的嘴唇就紧紧贴在一起了。她紧挨在他身上，她的嘴慢慢地张开了一点，他拥抱着她，突然感到从来没有过的喜悦，轻柔、亲切、欢心、内心的喜悦，无忧无虑，不再疲惫，不再焦虑，只感到一份莫大的喜悦。

她紧紧地抱着他，嘴唇在寻觅他的嘴唇，接着寻觅到了，就紧紧地吻着，他觉得她娇嫩、光滑、年轻、可爱、温暖发烫而又透着凉爽。他也紧紧拥抱着她，感到简直难以置信。之后，他们开始朝山下营地走去。

草坡的下端长着枞树林子，比拉尔就坐在那里，头伏在双臂上。从他们站着的地方望去，她好像一团深色的包袱，衬着棕色的树干，显得黑黝黝的。

"走吧，"罗伯特·乔丹说着就拔腿穿过齐膝高的石楠丛向她奔去。石楠长得密，他跑不快，才跑了一小段路，就放慢了脚步。他看得见妇人的头伏在交叉合抱的双臂上，在树干的衬托下显得又宽又黑。他走到她跟前，高声叫道："比拉尔！"

妇人抬起头来望着他。

"哦，"她说。"你们说完了？"

"你不舒服吗？"他俯身凑在她身边问道。

"我睡着了，"她说。

"比拉尔，"玛丽亚走上前来说，在她身旁跪下。"你身体好吗？没病吧？"

"好得很，"比拉尔说着，站了起来。她望着他们俩。"好啊，英国人，"她说，"你在耍男人的那套花招了？"

"你身体可好？"罗伯特·乔丹问，不接话茬。

"干吗不好？我刚才睡着了。"

At the lower edge of the meadow where the fir trees grew Pilar was sitting, her head on her arms. She looked like a dark bundle from where they stood; black against the brown of the tree trunk.

"Come on," Robert Jordan said and started to run toward her through the knee-high heather. It was heavy and hard to run in and when he had run a little way, he slowed and walked. He could see the woman's head was on her folded arms and she looked broad and black against the tree trunk. He came up to her and said, "Pilar!" sharply.

The woman raised her head and looked up at him.

"Oh," she said. "You have terminated already?"

"Are you ill?" he asked and bent down by her.

"I was asleep," she said.

"Pilar," Maria, who had come up, said and kneeled down by her. "How are you? Are you all right?"

"I'm magnificent," Pilar said and got up. She looked at the two of them. "Well, English," she said. "You have been doing manly tricks again?"

"You are all right?" Robert Jordan asked, ignoring the words.

"Why not? I slept."

Pilar laughed and laughed and stood looking at Robert Jordan laughing.

"Oh, English. English," she said laughing. "You are very comical. You must do much work now to regain your dignity."

The Hell with you, Robert Jordan thought. But he kept his mouth shut. While they had spoken the sun had clouded over and as he looked back up toward the mountains the sky was now heavy and gray.

"Sure," Pilar said to him, looking at the sky. "It will snow."

"Now? Almost in June?"

"Why not? These mountains do not know the names of the months. We are in the moon of May."

"It can't snow," he said. "It can't snow."

"Just the same, English," she said to him, "it will snow."

Robert Jordan looked up at the thick gray of the sky with the sun gone faintly yellow, and now as he watched gone completely and the gray becoming uniform so that it was soft and heavy; the gray now cutting off the tops of the mountains.

"Yes," he said. "I guess you are right."

By the time they reached the camp it was snowing and the flakes were dropping diagonally through the pines.

比拉尔笑了又笑,站在那里,望着罗伯特·乔丹笑。

“噢,英国人。英国人呀,”她笑着说,“你这人真滑稽。你再要装得一本正经可不容易了。”

见鬼去吧,罗伯特·乔丹想。但是他默不作声。他们刚才说话的时候,太阳被乌云遮住了。他回头仰望群山,只见天空阴霾密布。

“我确定,”比拉尔望着天空对他说,“要下雪了。”

“现在吗?快到6月还下雪?”

“为什么不能?山区是不分月份的。现在还是阴历5月份。”

“不可能下雪,”他说。“千万不要下雪。”

“不管怎么说,英国人,”她对他说,“会下的。”

罗伯特·乔丹仰望着灰蒙蒙的天空,只见太阳已经变得昏黄。他看见太阳完全消失,天际一片灰暗,显得模糊阴沉;乌云随即把山峰都遮住了。

“是啊,”他说,“看来你说对了。”

他们到达营地时,开始下雪了,雪片从松林间斜斜地飘落下来。

The flakes slanted through the trees, sparse at first and circling as they fell, and then, as the cold wind came driving down the mountain, they came whirling and thick and Robert Jordan stood in front of the cave in a rage and watched them.

"We will have much snow," Pablo said. His voice was thick and his eyes were red and bleary.

"Has the gypsy come in?" Robert Jordan asked him.

"No," Pablo said. "Neither him nor the old man."

"Will you come with me to the upper post on the road?"

"No," Pablo said. "I will take no part in this."

"I will find it myself."

"In this storm you might miss it," Pablo said. "I would not go now."

"It's just downhill to the road and then follows it up."

"You could find it. But your two sentries will be coming up now with the snow and you would miss them on the way."

"The old man is waiting for me."

"No. He will come in now with the snow."

Pablo looked at the snow that was blowing fast now past the mouth of the cave and said, "You do not like the snow, English?"

Robert Jordan swore and Pablo looked at him through his bleary eyes and laughed.

先是小雪斜穿过树林，盘旋而下，接着山上刮起寒风，大雪纷飞，这时罗伯特·乔丹站在山洞口，愤怒地望着风雪狂舞。

"我们要遇到大雪了，"巴勃罗说。他嗓音沙哑，眼睛发红，视线模糊。

"吉卜赛人回来了没有？"罗伯特·乔丹问他。

"没有，"巴勃罗说。"他和老头子都没回来。"

"你能陪我到公路上段的哨所去吗？"

"不，"巴勃罗说。"这事我不插手。"

"我自己去找。"

"这样大的风雪你会错过他们的，"巴勃罗说。"要是我，现在可不去。"

"只要下坡到了公路边，然后顺路走去就是了。"

"你能找到的。不过，下了雪，你的两个侦察员会在回来的路上，你可能会错过他们。"

"老头子正在等我。"

"不。现在下了雪，他会回来的。"

巴勃罗望着飞扫过洞口的风雪说："你不喜欢下雪吧，英国人？"

罗伯特·乔丹咒骂了一声，巴勃罗用迷糊的眼睛望着他笑。

Robert Jordan sat by the fire. "Let me take your shoes and dry them," Maria said. "I will hang them here in the smoke of the fire."

"Watch out you don't burn them," Robert Jordan told her. "I don't want to go around here barefoot." He took off his shoes and socks, standing in his bare feet on the dirt floor. "Hunt me a pair of socks, Maria."

"The Lord and Master," Pilar said and poked a piece of wood into the fire.

"You have to take advantage of what time there is," Robert Jordan told her.

"It is locked," Maria said.

"Here is the key," and he tossed it over.

"It does not fit this sack."

"It is the other sack. They are on top and at the side."

The girl found the pair of socks, closed the sack, locked it and brought them over with the key.

"Sit down and put them on and rub your feet well," she said. Robert Jordan grinned at her.

"You can not dry them with your hair?" he said for Pilar to hear.

"What a swine," she said. "First he is the Lord of the Manor. Now he is our ex-Lord Himself. Hit him with a chunk of wood, Maria."

罗伯特·乔丹坐在炉火边。"我把你的鞋拿去烤烤干，"玛丽亚说。"我把它挂在这炉灶的火边。"

"留心别把鞋烧了，"罗伯特·乔丹对她说。"我不想在这里光着脚走路。"他脱下鞋子和袜子，光着脚踏在泥地上。"给我找双袜子，玛丽亚。"

"夫君吩咐啦"，比拉尔说着，向火里添了块柴火。

"你得抓紧时间，"罗伯特·乔丹对她说。

"背包上着锁呢，"玛丽亚说。

"这是钥匙，"他把钥匙扔过去。

"不是这只包上的钥匙。"

"打开另一只包。袜子就在最上面的边上。"

姑娘找到了袜子，合上背包，上好锁，把袜子和钥匙一起拿过来。

"坐下来穿上袜子，把脚好好揉揉，"她说。罗伯特·乔丹咧嘴朝她笑笑。

"你不能用你的头发来把他们擦干吗？"他这话是故意说给比拉尔听的。

"真是个畜生，"她说，"开头当庄园主，现在是我们的前任上帝啦。拿块木柴揍他，玛丽亚。"

At the same time, Anselmo and Gypsy came back to the cave.

"Any movement?" He asked the gypsy.

"Six-hour watches, two men at a time on the big bridge," the gypsy said. "There are eight men and a corporal at the road mender's hut. Here is your chronometer."

"What about the sawmill post?" he asked to Anselmo.

"Not much Robert. It's all marked on the papers."

"And the road?" Robert Jordan asked.

"The same movement as always," the gypsy said. "Nothing out of the usual. Several motor cars."

The gypsy looked cold, his dark face was drawn with the cold and his hands were red. Standing in the mouth of the cave he took off his jacket and shook it.

"I stayed until they changed the watch," he said. "It was changed at noon and at six. That is a long watch. I am glad I am not in their army."

"Give a cup to Anselmo," Robert Jordan said to Maria. "It is he who is cold."

"How do you like it?" he asked Anselmo.

The old man was sitting by the fire with a smile on his face, his big hands holding the cup. He shook his head.

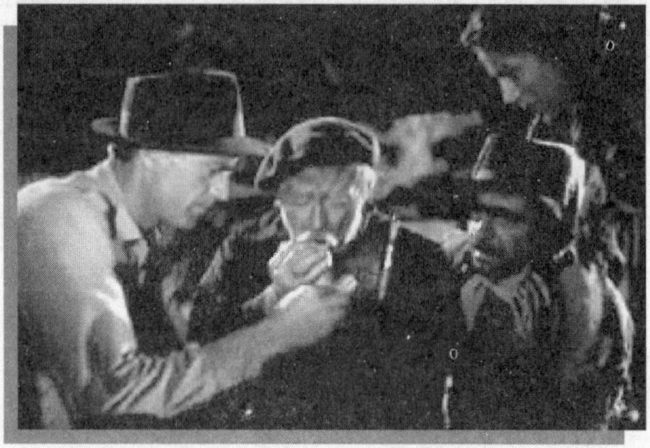

正在这时，安塞尔莫和吉卜赛人回到了山洞。

"情况怎么样？"他问吉卜赛人。

"大桥上每岗两个人，六小时换一次，"吉卜赛人说。"养路工小屋那边有八个人和一个班长。这是你的手表。"

"锯木厂边的哨所的情况怎么样？"他问安塞尔莫。

"没有特别的情况。都记下来了。"

"公路上呢？"罗伯特·乔丹问。

"还那样，"吉卜赛人说。"没什么特别情况。有几辆汽车。"

吉卜赛人浑身透出寒意，黑黑的脸冻得皮肤都绷紧了，两手发红。他站在洞口，脱下外衣把雪抖掉。

"我一直待到他们换岗的时候，"他说。"换岗的时间是中午十二点和下午六点。这一岗可不短。幸亏我不在他们部队里当兵。"

"给安塞尔莫来一杯，"罗伯特·乔丹对玛丽亚说。"挨冻的是他。"

"你觉得酒怎么样？"他问安塞尔莫。

老人坐在炉边，脸上堆着笑，两只大手捧着杯子，直摇头。

战地钟声 For Whom the Bell Tolls

"No?" Robert Jordan asked him.

"The child put water in it," Anselmo said.

"Exactly as Robert takes it," Maria said. "Are you something special?"

"No," Anselmo told her. "Nothing special at all. But I like to feel it burn as it goes down."

"Give me that," Robert Jordan told the girl, "and pour him some of that which burns."

He tipped the contents of the cup into his own and handed it back empty to the girl, who poured carefully into it from the bottle.

"Ah," Anselmo took the cup, put his head back and let it run down his throat. He looked at Maria standing holding the bottle and winked at her, tears coming from both eyes. "That," he said. "That." Then he licked his lips. "That is what kills the worm that haunts us."

"Robert," Maria said and came over to him, still holding the bottle. "Are you ready to eat?"

"Is it ready?"

"It is ready when you wish it."

"Have the others eaten?"

"All except you, Anselmo and the gypsy."

"Let us eat then," he told her.

"不喜欢？"罗伯特·乔丹问他。

"小丫头在里头兑了水，"安塞尔莫说。

"罗伯特就是这样喝的嘛，"玛丽亚说。"你就跟人家不一样？"

"不，"安塞尔莫对她说。"没什么不一样。我只是喜欢酒下肚时火辣辣的劲头。"

"把杯子给我，"罗伯特·乔丹对姑娘说，"给他来点火辣辣的玩意儿。"

他把杯里的酒倒在自己的杯子里，把空杯给姑娘，她小心翼翼地把酒瓶里的酒倒在杯里。

"啊，"安塞尔莫拿起酒杯，一仰脖灌进喉咙。他望望拿着酒瓶站在那儿的玛丽亚，对她眨眨眼睛，眼睛里涌出泪水。"就是这个劲，"他说，"就是这个劲。"然后他舔舔嘴唇。"这才能把我们肚子里作怪的蛔虫杀死。"

"罗伯特，"玛丽亚走到他身边说，仍然拿着酒瓶。"吃饭吗？"

"饭做好了吗？"

"做好了，你什么时候吃都行。"

"别人吃过了吗？"

"只有你、安塞尔莫和吉卜赛人还没吃。"

"让我们吃吧。"他对她说。

"And this snow," Robert Jordan said. "You think there will be much?"

"Much," Pablo said contentedly. Then called to Pilar, "You don't like it, woman, either? Now that you command you do not like this snow?"

"If it snows it snows," Pilar said, over her shoulder.

"Drink some wine, English," Pablo said. "I have been drinking all day waiting for the snow."

"Give me a cup," Robert Jordan said.

"To the snow," Pablo said and touched cups with him. Robert Jordan looked him in the eyes and clinked his cup. You bleary-eyed murderous sod, he thought. I'd like to clink this cup against your teeth. Take it easy, he told himself, take it easy.

"It is very beautiful the snow," Pablo said. "You won't want to sleep outside with the snow falling."

So that's on your mind too is it? Robert Jordan thought. You've a lot of troubles, haven't you, Pablo?

"No?" he said, politely.

"No. Very cold," Pablo said. "Very wet."

"Then I should sleep in here?" he asked politely.

"Yes."

"Thanks," Robert Jordan said. "I'll be sleeping outside."

"这场雪，"罗伯特·乔丹说，"你觉得会下大吗？"

"会的，"巴勃罗满意地说。然后他对比拉尔喊道，"你也不喜欢下雪吧，老婆?现在你当家，你不喜欢这场雪吧？"

"要下就下吧，"比拉尔转过头来说。

"喝点酒吧，英国人，"巴勃罗说，"我喝了一整天就等着下雪。"

"给我来一杯，"罗伯特·乔丹说。

"为雪干杯，"巴勃罗说，和他碰杯。罗伯特·乔丹盯着他的眼睛，"叮"的一声碰了杯。他想，你这个醉眼蒙眬的挨刀的家伙，我恨不得用这杯子把你的牙齿磕得叮叮响。别急，他对自己说，别急。

"雪真美，"巴勃罗说，"天在下雪，你不想睡在外面了吧。"

罗伯特·乔丹想，原来你也在想这个问题。巴勃罗，你操心的事也不少啊，对不对?

"不睡在外面？"他客气地说。

"不睡在外面。很冷，"巴勃罗说，"很潮湿。"

"那么我该睡在这里啦？"他客气地问。

"是啊。"

"谢谢，"罗伯特·乔丹说，"我还是睡在外面吧。"

战地钟声 For Whom the Bell Tolls

"Let me have a cup of wine, please," Robert Jordan said in Spanish. Then, "Lots of snow? Eh?" he said to Pablo.

The drunken man looked up at him and grinned. He nodded his head and grinned again.

"No offensive. No planes. No bridge. Just snow," Pablo said.

"You expect it to last a long time?" Robert Jordan sat down by him. "You think we're going to snow in all summer, Pablo, old boy?"

"All summer, no," Pablo said. "Tonight and tomorrow, yes."

"What makes you think so?"

"There are two kinds of storms," Pablo said, heavily and judiciously. "One comes from the Pyrenees. With this one there is great cold. It is too late for this one."

"Good," Robert Jordan said. "That's something."

"This storm comes from the Cantabrico," Pablo said. "It comes from the sea. With the wind in this direction there will be a great storm and much snow."

"Where did you learn all this, old timer?" Robert Jordan asked.

"I was a cart driver for many years," Pablo said. Robert Jordan didn't care him any more.

"请给我来一杯酒，"罗伯特·乔丹用西班牙语说。接着对巴勃罗说："雪下得不小，呃？"

醉汉抬起头来看他，露齿笑笑。他点点头，也呲着牙笑笑。

"进攻完蛋啦。飞机不来啦。桥炸不成啦。只有雪啦，"巴勃罗说。

"你盼望下很久？"罗伯特·乔丹在他旁边坐下。"巴勃罗，你以为整个夏天我们都会被雪困住吗，老兄？"

"整个夏天，不会，"巴勃罗说，"可今天晚上和明天，是这样的。"

"你凭什么这样认为？"

"暴风雪有两种，"巴勃罗一本正经而富有见识地说，"一种是从比利牛斯山刮来的。来了这种暴风雪，天就会极冷。现在已过了那个时候，所以不是这种。"

"不错，"罗伯特·乔丹说，"有道理。"

"现在这场风雪是从坎塔布里科刮来的，"巴勃罗说，"是从海上来的。风朝这个方向刮，会有大的暴风雪。"

"你是从哪里学来的这些，老资格？"罗伯特·乔丹问。

"我赶过好多年牲口，"巴勃罗说。罗伯特·乔丹不再理他。

"Maria," Pablo said from the table where he was sitting.

"What?" the girl asked.

"Wipe the table clean, Maria," Pablo said and grinned at Robert Jordan.

"Wipe your own spilling," Pilar said to him. "Wipe first your chin and your shirt and then the table."

"Maria," Pablo called.

"Pay no heed to him. He is drunk," Pilar said.

"Maria," Pablo called. "It is still snowing and the snow is beautiful."

"Want to make snowballs?" he said to Pablo. "Want to have a snowball fight?"

"What?" Pablo asked. "What do you propose?"

"Nothing," Robert Jordan said. "Got your saddles covered up good?"

"Yes."

Then in English Robert Jordan said, "Going to grain those horses or peg them out and let them dig for it?"

"What?"

"Nothing."

"Why do you speak in English?" Pablo asked.

"I don't know," Robert Jordan said. "When I get very tired sometimes I speak English. Or when I get very disgusted. Or baffled, say. When I get highly baffled I just talk English to hear the sound of it."

"玛丽亚，"坐在桌边的巴勃罗说。

"什么事？"姑娘问。

"把桌子擦干净，玛丽亚，"巴勃罗说，对罗伯特·乔丹露齿笑笑。

"把你自己泼出的酒抹掉吧。"比拉尔对他说。"先抹你自己的下巴和你的衬衫，再抹桌子。"

"玛丽亚，"巴勃罗喊着。

"别理他。他醉了，"比拉尔说。

"玛丽亚，"巴勃罗喊着，"雪还在下，真美呀。"

"想做雪球吗？"他对巴勃罗说，"想玩雪战吗？"

"什么？"巴勃罗问，"你打算干什么？"

"没什么，"罗伯特·乔丹说，"你的马鞍都盖好了？"

"对。"

罗伯特·乔丹然后用英语说，"打算去喂马吗？还是把它们拴在外面让它们自己扒开雪啃草吃？"

"你说什么？"

"没什么。"

"你干吗说英国话？"巴勃罗问。

"不知道，"罗伯特·乔丹说，"我非常疲乏的时候往往讲英语。或者在十分厌烦的时候，要不，在举棋不定的时候，我都会说英语。在我举棋不定时，说英语就是为了听听它的声音。"

战地钟声 *For Whom the Bell Tolls*

“听着，英国人，”奥古斯丁改变了话题。“你怎么到西班牙来的？别理睬巴勃罗。他喝多了。”

“我第一次来是在十二年前，为了研究这个国家和它的语言。”罗伯特·乔丹说，“我在大学里教授西班牙语。”

“你看着可不像教授啊，”普里米蒂伏说。

“他没有胡子，”巴勃罗说。“看他，他没长胡子。”

“你真的是个教授？”

“是讲师。”

“反正你教课？”

“是的。”

“可是为什么教西班牙语呢？”安德烈斯问。“你既然是英国人，教英语不是更容易些？”

“他的西班牙语说得跟我们一样，”安塞尔莫说。“为什么不教西班牙语？”

“对。不过外国人教西班牙语可多少有点自不量力，”费尔南多说。“我可没有反对你的意思，堂·罗伯特（只有西班牙贵族才被称为‘堂’，以示尊敬）。”

“他是个冒牌教授，”巴勃罗自得其乐地说，“他没长胡子。”

“你的英语肯定更好些，”费尔南多说。“教英语不是更好、更容易、更清楚吗？”

“Listen, English,” Agustín changed the subject. “How did you happen to come to Spain? Pay no attention to Pablo. He is drunk.”

“I came first twelve years ago to study the country and the language,” Robert Jordan said. “I teach Spanish in a university.”

“You look very little like a professor,” Primitivo said.

“He has no beard,” Pablo said. “Look at him. He has no beard.”

“Are you truly a professor?”

“An instructor.”

“But you teach?”

“Yes.”

“But why Spanish?” Andrés asked. “Would it not be easier to teach English since you are English?”

“He speaks Spanish as we do,” Anselmo said. “Why should he not teach Spanish?”

“Yes. But it is, in a way, presumptuous for a foreigner to teach Spanish,” Fernando said. “I mean nothing against you, Don Robert. (Only Spanish nobles can be called with ‘Don’ for respect.)”

“He's a false professor,” Pablo said, very pleased with himself. “He hasn't got a beard.”

“Surely you know English better,” Fernando said. “Would it not be better and easier and clearer to teach English?”

"He doesn't teach it to Spaniards—" Pilar started to intervene.

"I should hope not," Fernando said.

"Let me finish, you mule," Pilar said to him. "He teaches Spanish to Americans. North Americans."

"Can they not speak Spanish?" Fernando asked. "South Americans can."

"Mule," Pilar said. "He teaches Spanish to North Americans who speak English."

"Still and all I think it would be easier for him to teach English if that is what he speaks," Fernando said.

"Can't you hear he speaks Spanish?" Pilar shook her head hopelessly at Robert Jordan.

"Yes. But with an accent."

"Of where?" Robert Jordan asked.

"Of Estremadura," Fernando said primly.

"Oh my mother," Pilar said. "What a people!"

"It is possible," Robert Jordan said. "I have come here from there."

"As he well knows," Pilar said. She turned to Fernando. "Have you had enough to eat?"

"I could eat more if there is a sufficient quantity," Fernando told her. "And do not think that I wish to say anything against you, Don Robert—"

"他不是教西班牙人。"比拉尔开始插嘴了。

"但愿如此,"费尔南多说。

"让我把话说完,你这个杂种,"比拉尔对他说。"他教美洲人西班牙语。北美人。"

"他们不会讲西班牙语吗?"费尔南多问。"南美人是会讲的。"

"杂种,"比拉尔说。"他教说英语的北美人西班牙语。"

"不管怎么样,他既然讲英语,我看还是教英文容易些,"费尔南多说。

"难道你没听到他说的西班牙语吗?"比拉尔无可奈何地对罗伯特·乔丹摇摇头。

"不错。不过带点口音。"

"哪里的口音?"罗伯特·乔丹问。

"埃斯特雷马杜拉的,"费尔南多一本正经地说。

"我的妈呀,"比拉尔说,"这种人哪!"

"这很可能的,"罗伯特·乔丹说。"我是从那里来的。"

"他自己很清楚,"比拉尔说。她扭头对费尔南多说,"你吃够了吗?"

"东西多的话,我还能吃,"费尔南多对她说。"别以为我的话是反对你,堂·罗伯特……"

战地钟声 *For Whom the Bell Tolls*

"Don Robert has no beard," Pablo said. "He is a false professor."

"What do you mean, I have no beard?" Robert Jordan said. "What's this?" He stroked his chin and his cheeks where the three-day growth made blond stubble.

"Not a beard," Pablo said. He shook his head. "That's not a beard." He was almost jovial now. "He's a false professor."

"If it does not seem like a lunatic asylum here," Agustín said.

"You should drink," Pablo said to him. "To me everything appears normal. Except the lack of beard of Don Robert."

Maria ran her hand over Robert Jordan's cheek. "He has a beard," she said to Pablo.

"You should know," Pablo said.

Robert Jordan looked at him. "You," he said to Pablo. "Do you think this snow will last?"

"What do you think?"

"I asked you."

"Ask another," Pablo told him. "I am not your service of information. You have a paper from your service of information. Ask the woman. She commands."

"I asked you."

"You and the woman and the girl go to hell."

"He is drunk," Primitivo said. "Pay him no heed, English."

"堂·罗伯特没长胡子，"巴勃罗说。"他是冒牌教授。"

"你说我没胡子是什么意思？"罗伯特·乔丹说。"这是什么？"他摸摸下巴和脸颊。三天没刮脸，长了一片黄色的短胡须。

"不是胡子，"巴勃罗说。他摇摇头。"那不算胡子。"他这时简直快活极了。"他是个冒牌教授。"

"这里简直像个疯人院，"奥古斯丁说。

"你该喝酒，"巴勃罗对他说。"依我看，什么都正常，除了堂·罗伯特没长胡子。"

玛丽亚伸手摸摸罗伯特·乔丹的脸颊。"他有胡子，"她对巴勃罗说。

"你当然知道，"巴勃罗说。

罗伯特·乔丹望着他。"你，"他对巴勃罗说，"你看这场雪会一直下吗？"

"你说呢？"

"我问你。"

"问别人吧，"巴勃罗对他说，"我不是你的情报部。你有情报部的证明文件。问那女人。她做主。"

"我问你。"

"你和这女人和这丫头，全见鬼去吧。"

"他喝醉了，"普里米蒂伏说。"别理他，英国人。"

"I don't believe you can drink," Robert Jordan said to Pablo. "Nor that you're drunk."

"I am drunk," Pablo said with dignity. "To drink is nothing. It is to be drunk that is important."

"I doubt it," Robert Jordan told him. "Cowardly, yes."

Pablo grinned at him and put one finger up and wiped it across his throat. He shook his head that turned only a little each way on his thick, short neck.

"No, English," he said. "Do not provoke me." He looked at Pilar and said to her, "It is not thus that you get rid of me."

"Shameless," Robert Jordan said to him, committed now in his own mind to the action. "Coward."

"It is very possible," Pablo said. "But I am not to be provoked. Take something to drink, English, and signal to the woman it was not successful."

"Shut your mouth," Robert Jordan said. "I provoke you for myself."

"It is not worth the trouble," Pablo told him. "I do not provoke."

He's rare, all right, Robert Jordan thought, and smart, and very complicated.

"我看你不会喝酒,"罗伯特·乔丹对巴勃罗说,"我看你也没有醉。"

"我醉了,"巴勃罗神气地说。"喝酒没什么。醉了才有意思。"

"我怀疑,"罗伯特·乔丹对他说,"胆小鬼,倒是真的。"

巴勃罗朝他露齿笑笑,伸出一个手指在咽喉上一划。他摇摇头,可是脑袋在又粗又短的脖子上只微微晃动了一下。

"不行,英国人,"他说。"别惹我发火。"他望着比拉尔,对她说,"你想这样把我干掉可不行。"

"无耻之徒,"罗伯特·乔丹对他说,心里想动手。"胆小鬼。"

"很可能,"巴勃罗说。"可我是不会被激怒的。喝点儿什么吧,英国人,给妇人打个手势,告诉她这套行不通。"

"闭嘴,"罗伯特·乔丹说。"是我要向你寻衅滋事。"

"不值得费心,"巴勃罗对他说。"我是不会恼火的。"

罗伯特·乔丹想,是啊,他这个人很奇怪,很机灵,很不简单。

战地钟声 *For Whom the Bell Tolls*

“堂·罗伯特，”巴勃罗狠狠地说。

“堂·巴勃罗，”罗伯特·乔丹说。

“你根本不是教授，”巴勃罗说，“你没长胡子。再说，要把我干掉，只能靠暗杀，但要这样干，你就不是男人。”

“干杯，巴勃罗。”罗伯特·乔丹说着，举起杯子，喝了一口。“我正从你那里学了不少东西。”

“我在教教授啦，” 巴勃罗点点头，“来吧，堂·罗伯特，我们做个朋友吧。”

“我们已经是朋友了，”罗伯特·乔丹说。

“现在我们可要做好朋友了。”

“我们已经是好朋友了。”

“我要离开这里了，”奥古斯丁说。“一点不错，人家说我们活一辈子至少要听到一吨假话，刚才这一会儿我每个耳朵里就灌进了二十五磅。”

“你怎么啦，黑鬼？”巴勃罗对他说，“你不喜欢看到堂·罗伯特跟我做朋友？”

“你嘴里可别不干不净地叫我黑鬼。”奥古斯丁走到他面前站住了，双手垂在身旁。

“人家就是这样叫你的嘛。”巴勃罗说。

“不要你叫。”

“Don Robert,” Pablo said heavily.

“Don Pablo,” Robert Jordan said.

“You're no professor,” Pablo said, “because you haven't got a beard. And also to do away with me you have to assassinate me and, for this, you are not a man.”

“Cheers, Pablo,” Robert Jordan said and raised the cup up and drank from it. “I am learning much from you.”

“I am teaching the professor,” Pablo nodded his head. “Come on, Don Robert, we will be friends.”

“We are friends already,” Robert Jordan said.

“But now we will be good friends.”

“We are good friends already.”

“I'm going to get out of here,” Agustín said. “Truly, it is said that we must eat a ton of it in this life but I have twenty-five pounds of it stuck in each of my ears this minute.”

“What is the matter, negro?” Pablo said to him. “Do you not like to see friendship between Don Robert and me?”

“Watch your mouth about calling me negro.” Agustín went over to him and stood in front of Pablo holding his hands low.

“So you are called,” Pablo said.

“Not by you.”

Agustín hit Pablo hard across the mouth with his left hand, bringing it forward in a slapping, backhand sweep. Pablo sat there. The corners of his mouth were wine-stained and his expression did not change, but Robert Jordan watched his eyes narrow, as a cat's pupils close to vertical slits in a strong light.

"Nor this," Pablo said. "Do not count on this, woman." He turned his head toward Pilar. "I am not provoked."

Agustín hit him again. This time he hit him on the mouth with his closed fist. Robert Jordan was holding his pistol in his hand under the table.

The round-headed man sat staring at Agustín from his flat little eyes. The pupils were even smaller now. He licked his lips then, put up an arm and wiped his mouth with the back of his hand, looked down and saw the blood on his hand. He ran his tongue over his lips, then spat.

"Nor that," he said. "I am not a fool. I do not provoke."

Agustín hit him again hard in the mouth and Pablo laughed at him, showing the yellow, bad, broken teeth in the reddened line of his mouth.

奥古斯丁举起左手,反手一挥,狠狠地抽了巴勃罗一耳光。巴勃罗坐在那里,嘴角上沾着酒,不动声色,但罗伯特·乔丹注意到,他眯起的双眼就像猫的瞳孔在强光照射下收缩成一条垂直的狭缝。

"这样也不行,"巴勃罗说。"别指望这样做啦,太太。"他转过头来朝着比拉尔。"我不会被激怒的。"

奥古斯丁又揍了他一下。他这次紧握了拳头,掴在他嘴上。罗伯特·乔丹在桌子下的手握住手枪。

这个圆脑袋的汉子坐着,没神的小眼睛瞪着奥古斯丁。这时,瞳孔竟变得更小了。他舔舔嘴唇,举起一条手臂,用手背擦擦嘴,低头看到了手上的血。他用舌头舔着嘴唇,接着唾了一口血水。

"还是不行,"他说,"我不是傻瓜。我不会生气。"

奥古斯丁又狠狠地给他嘴上一拳。巴勃罗冲着他哈哈大笑,有血红的一条线的嘴里露出一口黄色的坏牙。

"Leave it alone," Pablo said and reached with a cup to scoop some wine from the bowl.

"Coward," Agustín said.

"Nor words either," Pablo said and made a swishing noise rinsing the wine in his mouth. He spat on the floor. "I am far past words."

Agustín stood there looking down at him and cursed him, speaking slowly, clearly, bitterly and contemptuously and cursing as steadily as though he were dumping manure on a field, lifting it with a dung fork out of a wagon.

"Nor of those," Pablo said. "Leave it, Agustín. And do not hit me more. You will injure your hands."

Agustín turned from him and went to the door.

"Do not go out," Pablo said. "It is snowing outside. Make yourself comfortable in here."

"And you! You!" Agustín turned from the door and spoke to him, putting all his contempt in the single, "You".

"Yes, me," said Pablo. "I will be alive when you are dead."

Agustín walked over to him and, striking quickly with the side of his hand, knocked the cup out of his hand.

"I will be going out to see the horses," Pablo said.

"别管它！"巴勃罗说，用杯子从缸里舀了些酒。

"胆小鬼，"奥古斯丁说。

"骂我也是白搭，"巴勃罗说，用酒漱漱口，发出咕噜的声音，然后吐在地上。"骂我根本不起作用。"

奥古斯丁站在那里，低头望着他，慢吞吞地，一字一句地，刻薄而轻蔑地骂他，一迭连声地骂着，好像用粪叉从粪车里一下下地挑起粪肥，给地里施肥似的。

"再骂也是没用，"巴勃罗说，"算了，奥古斯丁。别再揍我啦。你会伤了自己的手的。"

奥古斯丁从他身旁走开，朝洞口走去。

"别出去，"巴勃罗说。"外面在下雪。你在里面待着舒服。"

"你！你！"奥古斯丁在门口转身对他说，把所有的轻蔑都放在"你"这个字上。

"对，就是我，"巴勃罗说。"等你完蛋的时候，我一定还活着。"

奥古斯丁走到他前面，用手的侧面极快地打掉了他手中的杯子。

"我要出去看看马了，"巴勃罗说。

"I go," said Pablo. "But I will be back shortly." He lifted the blanket over the door of the cave and stepped out. Then from the door he called, "It's still falling, English."

"Now, English," Pilar said, "you have seen how he is."

"What will he do?" Robert Jordan asked.

"Anything," the woman looked down at the table. "Anything. He is capable of doing anything."

"Where is the automatic rifle?" Robert Jordan asked.

"There in the corner wrapped in the blanket," Primitivo said. "Do you want it?"

"Later," Robert Jordan said. "I wished to know where it is."

"It is there," Primitivo said. "I brought it in and I have wrapped it in my blanket to keep the action dry. The pans are in that sack."

"He would not do that," Pilar said. "He would not do anything with the machine gun."

"I thought you said he would do anything."

"He might," she said. "But he has no practice with the machine gun. He could toss in a bomb. That is more his style."

"我走，"巴勃罗说，"不过我马上就会回来。"他撩起洞口的毯子，走到外面。接着他在洞外嚷嚷，"英国人，还在下雪。"

"现在，英国人，"比拉尔说，"你看到他的真实嘴脸了。"

"他会怎么干？"罗伯特·乔丹问。

"什么都干得出来，"妇人低头望着桌子。"什么都干得出来。他什么都能干得出来。"

"自动步枪在哪儿？"罗伯特·乔丹问。

"在角落那儿，包在毯子里，"普里米蒂伏说。"你用吗？"

"一会用，"罗伯特·乔丹说。"我想知道它放在哪儿。"

"就在那里，"普里米蒂伏说。"我把它拿进来，裹在我的毯子里，为保持干燥。弹药盘放在那只包里。"

"他不会动它的，"比拉尔说。"他不会在这支机关枪上做什么手脚。"

"我记得你刚才还说他这人什么都干得出来。"

"他可能会，"她说。"不过他没有使过机关枪。他会扔个炸弹进来。这才更符合他的风格。"

"It is an idiocy and a weakness not to have killed him," the gypsy said. He had taken no part in any of the talk all evening. "Last night Robert should have killed him."

"Kill him," Pilar said. Her big face was dark and tired looking. "I am for it now."

"I was against it," Agustín said. He stood in front of the fire, his long arms hanging by his sides, his cheeks, stubble-shadowed below the cheekbones, hollow in the firelight. "Now I am for it," he said. "He is poisonous now and he would like to see us all destroyed."

"Let all speak," Pilar said and her voice was tired. "You, Andrés?"

"Kill him," the brother with the dark hair growing far down in the point on his forehead said and nodded his head.

"Eladio?"

"Equally," the other brother said. "To me he seems to constitute a great danger. And he serves for nothing."

"Primitivo?"

"Equally."

"Fernando?"

"Could we not hold him as a prisoner?" Fernando asked.

"不把他干掉，就是愚蠢、胆小，"吉卜赛人说。在整个晚上这场谈话中，他还没开过口。"罗伯特昨晚就该把他杀掉。"

"杀了他吧，"比拉尔说。她那张大脸露出了阴郁而疲惫的神色。"我现在赞成这个做法了。"

"我本来是反对的，"奥古斯丁说。他站在炉灶前，两条长手臂垂在身体两侧，颧骨下满是胡子茬的两颊，在炉火映照下显得凹陷。"我现在赞成了，"他说。"他这个人现在很恶毒，他想毁了我们大家。"

"大家说说吧，"比拉尔说，但她的声音有气无力。"安得烈斯，你说呢？"

"杀掉他，"俩兄弟中那个大脑门说，还点点头。

"埃拉迪奥？"

"同样，"另一个兄弟说。"依我看，他是个大祸根，而且根本不中用了。"

"普里米蒂伏？"

"同样。"

"费尔南多？"

"我们不能把他关起来吗？"费尔南多问。

"Who would look after a prisoner?" Primitivo said. "It would take two men to look after a prisoner and what would we do with him in the end?"

"We could sell him to the fascists," the gypsy said.

"None of that," Agustín said. "None of that filthiness."

"It was only an idea," Rafael, the gypsy, said. "It seems to me that the fascist would be happy to have him."

"Leave it alone," Agustín said. "That is filthy."

"No filthier than Pablo," the gypsy justified himself.

"One filthiness does not justify another," Agustín said. "Well, that is all. Except for the old man and the English."

"They are not in it," Pilar said. "He has not been their leader."

"One moment," Fernando said. "I have not finished."

"Go ahead," Pilar said. "Talk until he comes back. Talk until he rolls a hand grenade under that blanket and blows this all up. Dynamite and all."

"I do not think so," Agustín said. "Because that would blow the wine up too and he will be back in a little while to the wine."

"谁来看守囚徒？"普里米蒂伏说。"一个囚徒得两个人看。再说，最后我们怎么处置他？"

"我们可以把他出卖给法西斯分子，"吉卜赛人说。

"这种事不能干，"奥古斯丁说。"这种卑鄙勾当不能干。"

"我不过是出个主意罢了，"吉卜赛人拉斐尔说。"依我看哪，法西斯分子会高兴把他弄到手的。"

"算了吧，"奥古斯丁说。"那太卑鄙了。"

"不会比巴勃罗更卑鄙吧，"吉卜赛人为自己辩护道。

"不能用卑鄙来对付卑鄙，"奥古斯丁说。"好；大家都

表态了。还有老头子和英国人没表态。"

"他们跟这事没关系，"比拉尔说。"他没有当过他们的头儿。"

"等一下，"费尔南多说。"我的话还没说完。"

"说啊，"比拉尔说。"一直说到他回来。说到他从毯子下面扔个手榴弹进来把我们全炸死，把炸药什么的全炸掉。"

"我不这样认为，"奥古斯丁说。"这一来把酒也要炸掉啦，可等一会儿他就要来喝酒的。"

“干吗不把他交给艾苏道，让艾苏道拿他去跟法西斯分子做交易？”拉斐尔提议说。“可以弄瞎他的眼睛，那就容易对付了。”

“闭嘴，”比拉尔说。“你一开口，我就觉得你这人实在也该杀。”

“法西斯分子反正不肯为了他给一分钱，”普里米蒂伏说。“这种事别人试过，他们不给钱，倒会把你也毙掉。”

“我认为，弄瞎了他的眼睛，倒能拿他做成交易，”拉斐尔说。

“闭嘴，”比拉尔说。“要是再说弄瞎眼睛，你可以跟他一起去。”

“我的话还没让说完哪，”费尔南多插嘴说。

“说完，”比拉尔对他说。“说下去。把话说完。”

“既然把巴勃罗关起来行不通，”费尔南多接着说，“而通过任何形式的谈判把他抛给敌人的做法又使人反感……”

“说完呀，”比拉尔说。“看在上帝的面上，快说完呀。”

“我认为，”费尔南多不慌不忙地说下去，“为了保证计划中的行动取得最大成功，也许最好是除掉他。”

“Why not turn him over to El Sordo and let El Sordo sell him to the fascists?” Rafael suggested. “You could blind him and he would be easy to handle.”

“Shut up,” Pilar said. “I feel something very justified against you too when you talk.”

“The fascists would pay nothing for him anyway,” Primitivo said. “Such things have been tried by others and they pay nothing. They will shoot you too.”

“I believe that blinded he could be sold for something,” Rafael said.

“Shut up,” Pilar said. “Speak of blinding again and you can go with the other.”

“I have not been allowed to finish,” Fernando interrupted.

“Finish,” Pilar told him. “Go on. Finish.”

“Since it is impractical to hold Pablo as a prisoner,” Fernando commenced, “and since it is repugnant to offer him—”

“Finish,” Pilar said. “For the love of God, finish.”

“—in any class of negotiation,” Fernando proceeded calmly, “I am agreed that it is perhaps best that he should be eliminated in order that the operations projected should be insured of the maximum possibility of success.”

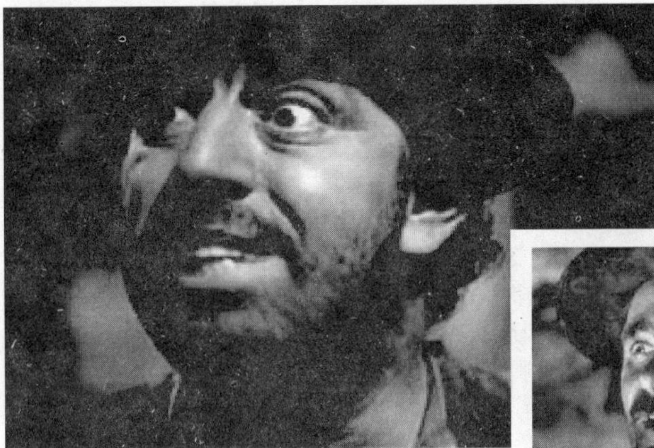

比拉尔望着费尔南多，摇摇头，咬着嘴唇，一声不吭。大家准备杀掉巴勃罗，比拉尔伤感地说："在革命初期，巴勃罗可不是胆小鬼。"

"革命开始的时候，你们在哪里？"罗伯特·乔丹问。

"在家乡。"

"阿维拉？"

"什么阿维拉！"

"巴勃罗说他是阿维拉人。"

"他吹牛。他想冒充自己是大城市里的人。他老家是……"她讲出了小镇的名字。

"当时出了什么事？"

Pilar looked at Fernando, shook her head, bit her lips and said nothing. They prepared to kill Pablo and Pilar said sadly, "Pablo wasn't a coward at the beginning of the revolution."

"Where were you at the start of the movement?" Robert Jordan asked.

"In my town."

"Avila?"

"What, Avila!"

"Pablo said he was from Avila."

"He lies. He wanted to take a big city for his town. It was this town," and she named a town.

"And what happened?"

"Much," the woman said. "Much. And all of it ugly. Even that which was glorious."

"Tell me about it," Robert Jordan said.

"It is brutal," the woman said. "I do not like to tell it before the girl."

"Tell it," said Robert Jordan. "And if it is not for her, that she should not listen."

"I can hear it," Maria said. She put her hand on Robert Jordan's. "There is nothing that I cannot hear."

"It isn't whether you can hear it," Pilar said. "It is whether I should tell it to you and make you have bad dreams."

"好多事，"妇人说，"好多事。可全都是丑陋不堪的。哪怕本来是光荣的事。"

"跟我讲讲吧，"罗伯特·乔丹说。

"太残忍啦，"妇人说。"我不想当着这姑娘的面讲。"

"讲吧，"罗伯特·乔丹说。"她不该听的，不听就是了。"

"我听了没事，"玛丽亚说。她把手搁在罗伯特·乔丹手上。"没有什么我不能听的。"

"问题不在你听得听不得，"比拉尔说。"而是我该不该对你讲，让你做噩梦。"

"I will not get bad dreams from a story," Maria told her. "You think after all that has happened with us I should get bad dreams from a story?"

"Maybe it will give the English bad dreams."

"Try it and see."

"No, English, I am not joking. Did you see the start of the movement in any small town?"

"No," Robert Jordan said.

"Then you have seen nothing. You have seen the ruin that now is Pablo, but you should have seen Pablo on that day."

"Tell it."

"No. I do not want to."

"Tell it."

"All right, then. I will tell it truly as it was. But you, beautiful girl, if it reaches a point that it molests you, tell me."

"I will not listen to it if it molests me," Maria told her. "It cannot be worse than many things."

"I believe it can," the woman said.

He reached out and found Maria's hand and held it in his, while she opened her hand and laid it flat on top of his as they listened.

"我不会听了个故事就做噩梦,"玛丽亚对她说。"我们经历了这许多事情,你以为我听了个故事还会做噩梦?"

"说不定会叫英国人做噩梦。"

"试试看吧。"

"不,英国人,我不是开玩笑。你见过小城镇挑头闹革命时的情景吗?"

"没见过,"罗伯特·乔丹说。

"那么你根本没有见过世面。你看到巴勃罗现在垮了的模样,可是你该看看巴勃罗当日的威风。"

"讲吧。"

"不,我不想讲。"

"讲吧。"

"好吧。我要把它真实地讲出来。可你,漂亮姑娘,假如讲到你受不了的地方,跟我说。"

"假如我受不了,我就不听,"玛丽亚对她说。"不见得会比那许多悲惨的事更糟吧。"

"我看会,"妇人说。

他伸手摸到了玛丽亚的手,握在自己手中,她摊开手掌,平放在他手上,俩人就这样听着。

"It was early in the morning when the civil guard surrendered at the barracks," Pilar began.

"You had assaulted the barracks?" Robert Jordan asked.

Pilar said, "Pablo had surrounded it in the dark, cut the telephone wires, placed dynamite under one wall and called on the civil guard to surrender. They would not. And at daylight he blew the wall open. There was fighting. Two civil guards were killed. Four were wounded and four surrendered.

We all lay on roofs and on the ground and at the edge of walls and of buildings in the early morning light and the dust cloud of the explosion had not yet settled, for it rose high in the air and there was no wind to carry it, and all of us were firing into the broken side of the building, loading and firing into the smoke, and from within there was still the flashing of rifles and then there was a shout from in the smoke not to fire more, and out came the four civil guard with their hands up. A big part of the roof had fallen in and the wall was gone and they came out to surrender.

'Are there more inside?' Pablo shouted.

'There are wounded.'

'Guard these,' Pablo said to four who had come up from where we were firing. 'Stand there. Against the wall.' he told the civil guard."

"那天大清早，兵营里的民防军投降了，"比拉尔开始讲。

"你们袭击了兵营？"罗伯特·乔丹问。

比拉尔说："巴勃罗乘着黑夜包围了兵营，割断了电话线，在一堵墙脚下放了炸药包，命令民防军投降。他们不肯。天亮时他就把那堵墙炸开，接着就开火了。打死了两个民防军。四个民防军受伤，四个投降。在朦胧的清早，我们大家伏在房顶上、地上、墙脚边和建筑旁。爆炸引起的尘土没有马上从空中掉下来，因为扬得很高，没有风吹散它。我们大家朝着建筑被炸开的那一面开火，边装子弹，边向烟雾里开枪，屋里仍有步枪发射的闪光，接着烟雾里有人叫喊别再开枪，四个民防军举着双手走出来了。一大片屋顶已经坍塌下来，一边的墙已经炸没了，于是他们出来投降。

'里面还有人吗？'巴勃罗喊着。

'有些受伤的。'

'看住他们，'巴勃罗对从我们射击的方向走过来的四个人说。'站在那儿，靠着墙。'他对民防军说。"

比拉尔接着说："四个民防军贴墙站着，脏兮兮的，浑身是土，给硝烟熏得漆黑，那四个看守用枪口对准了他们，巴勃罗和别的人就到屋里去干掉那些受伤的人。

'你打算把我们怎么办？'有一个人问他。

'毙了你们！跪下，'巴勃罗说。

'那我们就跪下，'第一个民防军说。四人都跪下，脑袋顶着墙，双手垂在身体两侧，模样很别扭。巴勃罗走到他们背后，用枪口逐个抵着他们的后脑勺开了枪。枪声响处，一个个倒下了。我现在好像还能听到那尖厉而沉闷的枪声，还能看到那枪筒猛地一颤，那人的脑袋向前耷拉下去。手枪抵着后脑勺的时候，有一个脑袋一动不动，有一个脑袋向前一冲，前额抵在石墙上，有一个浑身哆嗦，脑袋直晃，只有一个用双手捂住了眼睛，那是最后一个。那四具尸体都倒在墙脚边，巴勃罗手里仍旧握着枪，转身朝我们走来。"

Pilar continued, "The four civil guards stood against the wall, dirty, dusty, smoke-grimed, with the four who were guarding them pointing their guns at them and Pablo and the others went in to finish the wounded.

'What are you going to do with us?' one asked him.

'Shoot you! Kneel,' Pablo said.

'Then let us kneel,' the first civil guard said, and the four knelt, looking very awkward with their heads against the wall and their hands by their sides, and Pablo passed behind them and shot each in turn in the back of the head with the pistol, going from one to another and putting the barrel of the pistol against the back of their heads, each man slipping down as he fired. I can hear the pistol still, sharp and yet muffled, and see the barrel jerk and the head of the man drop forward. One held his head still when the pistol touched it. One pushed his head forward and pressed his forehead against the stone. One shivered in his whole body and his head was shaking. Only one put his hands in front of his eyes, and he was the last one, and the four bodies were slumped against the wall when Pablo turned away from them and came toward us with the pistol still in his hand."

"What happened to the others?" Robert Jordan asked. "Were there no other fascists in the village?"

"Were there no other fascists? There were more than twenty. But none was shot."

"What was done?"

"Pablo had them beaten to death with flails and thrown from the top of the cliff into the river."

"All twenty?"

"I will tell you. It is not so simple. And in my life never do I wish to see such a scene as the flailing to death in the plaza on the top of the cliff above the river. The town is built on the high bank above the river and there is a square with a fountain and there are benches and big trees that give a shade for the benches. The balconies of the houses look out on the plaza. Six streets enter on the plaza and there is an arcade from the houses that goes around the plaza so that one can walk in the shade of the arcade when the sun is hot. On three sides of the plaza is the arcade and on the fourth side is the walk shaded by the trees beside the edge of the cliff with, far below, the river. It is three hundred feet down to the river."

"其他人怎么样?"罗伯特·乔丹问。"镇上难道没有别的法西斯分子吗?"

"没有别的法西斯分子?还有二十多个呢。可是一个也没有被枪杀。"

"那是怎么回事?"

"巴勃罗命令用连枷把他们活活打死,然后从峭壁上把他们扔进江里。"

"二十多个都这样?"

"我跟你讲吧。事情不那么简单。我这一辈子也不想看这种情景了,那就是在江边峭壁上的广场上用连枷把人活活打死。那小镇建在江岸边,离江面很高,那里有一个广场,广场上有喷泉,还有几条长椅和为长椅遮阴的大树。房子的阳台都对着广场。六条街道通向广场,周围有一条和每座房子相通的拱廊,阳光灼热的时候,人们可以在廊荫下行走。广场三边都是拱廊,第四边是峭壁边上的一条有树木遮阴的走道,下面是相距 300 英尺的江面。"

"Pablo organized it all as he did the attack on the barracks. First he had the entrances to the streets blocked off with carts as though to organize the plaza for an amateur bullfight. The fascists were all held in the city hall, the city hall, which was the largest building on one side of the plaza. It was there the clock was set in the wall and it was in the buildings under the arcade that the club of the fascists was. And under the arcade on the sidewalk in front of their club were their chairs and tables for their club. Pablo placed them in two lines as you would place men for a rope pulling contest, or as they stand in a city to watch the ending of a bicycle road race with just room for the cyclists to pass between, or as men stood to allow the passage of a holy image in a procession. Two meters was left between the lines and they extended from the door of the city hall clear across the plaza to the edge of the cliff. So that, from the doorway of the city hall, looking across the plaza, one coming out would see two solid lines of people waiting."

"当时的安排由巴勃罗一手组织，就像安排袭击兵营时一样。他先用大车堵住通向各条大街的路口，仿佛在广场上准备举行业余斗牛似的。法西斯分子统统被关在镇公所里，这是广场一边最大的房子。有只大钟就是安在镇公所的墙上，法西斯分子的俱乐部就在那拱廊下的房屋里。在拱廊下的俱乐部门前的人行道上有一些桌椅。巴勃罗叫大家排成两行，就像叫人们排好了准备来一场拔河比赛，或者像人们在城里站着观看自行车比赛到达终点时那样，只给自行车运动员留出一条窄路从中通过，或者像人们站着让路给圣像仪仗队通过一样。两排人之间空出两米宽的一条过道，人们从镇公所门口排起，穿过整个广场，一直排到峭壁边。这样，从镇公所大门出来的人朝广场一看，只见两行排得很紧密的人在等待。"

"They were armed with flails used to beat out the grain and they were a good flail's length apart. All did not have flails, as enough flails could not be obtained. But most had flails obtained from the store of Don Guillermo Martin, who was a fascist and sold all sorts of agricultural implements. And those who did not have flails had heavy herdsman's clubs, or ox-goads, and some had wooden pitchforks; those with wooden tines that are used to fork the chaff and straw into the air after the flailing. Some had sickles and reaping hooks but these Pablo placed at the far end where the lines reached the edge of the cliff. These lines were quiet and it was a clear day, as today is clear, and there were clouds high in the sky, as there are now, and the plaza was not yet dusty for there had been a heavy dew in the night, and the trees cast a shade over the men in the lines. Only near the city hall, where the priest was complying with his duties with the fascists, was there any ribaldry, and that came from those worthless ones who, as I said, were already drunk and were crowded around the windows shouting obscenities and jokes in bad taste through the iron bars of the windows."

"他们用打谷的连枷武装自己，两排之间有足够抡起连枷的空地。搞不到足够的连枷，不是所有的人都拿着连枷。法西斯分子堂·吉列尔莫·马丁的店铺里卖各种各样的农具，大多数人从那里搞来了连枷。没有连枷的人就拿着粗大的牧羊棍或赶牛棒，有的拿着木制的干草叉，那是打谷后把干草和麦秆挑向空中的木叉，有的拿着收割用的镰钩和大镰刀，不过巴勃罗把这些人安排在队伍靠近峭壁的一边。两排人静悄悄的，那天就像今天一样晴朗，就像现在一样天高云淡，前一天晚上露水很浓，广场上那时还没有灰尘，两排人的身上被树荫遮着。只有在神父给法西斯分子做圣事的镇公所附近有下流的叫骂声；那些人，我已说过，是已经喝醉的二流子，他们挤在窗外，隔着窗上的铁栅栏，对里面大骂粗话，开些低级下流的玩笑。"

战地钟声 For Whom the Bell Tolls

"And as we were at the far end of the line where the walk runs along the cliff by the river, Pablo took the hat in his hand and sailed it off over the cliff with the motion a herdsman makes throwing a stone underhand at the bulls to herd them. The hat sailed far out into space and we could see it smaller and smaller, the patent leather shining in the clear air, sailing down to the river. I looked back over the square and at all the windows and all the balconies there were people crowded and there was the double line of men across the square to the doorway of the city hall and the crowd swarmed outside against the windows of that building and there was the noise of many people talking, and then I heard a shout and some one said 'Here comes the first one,' and it was Don Benito Garcia, the Mayor. He came out bareheaded walking slowly from the door and down the porch and nothing happened; and he walked between the line of men with the flails and nothing happened. He passed two men, four men, eight men, ten men and nothing happened and he was walking between the lines of men, his head up, his fat face gray, his eyes looking ahead and then flickering from side to side and walking steadily. And nothing happened."

"我们那时正站在这两排人的尽头，沿江峭壁边缘的走道上，巴勃罗伸手拿了帽子，从峭壁上扔下去，就像牧人低手扔石块赶牛似的。帽子远远地飘在空中，大家眼看它变得越来越小，帽子的漆皮在清澈的空中闪闪发亮，直落到江里。我回头望着广场，只见所有的窗口和阳台上都挤满了人，两排人在广场上排到镇公所门口，大楼窗前也都是人，挤来挤去，七嘴八舌，只听得一声大叫，有人说，'头一个出来啦。'原来是镇长堂·贝尼托·加西亚。他不戴帽子从大门里慢吞吞走出来，穿过门廊，但什么也没发生；他走到两排拿着连枷的人中间，还是什么也没发生。他在两个人、四个人、八个人、十个人中间走过，还是什么也没发生。他在这两排人中间走着，抬起了头，他的胖脸阴郁，眼睛先是望着前方，接着举目四望，稳稳当当地走着。还是什么也没发生。"

"From a balcony some one cried out, 'What is the matter, cowards?' and still Don Benito walked along between the men and nothing happened. Then I saw a man three men down from where I was standing and his face was working and he was biting his lips and his hands were white on his flail. I saw him looking toward Don Benito, watching him come on. And still nothing happened. Then, just before Don Benito came abreast of this man, the man raised his flail high so that it struck the man beside him and smashed a blow at Don Benito that hit him on the side of the head and Don Benito looked at him and the man struck again and shouted, 'That for you,' and the blow hit Don Benito in the face and he raised his hands to his face and they beat him until he fell. The man who had struck him first called to others to help him and he pulled on the collar of Don Benito's shirt and others took hold of his arms and with his face in the dust of the plaza, they dragged him over the walk to the edge of the cliff and threw him over and into the river."

战地钟声 *For Whom the Bell Tolls*

“有人在露台上喊叫：‘怎么搞的，你们这些胆小鬼？’堂·贝尼托仍旧在两排人中间走着，还是什么也没发生。我看到一个男人，我们之间隔着三个人，他脸上的肌肉在抽动，他咬着嘴唇，使劲握住连枷的手失去了血色。我看他朝堂·贝尼托的方向望去，等着他走过来。仍旧没有动静。等到堂·贝尼托正要走到此人身旁，那人高高地抡起了连枷，竟然打到了旁边的人，然后一下子照堂·贝尼托砸过去，打在他脑袋一侧，堂·贝尼托瞅了他一眼，这人又举起连枷砸过去，一边嚷道：‘给你点颜色看看，’这一下打在堂·贝尼托脸上，他举起双手捂住脸，于是大家纷纷动手，直到把他打翻在地。最早动手的那个人叫其他人帮忙，他一把抓住堂·贝尼托的衬衫领子，其他人抓住他的胳膊，他的脸贴在广场的泥地上，大家把他一路拖着，经过走道，拖到峭壁边，向外扔到江里。”

"It was then that we saw a disgraceful sight, for the man who walked out of the doorway of the city hall was Don Faustino Rivero, the oldest son of his father, Don Celestino Rivero, a land owner. He was tall and his hair was black and it was freshly combed back from his forehead for he always carried a comb in his pocket and he had combed his hair now before coming out. He was a great annoyer of girls, and he was a coward, and he had always wished to be an amateur bullfighter. He went much with gypsies and with bullfighters and with bull raisers and delighted to wear the Spanish Southern Andalucian costume, but he had no courage and was considered a joke. One time he was announced to appear in an amateur benefit fight for the old people's home in Avila and to kill a bull from on horseback in the Andalucian style, which he had spent much time practicing, and when he had seen the size of the bull that had been substituted for him in place of the little one, weak in the legs, he had picked out himself, he had said he was sick and, some said, put three fingers down his throat to make himself vomit."

"我们看到了一幕丢人的景象，因为从镇公所大门里出来的是堂·福斯蒂诺·里维罗，也就是地主堂·塞莱斯蒂诺·里维罗的大儿子。他是个高个儿，一头黑发，而且刚向后梳理过，他口袋里总是揣着一把梳子，这次出来之前也梳了头发。他老是和姑娘们纠缠不清，还是个胆小鬼，却总想当个业余斗牛士。他常和吉卜赛人、斗牛士和养牛人混在一起，还爱穿那种西班牙南部地区安达卢西亚式斗牛服，可是他没胆量，被人当笑柄。有一次在替阿维拉养老院募捐而举行的业余斗牛表演中，传言他要出场，照安达卢西亚的方式，骑在马背上把牛杀死。他已经花了很多时间练习，事先挑了一头没有腿力的小牛，但到场上发现换了一头大牛，马上借口说自己恶心，而且据说用三个手指伸进自己的嗓子眼催吐。"

战地钟声 For Whom the Bell Tolls

"Don Faustino could not walk alone and the peasant in a black smock helped him on one side and another peasant in a black smock and herdsman's boots helped him on the other, supporting him by the arms and Don Faustino walking along between the lines with his hands over his eyes, his lips never quiet, and his black hair slicked on his head and shining in the sun, and as he passed the peasants would say, 'Don Faustino, that you should have a good appetite,' and one, who had failed at bullfighting himself, said, 'Don Faustino, bullfighter, at your orders.' and another said, 'Don Faustino, there are beautiful girls in heaven.' And they walked Don Faustino through the lines, holding him close on either side, holding him up as he walked, with him with his hands over his eyes. But he must have looked through his fingers, because when they came to the edge of the cliff with him, he knelt again, throwing himself down and clutching the ground and holding to the railing, saying, 'No. No. No. Please. NO. Please. Please. No. No.'"

"堂·福斯蒂诺没法自己走路，有个穿黑罩衣的农民就在一边架着他，另一个身穿黑罩衣和牧人靴的农民在另一边架着他，在两排人中间朝前走。堂·福斯蒂诺两手挡在眼前，嘴唇一直在哆嗦，黑发滑溜溜的，在阳光中闪亮。他走过的时候，农民们说，'堂·福斯蒂诺，祝你好胃口。'有一个自己斗牛也没有成功的人说，'堂·福斯蒂诺，斗牛士，听您吩咐。'另一个说，'堂·福斯蒂诺，天堂里有的是漂亮姑娘。'他们在两旁紧紧架着他在两排人中间走，双脚几乎离地，而他只顾用手遮住眼睛。不过，他准在指缝中偷看，拖到峭壁边时，他双膝跪下，扑倒在地，抓住了栏杆，死也不肯起身，他说，'别。别。别。求求你们。千万别。求求你们。求求你们。不要。不要。'"

"When the square had been closed off and the lines formed, I had admired and understood it as a conception of Pablo, although it seemed to me to be somewhat fantastic and that it would be necessary for all that was to be done in good taste if it were not to be repugnant. Certainly if the fascists were to be executed by the people, it was better for all the people to have a part in it, and I wished to share the guilt as much as any, just as I hoped to share in the benefits when the town should be ours. But after their death I felt a feeling of shame and distaste, and with the coming of the drunkards and the worthless ones into the lines, and the abstention of those who left the lines as a protest after their death, I wished that I might disassociate myself altogether from the lines, and I walked away, across the square, and sat down on a bench under one of the big trees that gave shade there.

Two peasants from the lines walked over, talking together, and one of them called to me, 'What passes with you, Pilar?'

'Nothing, man,' I told him.

'Yes,' he said. 'Speak. What passes?'

'I think that I have a belly-full,' I told him."

"当广场被堵住、人们排成队伍时，我很佩服巴勃罗的这个主意，并且也理解，尽管我认为有点荒唐，觉得如果这一切是必不可少的，就得干得体面些，别叫人受罪。如果百姓动手处决法西斯分子，最好人人动手；我希望跟大家一起承担良心的谴责，正像我希望等这个镇子由我们管理的时候跟大家一起分享胜利果实一样。可是，他们被杀之后，我觉得害臊、难堪，再加上队伍里面来了醉汉和二流子，有些人看到他们被杀的情况，离开了队伍表示抗议，我希望自己也和这两排人完全脱离关系，我一边穿过广场，在一棵大树树荫里的长凳上坐下。

队伍里有两个农民，一边说话，一边走过来，其中一个叫我：'比拉尔，你怎么啦？'

'没什么，伙计，'我对他说。

'肯定有事，'他说。'说吧。出了什么事。'

'我看我受够了，'我对他说。"

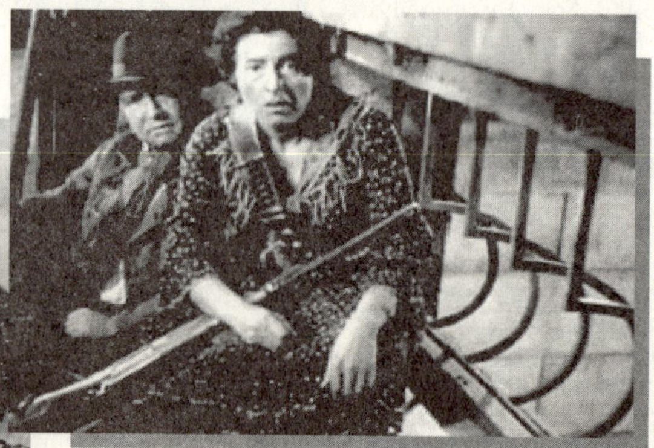

"Do not tell me about it," said Maria. "I do not want to hear it. This is enough. This was too much."

"I told you that you should not have listened," Pilar said. "See. I did not want you to hear it. Now you will have bad dreams."

"No," said Maria. "But I do not want to hear more."

"I wish you would tell me of it sometime," Robert Jordan said.

"I will," Pilar said. "But it is bad for Maria."

"I don't want to hear it," Maria said pitifully. "Please, Pilar. And do not tell it if I am there, for I might listen in spite of myself."

Her lips were working and Robert Jordan thought she would cry.

"Please, Pilar, do not tell it."

"Do not worry, little cropped head," Pilar said. "Do not worry. But I will tell the English sometime."

"But I want to be there when he is there," Maria said. "Oh, Pilar, do not tell it at all."

"I will tell it when you are working."

"No. No. Please. Let us not tell it at all," Maria said.

"别说那天的情形了,"玛丽亚说,"我不要听了。够啦。叫人太难受了。"

"我早对你说你不该听,"比拉尔说,"瞧,我本来不希望你听,现在你要做噩梦啦。"

"不会的,"玛丽亚说,"不过我不想再听了。"

"我倒希望你以后有时间给我讲讲,"罗伯特·乔丹说。

"我一定讲,"比拉尔说。"不过玛丽亚听了没好处。"

"我不要听,"玛丽亚可怜巴巴地说道,"求求你,比拉尔。我在场的时候别讲,我会忍不住要听的。"

她的嘴唇在哆嗦,罗伯特·乔丹觉得她要哭了。

"求求你,比拉尔,别讲了。"

"别担心,短头发的小东西,"比拉尔说,"别担心。不过我以后要讲给英国人听的。"

"可我要和他在一起,"玛丽亚说,"啊,比拉尔,你干脆别讲了。"

"以后等你干活的时候,我讲。"

"不要。不要。求求你。千万别讲了,"玛丽亚说。

Robert Jordan saw Pilar looking at him, her fingers on her lips. She was looking toward the door.

The blanket fastened across the opening of the cave was lifted and Pablo put his head in. He grinned at them all, pushed under the blanket and then turned and fastened it again. He turned around and stood there, then pulled the blanket cape over his head and shook the snow from it.

"You were speaking of me?" he addressed them all. "I am interrupting?"

No one answered him and he hung the cape on a peg in the wall and walked over to the table.

He picked up his cup which had stood empty on the table and dipped it into the wine bowl. "There is no wine," he said to Maria. "Go draw some from the skin."

"Be careful," he said to her. "The wine's below the chest now."

No one said anything.

"I drank from the belly-button to the chest today," Pablo said. "It's a day's work. What's the matter with you all? Have you lost your tongues?"

No one said anything at all.

"Screw it up, Maria," Pablo said. "Don't let it spill."

"There'll be plenty of wine," Agustín said. "You'll be able to be drunk."

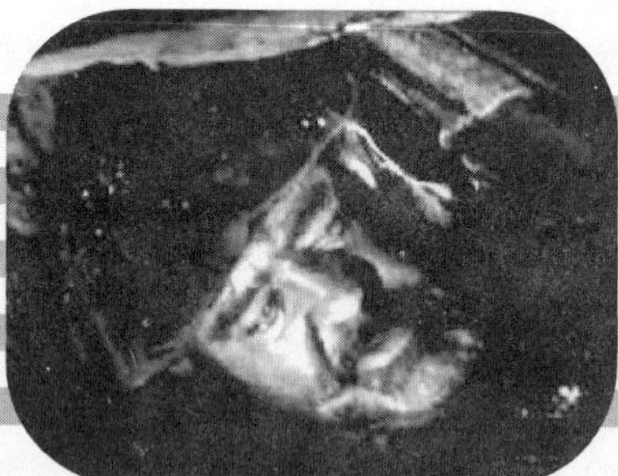

罗伯特·乔丹看到比拉尔看着他，她的手指放在嘴唇上。她正望着洞口。

系在洞口的毯子撩起来了，巴勃罗探进头来。他呲着牙朝大家笑笑，撩开毯子挤了进来，然后回身系上挂毯。他转身站在那里，脱掉从头上套上的毯子式披风，抖掉上面的雪。

"你们在聊我吧?"他对大伙说。"我把你们的话打断啦? "

没人接他的话茬；他把披风挂在洞壁的木钉上，向桌边走去。

他拿起桌上他那只空杯子从酒缸里舀酒。"没有酒了，"他对玛丽亚说，"去，从酒袋里倒些来。"

"小心点，"他对她说。"袋里只剩一半酒了。"

没人言语。

"我今天从皮酒袋的肚脐那儿喝到了胸口，"巴勃罗说。"一天工夫。你们大伙儿怎么啦? 丢了舌头啦? "

大家一句话也没说。

"把塞子拧紧，玛丽亚，"巴勃罗说。"别弄酒了。"

"酒多的是哪，"奥古斯丁说。"够你喝个醉。"

战地钟声 *For Whom the Bell Tolls*

"Do you think it will clear tomorrow?" Robert Jordan asked him.

"Yes, I believe it will be cold and clear. This wind is shifting. We will have good weather for it, English," Pablo said to Robert Jordan.

"We," Pilar said. "We?"

"Yes, we," Pablo grinned at her and drank some of the wine. "Why not? I thought it over while I was outside. Why should we not agree?"

"In what?" the woman asked. "In what now?"

"In all," Pablo said to her. "In this of the bridge. I am with you now."

"You are with us now?" Agustín said to him. "After what you have said?"

"Yes," Pablo told him. "With the change of the weather I am with you."

Agustín shook his head. "The weather," he said and shook his head again. "And after me hitting you in the face?"

"Yes," Pablo grinned at him and ran his fingers over his lips. "After that too."

Robert Jordan was watching Pilar. She was looking at Pablo as at some strange animal.

"你看明天会放晴吗？"罗伯特·乔丹问他。

"会的，看来明天要转冷放晴了。风向在变。我们行动时会遇上好天气，英国人。"巴勃罗对罗伯特·乔丹说。

"我们，"比拉尔说，"我们？"

"是的，我们，"巴勃罗露齿对她笑笑，喝了几口酒。"为什么不？我刚才在外面把这个问题想过了。干吗我们要不一致？"

"关于什么事？"妇人问。"到底关于什么事？"

"所有的事都保持一致，"巴勃罗对她说。"关于这次炸桥行动，现在我和你们一起干。"

"你和我们一起干？"奥古斯丁对他说。"在你说过哪些话之后？"

"不错，"巴勃罗对他说。"天气变了，我和你们一起干了。"

奥古斯丁摇摇头，"天气，"他说，又摇摇头，"即使我打过你的脸？"

"对，"巴勃罗朝他露齿笑笑，用手指摸摸嘴唇。"即使这样也干。"

罗伯特·乔丹注视着比拉尔。她正望着巴勃罗，仿佛他是头怪物。

"Listen," she said to Pablo.

"Yes, woman."

"What passes with you?"

"Nothing," Pablo said. "I have changed my opinion. Nothing more."

"You were listening at the door," she told him.

"Yes," he said. "But I could hear nothing."

"You fear that we will kill you."

"No," he told her. "I do not fear that. You know that."

"Well, what passes with you?" Agustín said. "One moment you are drunk and putting your mouth on all of us and disassociating yourself from the work in hand and speaking of our death in a dirty manner and insulting the women and opposing that which should be done—"

"I was drunk," Pablo told him.

"And now—"

"I am not drunk," Pablo said. "And I have changed my mind."

"Let the others trust you. I do not," Agustín said.

"Trust me or not," Pablo said. "But there is no one who can take you to Gredos as I can."

"Gredos?"

"It is the only place to go after this of the bridge."

Now, they made peace with Pablo again, but this compromise probably led to a more serious result. The second day seemed to pass placidly.

“听着，”她对巴勃罗说。

“是，太太。”

“你这是怎么啦？”

“没什么，”巴勃罗说。“我改了主意。就是这么回事。”

“你在洞口偷听了吧？”她对他说。

“是啊，”他说。“不过我什么也没听到。”

“你怕我们杀了你。”

“不，”他对她说。“我不怕这个。这你知道。”

“噢，那你是怎么啦？”奥古斯丁说，“你刚才还是喝得醉醺醺的，数落我们大家，不愿卷入我们当前的任务，恶毒地咒我们死，辱骂妇女，反对该做的事。”

“我刚才醉了，”巴勃罗对他说。

“那么现在？”

“我不醉了，”巴勃罗说。“我改了主意。”

“让别人听信你说的话吧。我可不信，”奥古斯丁说。

“信不信由你，”巴勃罗说，“可除了我没人能把你们带到格雷多斯山区去。”

“格雷多斯？”

“炸桥后只有这条路可走。”

现在，他们又一次和巴勃罗妥协，但这次妥协可能会酿成更大的恶果。第二天似乎平静地过去了。

A warm wind came with daylight and Robert Jordan could hear the snow melting in the trees and the heavy sound of its falling. It was a late spring morning. He knew with the first breath he drew that the snow had been only a freak storm in the mountains and it would be gone by noon. Then he heard a horse coming, the hoofs balled with the wet snow thumping dully as the horseman trotted. He heard the noise of a carbine scabbard slapping loosely and the creak of leather.

He buttoned his shirt with one hand and held the automatic pistol in the other loosening the safety catch with his thumb. He saw the horseman coming through the trees. He crouched now in the robe and holding the pistol in both hands aimed it at the man as he rode toward him. He had never seen this man before.

The horseman was almost opposite him now. He was riding a big gray gelding and he wore a khaki beret, a blanket cape like a poncho, and heavy black boots. From the scabbard on the right of his saddle projected the stock and the long oblong clip of a short automatic rifle. He had a young, hard face and at this moment he saw Robert Jordan.

黎明带来一阵温暖的风，罗伯特·乔丹听到树上的积雪融化了，啪嗒落在地上。那是个暮春的早晨。他吸了一口气就知道，这场暴风雪只不过是山区里的反常现象，到中午雪就会融化。他接着听到有匹马过来了，骑手策马小跑，马蹄带踩着已经融化的雪，发出咄咄的脚步声。他听到卡宾枪套摇晃时的拍打声和皮马鞍的咯吱咯吱声。

他一手扣上衬衫扣，一手拿起自动手枪，用大拇指松开保险。他看到了骑手从树林里过来了，他匍匐在睡袋里，两手握住枪，瞄准朝他骑马过来的人。他从来没见过这个人。

这时，骑手几乎就在他对面了。他骑着一匹灰色大阉马，头戴卡其贝雷帽，穿着毯子式披风和笨重的黑靴，马鞍右侧的枪套里撅出一支短把自动步枪的枪托和狭长的子弹夹。他长着一张年轻而冷酷的脸，与此同时他也看到了罗伯特·乔丹。

The horseman reached his hand down toward the scabbard and as he swung low, turning and jerking at the scabbard, Robert Jordan saw the scarlet of the formalized device he wore on the left breast of his khaki blanket cape.

Aiming at the center of his chest, a little lower than the device, Robert Jordan fired.

The pistol roared in the snowy woods.

The horse plunged as though he had been spurred and the young man, still tugging at the scabbard, slid over toward the ground, his right foot caught in the stirrup. The horse broke off through the trees dragging him, bumping, face downward, and Robert Jordan stood up holding the pistol now in one hand.

The big gray horse was galloping through the pines. There was a broad swath in the snow where the man dragged with a scarlet streak along one side of it. People were coming out of the mouth of the cave. Robert Jordan reached down and unrolled his trousers from the pillow and began to put them on.

Overhead he heard the noise of a plane flying very high. Through the trees he saw where the gray horse had stopped and was standing, his rider lied on the snow, dead.

骑手一手朝下伸向枪套，当他弯腰转身从枪套里急速拔枪的时候，罗伯特·乔丹看到他卡其披风的左胸前佩戴着鲜红色的统一标记。

罗伯特·乔丹朝着这标记的下方一点瞄准，朝他当胸开了一枪。

枪声在积雪的树林里震响着。

那匹马仿佛突然被马刺踢了一下，向前猛地一冲；那年轻人还在拉扯枪套，身子同时朝地面溜下去，右脚被马镫勾住了。那匹马撒开四蹄拖着脸朝下的骑手颠簸碰撞，在林中奔驰而去。罗伯特·乔丹一手握枪，站起身来。

大灰马在松林中狂奔。骑手的身子在雪地上拖出了一条宽阔的痕迹，一边是一道深红色的血迹。大家从山洞里走出来。罗伯特·乔丹伸手把当枕头用的裤子展开，开始往身上穿。

他听到头顶上一架飞机飞得很高。他透过树林看见大灰马停下来站在那里，骑手躺在雪地上，死了。

"There's cavalry out," Robert Jordan said. "Get your damned gun up there."

He heard Pilar call, "Agustín," into the cave. Then she went into the cave and then two men came running out, one with the automatic rifle with its tripod swung on his shoulder; the other with a sackful of the pans.

"Get up there with them," Robert Jordan said to Anselmo. "You lie beside the gun and hold the legs still," he said.

"I will put him with the others," Pablo said.

"No," Robert Jordan said. "He has made tracks into here. He must make them out."

"True," agreed Pablo. "I will ride him out and will hide him and bring him in when the snow is melted. You have much head today, English."

Robert Jordan looked back and saw Maria now standing with Pilar. Then she came running up the trail. He dropped behind Primitivo to speak to her.

"You," she said. "Can I go with you?"

"No. Help Pilar."

She was walking behind him and put her hand on his arm.

"I'm coming."

"No."

She kept on walking close behind him.

“骑兵来了，”罗伯特·乔丹说，“把该死的机枪架在山上。”

他听到比拉尔冲着山洞叫“奥古斯丁”。接着她走进山洞，然后两个男人跑出来，一个拿着自动步枪，三脚架搭在肩上；另一个拿着一口袋子弹盘。

“跟他们一起上山，”罗伯特·乔丹对安塞尔莫说。“你伏在枪边，抓住枪架别动，”他说。

“我来把它和别的马放在一起，”巴勃罗说。

“不行，”罗伯特·乔丹说，“它留下了来这里的马蹄印，还得踩出一条回去的蹄印。”

“对，”巴勃罗同意。“我骑它出去，把它藏起来，等雪化了再带回来。你今天很有头脑，英国人。”

罗伯特·乔丹回过头来，看见玛丽亚和比拉尔一起站着。接着她从山路上跑来。他有意落在普里米蒂伏的后面，跟她说话。

“你，”她说，“我可以跟你去吗？”

“不行。去帮比拉尔做事。”

她跟着他走，一只手搭在他胳膊上。

“我要去。”

“不行。”

她还是紧跟他走着。

"I could hold the legs of the gun in the way you told Anselmo."

"You will hold no legs. Neither of guns nor of nothing."

Walking beside him she reached forward and put her hand in his pocket.

"No," he said.

"Kiss me," she said, "if you go."

"You are shameless," he said.

"Yes," she said. "Totally."

"Get you back now. There is much work to do. We may fight here if they follow these horse tracks."

"You," she said. "Did you see what he wore on his chest?"

"Yes. Why not?"

"It was the Sacred Heart."

"Yes. All the people of Navarre wear it."

"And you shot for that?"

"No. Below it. Get you back now."

"You," she said. "I saw all."

"You saw nothing. One man. One man from a horse. Get you back."

"Say that you love me."

"No. Not now."

"Not love me now?"

"Stop. Get you back. One does not do that and love all at the same moment."

"我可以按住枪架,就像你叫安塞尔莫做的那样。"

"不要你按枪架。不管是枪架还是别的,什么也不要你做。"

她向前走在他身边,把手插进他的口袋。

"别,"他说。

"亲亲我,"她说,"如果你要走。"

"你真不知害臊,"他说。

"对,"她说。"一点也不。"

"你现在回去。要做的事很多。如果他们循着这些马蹄印来,我们说不定要在这里开火。"

"你,"她说,"你看到他胸前佩戴着什么了?"

"看到。怎么会看不到?"

"那是圣心啊。"

"不错。所有的纳瓦拉人都佩戴圣心。"

"你就瞄着它开枪?"

"不。瞄准了圣心下面。你现在回去吧。"

"你,"她说,"我全都看到了。"

"你什么也没有看到。一个男人,一个从马背上摔下来的男人。你回去吧。"

"说你爱我。"

"不。现在不行。"

"现在不爱我了?"

"别说了。你回去吧。一个人不能一边打仗一边谈恋爱啊。"

"I want to go to hold the legs of the gun and while it speaks love you all in the same moment."

"You are crazy. Get you back now."

"I am crazy," she said. "I love you."

"Then get you back."

"Good. I go. And if you do not love me, I love you enough for both."

He looked at her and smiled through his thinking.

"When you hear firing," he said, "come with the horses. Aid Pilar with my sacks. It is possible there will be nothing. I hope so."

"I go," she said. "Look what a horse Pablo rides."

The big gray was moving ahead up the trail.

"Yes. But go."

"I go."

Her fist, clenched tight in his pocket, beat hard against his thigh. He looked at her and saw there were tears in her eyes. She pulled her fist out of his pocket and put both arms tight around his neck and kissed him.

"I go," she said. "I go."

He looked back and saw her standing there, the first morning sunlight on her brown face and the cropped, tawny, burned-gold hair. She lifted her fist at him and turned and walked back down the trail, her head down.

"我要去按住枪架，一边听枪响，一边说爱你。"

"你疯了。你现在回去。"

"我就是疯了,"她说,"我爱你。"

"那么你回去。"

"好。我走了。你要是不爱我,我对你的爱够我们俩消受的。"

他望着她,想了一想,不禁微笑了。

"你听到了枪声,"他说,"就跟那些马匹一起走,帮比拉尔背我的背包。说不定平安无事。但愿这样。"

"我走了,"她说。"瞧,巴勃罗骑的马多棒。"

大灰马在山路上一直跑在前面。

"对。走吧。"

"我走了。"

她把手在他口袋里紧握成拳头,使劲地捶了他大腿一下。他看看她,看到她眼睛里噙着泪水。她从他口袋里抽出拳头,张开双臂紧紧搂着他的脖子,亲吻他。

"我走了,"她说。"我走了。"

他回过头来,看到她站在那儿,黎明的曙光照着她褐色的脸和一头闪着金光的黄褐色短发。她向他举举拳头,垂下头去,转身沿着小路往回走了。

Robert Jordan caught up with Primitivo and said "Cut me pine branches and bring them quickly."

"I do not like the gun there," he said to Agustín.

"Why?"

"Place it over there," Robert Jordan pointed, "and later I will tell you."

"Here, thus. Let me help you. Here," he said, then squatted down.

He looked out across the narrow oblong, noting the height of the rocks on either side.

"It must be farther," he said, "farther out. Good. Here. That will do until it can be done properly. There. Put the stones there. Here is one. Put another there at the side. Leave room for the muzzle to swing. The stone must be farther to this side. Anselmo. Get you down to the cave and bring me an ax. Quickly."

Primitivo brought the pine branches and Robert Jordan stuck them through the snow into the unfrozen earth, arching them over the gun from either side.

"Bring more," he said. "There must be cover for the two men who serve it. This is not good but it will serve until the ax comes. Listen," he said, "if you hear a plane lie flat wherever you are in the shadows of the rocks. I am here with the gun."

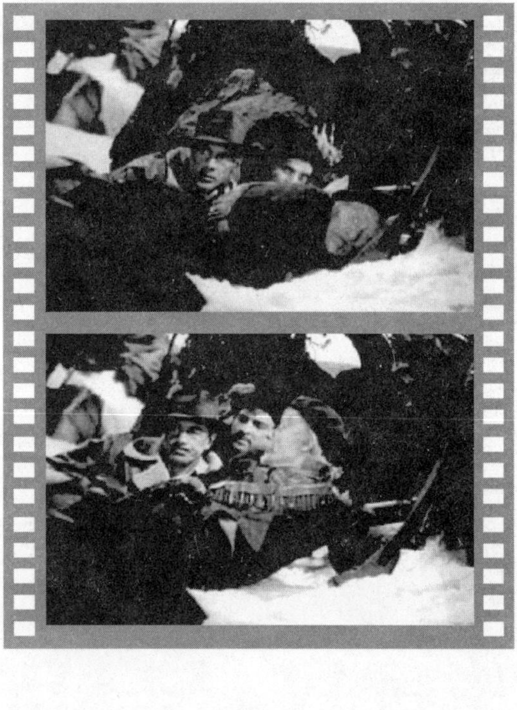

罗伯特·乔丹赶上了普里米蒂伏并对他说："给我砍些松枝，快点拿来。"

"枪架在那里不对劲，"他对奥古斯丁说。

"为什么？"

"挪到那边去吧，"罗伯特·乔丹指点着，"我以后告诉你。"

"架在这儿。我来帮你搬。这儿，"他说着就蹲下来。

他眺望着对面一块狭长地带，打量着两边岩石的高度。

"要放远点，"他说，"再远一点。好。架在这儿。这样放行了，以后再好好调整。那儿，把石块放在那儿。这儿放一块。边上再放一块。给枪口留些转动的地方。这石头还得朝这边挪过来一点。安塞尔莫，到下面山洞里给我拿把斧头。快。"

普里米蒂伏拿来了松枝，罗伯特·乔丹把它们插在积雪下尚未冻结的泥土里，窝成拱形遮住了枪身。

"再弄点来，"他说。"必须掩护那两个射击的人。这不管什么用，不过在斧子拿来之前能将就。听着，"他说，"如果你们听到飞机的声音，就地卧倒在岩石的阴影里。我在这里守着枪。"

战地钟声 *For Whom the Bell Tolls*

Just then, while Robert Jordan was watching all of the country that was visible, he saw the gypsy coming through the rocks to the left. He was walking with a loose, high-hipped, sloppy swing, his carbine was slung on his back, his brown face was grinning and he carried two big hares, one in each hand.

"Hello, Robert," he called cheerfully.

Robert Jordan put his hand to his mouth, and the gypsy looked startled. He slid over behind the rocks to where Robert Jordan was crouched beside the brush-shielded automatic rifle. He crouched down and laid the hares in the snow. Robert Jordan looked up at him.

"Where have you been?" he lowered his voice.

"I tracked them," the gypsy said.

"And your post?"

"It was not for long," the gypsy whispered. "Is there an alarm?"

"There is cavalry out."

"Have you seen them?" The gypsy said.

"There is one at the camp now," Robert Jordan said. "He came for breakfast."

"I thought I heard a shot or something like one," the gypsy said. "Did he come through here?"

"Here. Your post."

"I am a poor, unlucky man."

"Take your hares to camp and bring us up some breakfast." The gypsy followed his order and left there.

正在罗伯特·乔丹极目眺望山野时，看到那吉卜赛人穿过山岩从左边过来了。他扭着屁股，漫不经心，大摇大摆地走过来，卡宾枪挎在背上，褐色的脸上咧嘴笑着，双手各提着一只大兔子。

"喂，罗伯特，"他兴高采烈地喊着。

罗伯特·乔丹把手按在嘴上，吉卜赛人显然怔了一下。他一溜烟闪到山岩后面，来到伏在树枝掩护后守着自动步枪的罗伯特·乔丹身边。他蹲下身子，把兔子放在雪地上。罗伯特·乔丹抬头看着他。

"你到哪儿去了？"他低声说。

"我去追兔子，"吉卜赛人说。

"你不是在放哨吗？"

"捉兔子时间不长，"吉卜赛人低声说。"有警报吗？"

"骑兵来了。"

"你看见他们了？"吉卜赛人说。

"有一个在营地，"罗伯特·乔丹说。"他来吃早饭的。"

"我好像听到了一声枪响什么的，"吉卜赛人说。"他从这儿过去的？"

"这儿。从你的岗哨上来的。"

"我这个倒霉的可怜虫。"

"把兔子带到营地去，带点早饭过来。"吉卜赛人按照他说的做了，离开了那里。

Agustín and Primitivo came up with the brush and Robert Jordan built a good blind for the automatic rifle, a blind that would conceal the gun from the air and that would look natural from the forest.

He showed them where to place a man high in the rocks to the right where he could see all the country below and to the right, and another where he could command the only stretch where the left wall might be climbed.

"Do not fire if you see any one from there," Robert Jordan said. "Roll a rock down as a warning, a small rock, and signal to us with your rifle, thus," he lifted the rifle and held it over his head as though guarding it. "Thus for numbers," he lifted the rifle up and down. "If they are dismounted point your rifle muzzle at the ground. Thus. Do not fire from there until you hear the machine gun fire. Shoot at a man's knees when you shoot from that height. If you hear me whistle twice on this whistle get down, keeping behind cover, and come to these rocks where the machine gun is."

奥古斯丁和普里米蒂伏带来了树枝。罗伯特·乔丹给自动步枪筑了个很好的掩体，从空中一点也看不出来，从树林那边望过来很自然。

他指给他们看，该在右边山岩顶上布置一个人，能望到下面的整个山野和右侧，另外再布置一个人来控制住左边山崖唯一可以爬上来的要道。

“要是看到有人从那里过来，别开枪，”罗伯特·乔丹说。“丢块石头，一块小石头下来警告，再用步枪，这样给我们打信号。”他提起步枪，平举过头，好像在保护自己的脑袋。“有几个敌人就举几次，”他上上下下举着步枪。“要是他们下马，你把枪口朝向地面。这样。要听到机枪响了，你才能在那里开枪。从上面射击，要瞄准对方的膝盖。如果听到我用这只哨子吹两遍，你就下山，注意掩护自己，跑到架机枪的岩石这边来。”

Primitivo raised the rifle.

"I understand," he said. "It is very simple."

"Send first the small rock as a warning and indicate the direction and the number. See that you are not seen."

"Yes," Primitivo said. "If I can throw a grenade?"

"Not until the machine gun has spoken. It may be that cavalry will come searching for their comrade and still not try to enter. They may follow the tracks of Pablo. We do not want combat if it can be avoided. Above all that we should avoid it. Now get up there."

Anselmo came up with the ax and crouched by the machine gun.

"Do you wish more branches?" he asked. "To me it seems well hidden."

"Not branches," Robert Jordan said. "Two small trees that we can plant here and there to make it look more natural. There are not enough trees here for it to be truly natural."

"I will bring them."

"Cut them well back, so the stumps cannot be seen."

Robert Jordan heard the ax sounding in the woods behind him. He looked up at Primitivo above in the rocks and he looked down at the pines across the clearing.

普里米蒂伏提起步枪。

"我明白,"他说。"这很简单。"

"先丢下小石头警告,指明方向和人数。注意自己别被人发现。"

"是,"普里米蒂伏说。"我可以扔个手榴弹吗?"

"要等到机枪响了才行。也许骑兵队会来找他们的同伴,并不打算深入。他们会循着巴勃罗留下的马蹄印走。如果能避免的话,我们就不打。最重要的是应该避免交火。现在上山到那边去吧。"

安塞尔莫拿着斧头过来,蹲在机枪旁边。

"你还要树枝吗? "他问,"我看已经掩护得不错了。"

"不要树枝了,"罗伯特·乔丹说。"要两棵小树,这边插一棵,那边插一棵,看起来会更自然些。要使这儿显得真正自然,树还不够。"

"我去砍。"

"要齐根砍,别留下树桩给人家发现。"

罗伯特·乔丹听到身后树林里响起了砍树声。他抬头望望山岩上的普里米蒂伏, 又低头望望山下空地对面的松林。

"Get you down," Robert Jordan whispered to Agustín, and he turned his head and flicked his hand down, down, to Anselmo who was coming through the gap with a pine tree, carrying it over his shoulder like a Christmas tree. He saw the old man drop his pine tree behind a rock and then he was out of sight in the rocks and Robert Jordan was looking ahead across the open space toward the timber. He saw nothing and heard nothing but he could feel his heart pounding and then he heard the clack of stone on stone and the leaping, dropping clicks of a small rock falling. He turned his head to the right and looking up saw Primitivo's rifle raised and lowered four times horizontally.

Then there was nothing more to see but the white stretch in front of him with the circle of horse tracks and the timber beyond.

"Cavalry," he said softly to Agustín.

Agustín looked at him and his dark, sunken cheeks widened at their base as he grinned. Robert Jordan noticed he was sweating. He reached over and put his hand on his shoulder. His hand was still there as they saw the four horsemen ride out of the timber.

"卧倒,"罗伯特·乔丹对奥古斯丁低声说,转过头去,对安塞尔莫急速地摆手,示意他卧倒,卧倒;安塞尔莫肩上扛着一棵松树,像扛着一棵圣诞树似的,正从山凹走来。他看到老人把松树撂在一块岩石后面,自己也躲在岩石背后不见了。罗伯特·乔丹望着开阔的空地对面的树林。他没看到也没听到什么,只觉得自己的心怦怦地跳,接着听到石头和石头的碰撞声,有一块小石头蹦蹦跳跳地滚下石壁时的嗒嗒声。他转向右面抬头看见普里米蒂伏的步枪上下平举了四次。

他只见到面前的一片白色雪地,上面有一圈马蹄印以及远处的松林,别的什么也看不见。

"骑兵,"他轻声对奥古斯丁说。

奥古斯丁望着他龇牙笑笑,黑黝黝的凹陷的双颊下部显得更宽了。罗伯特·乔丹发觉他在冒汗,就伸手按在他的肩头上。他按着他的肩头,这时他们看到树林里跑出四个骑兵来。

战地钟声 *For Whom the Bell Tolls*

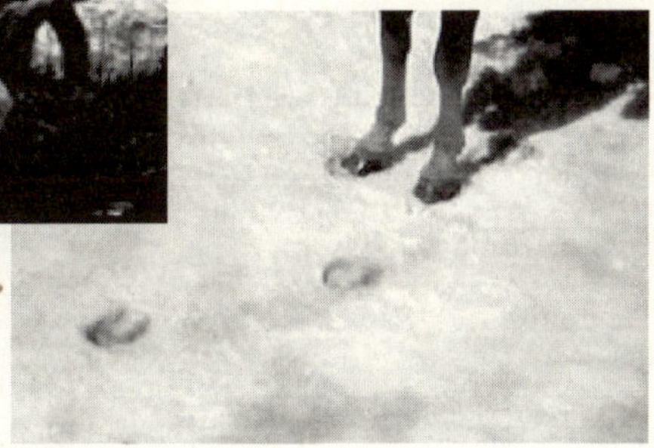

One horseman was ahead and three rode behind. The one ahead was following the horse tracks. He looked down as he rode. The other three came behind him, fanned out through the timber. They were all watching carefully. Robert Jordan felt his heart beating against the snowy ground as he lay, his elbows spread wide and watched them over the sights of the automatic rifle.

The man who was leading rode along the trail to where Pablo had circled and stopped. The others rode up to him and they all stopped.

Robert Jordan saw them clearly over the blued steel barrel of the automatic rifle. He saw the faces of the men, the sabers hanging, the sweat-darkened flanks of the horses, and the cone-like slope of the khaki capes, and the Navarrese slant of the khaki berets. The leader turned his horse directly toward the opening in the rocks where the gun was placed and Robert Jordan saw his young, sun and wind-darkened face, his close-set eyes, hawk nose and the overlong wedge-shaped chin.

The leader sat his horse there, the horse's chest toward Robert Jordan, the horse's head high, the butt of the light automatic rifle projecting forward from the scabbard at the right of the saddle.

一个骑兵领先，后面跟着三个。领先的那个循着马蹄印过来。他骑在马上低头察看着。其他三个跟在他后面，成扇形穿过树林。他们都在仔细观察着。罗伯特·乔丹匍匐着，觉得自己的心抵着雪地在怦怦地跳动，他撑开两肘，通过自动步枪的瞄准器注视着他们。

带头的那个沿着蹄印骑到巴勃罗打转的地方，停下来了。其他三人向他靠拢，也都停下来了。

罗伯特·乔丹顺着自动步枪蓝色的钢枪筒，清楚地看到了他们。他看到了他们的脸和身上挂着的马刀、被汗浸湿的黑色马腹、圆锥形的卡其披风和纳瓦拉人惯常歪戴着的卡其贝雷帽。领先的那个拨转马头，正对着架枪的岩石缺口。罗伯特·乔丹看清他那张饱经风霜的年轻的黑脸、两只相距很近的眼睛、鹰钩鼻子和过长的楔形下巴。

这个领头的骑兵骑在马背上，马头高昂着，胸脯朝着罗伯特·乔丹，马鞍右侧的枪套里露出了轻自动步枪的枪托。

"We could have killed all four," Agustín said quietly. He was still wet with sweat.

"Yes," Robert Jordan whispered. "But with the firing who knows what might have come?"

Just then he heard the noise of another rock falling and he looked around quickly. He looked at his wristwatch and then up to where Primitivo was raising and lowering his rifle in what seemed an infinity of short jerks. And then he heard the noise of a body of cavalry coming.

"Do not worry," he whispered to Agustín. "They will pass as the others."

They came into sight trotting along the edge of the timber in column of twos, twenty mounted men, armed and uniformed as the others had been, their sabers swinging, their carbines in their holsters; and then they went down into the timber as the others had.

"You see?" Robert Jordan said to Agustín.

"There were many," Agustín said.

"These would we have had to deal with if we had destroyed the others," Robert Jordan said very softly.

Robert Jordan looked up at Primitivo's post and saw him signal, "Nothing," crossing his two hands, palms down.

"我们可以把四个都干掉,"奥古斯丁悄悄地说。他仍然汗淋淋的。

"是啊,"罗伯特·乔丹悄声说。"可是开了火,谁知道会出现什么后果?"

正在这时,他又听到有块石头滚落下来的声音,立刻朝四周扫了一眼。他看看手表,接着抬头朝普里米蒂伏望望,只见他正在急速地上下举动步枪,举了无数次。他接着听到有一队骑兵骑马过来的声音。

"别急,"他对奥古斯丁耳语道,"他们会像刚才几个那样过去的。"

树林边缘出现了二十个骑兵,两个一排,和刚才那四个人一样的武器和服装,马刀晃动着,枪套里插着卡宾枪。他们和先前几个一样,朝树林中骑去了。

"你看到了?"罗伯特·乔丹对奥古斯丁说。

"人数很多,"奥古斯丁说。

"要是我们干掉了先前几个,现在就不得不对付这些了,"罗伯特·乔丹轻轻地说。

罗伯特·乔丹抬头望着普里米蒂伏的岗哨,看到他交叉双手,手掌朝下,示意"平安无事"。

As Robert Jordan spoke he heard something. It was a noise far off that came above the sound of the warm wind in the trees. He could not be sure and he held his mouth open and listened, glancing up at Primitivo as he did so. He thought he heard it but then it was gone. The wind was blowing in the pines and now Robert Jordan strained all of himself to listen. Then he heard it faintly coming down the wind.

"Shut up," he said, not listening, and lying beside him, his head having been turned away. Agustín looked over at him suddenly.

"What's up?" he asked.

Robert Jordan put his hand over his own mouth and went on listening. There it came again. It came faint, muted, dry and far away. But there was no mistaking it now. It was the precise, crackling, curling roll of automatic rifle fire. It sounded as though pack after pack of miniature firecrackers were going off at a distance that was almost out of hearing.

Robert Jordan looked up at Primitivo who had his head up now, his face looking toward them, his hand cupped to his ear. As Robert Jordan looked with his binoculars, Primitivo pointed up the mountain toward the highest country.

罗伯特·乔丹说话时听到了什么声音。这个遥远的声响盖过了暖风吹过树林子的声音。他听不真切，就张开了嘴倾听，同时抬头向普里米蒂伏瞥了一眼。他自以为听到了这声音，但接着这声音消失了。松林里，风在刮，罗伯特·乔丹全神贯注地细听着。接着他听到了随风飘来的微弱的声响。

“别出声，”他说。他伏在奥古斯丁身边，头转向别处，不听他说话。奥古斯丁突然看着他。

“怎么回事？”奥古斯丁问。

罗伯特·乔丹把手捂在自己嘴上，继续倾听。这声音又出现了，低弱而模糊，遥远而单调。但这一回是不会听错的。正是自动步枪射击时发出的一连串清脆的嗒嗒声，就像在遥远的地方成串成串地放小型爆竹，几乎听不到。

罗伯特·乔丹抬眼看着普里米蒂伏，见他这时正抬起了头，脸朝着他们，一手拢着耳朵倾听。罗伯特·乔丹用望远镜眺望时，普里米蒂伏朝地形最高的山峦指指。

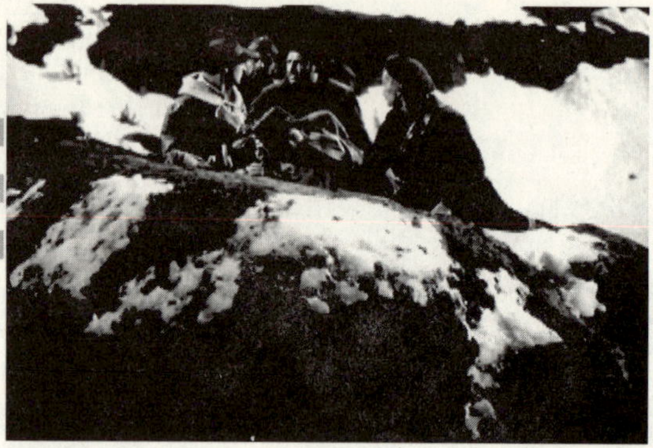

"They are fighting at El Sordo's," Robert Jordan said.

"Then let us go to aid them," Agustín said. "Collect the people."

"No," Robert Jordan said. "We stay here."

Robert Jordan looked up at where Primitivo stood now in his lookout post, holding his rifle and pointing. He nodded his head but the man kept pointing, putting his hand to his ear and then pointing insistently and as though he could not possibly have been understood.

"Stay with this gun and unless it is sure, sure, sure that they are coming in do not fire. And then not until they reach that shrub," Robert Jordan pointed. "Do you understand?"

"Yes. But—"

"No but. I will explain to you later. I go to Primitivo."

"We have to aid them," Primitivo said when Robert Jordan came to his post.

"It is impossible," Robert Jordan told him. "I have expected this all morning."

"How?"

"They went to steal horses last night. The snow stopped and they tracked them up there."

"But we have to aid them," Primitivo said. "We cannot leave them alone to this. Those are our comrades."

"艾苏道那边开火了，"罗伯特·乔丹说。

"我们去支援他们吧，"奥古斯丁说，"把人集合起来。"

"不行，"罗伯特·乔丹说。"我们待在这儿。"

罗伯特·乔丹抬头望着站在监视岗上握着步枪指点着的普里米蒂伏。他点点头，但普里米蒂伏仍旧指点着，把手搁在耳朵后面，接着又一股劲地指着，好像人家没明白他的意思似的。

"你守住这挺机枪，在确实肯定敌人过来之前，千万别开枪。即使开枪，也要等他们到了树丛那儿的时候，"罗伯特·乔丹指着。"你明白吗？"

"明白。但是……"

"没有但是。我待会再跟你解释。现在我到普里米蒂伏那儿去。"

"我们一定要支援他们，"当罗伯特·乔丹来到他的岗位，普里米蒂伏对他说。

"不可能，"罗伯特·乔丹说。"从早晨起我就料到这个了。"

"怎么呢？"

"他们昨晚去偷马。雪停了，人家跟着马蹄印追踪到那里。"

"我们可一定要支援他们，"普里米蒂伏说。"我们不能眼看着他们不管。他们是我们的同志啊。"

Robert Jordan put his hand on Primitivo's shoulder.

"We can do nothing," he said. "If we could I would do it."

"There is a way to reach there from above. We can take that way with the horses and the two guns. This one below and yours. We can aid them thus."

"Listen—" Robert Jordan said.

"That is what I listen to," Primitivo said.

The firing was rolling in overlapping waves. Then they heard the noise of hand grenades heavy and sodden in the dry rolling of the automatic rifle fire.

"They are lost," Robert Jordan said. "They were lost when the snow stopped. If we go there we are lost, too. It is impossible to divide what force we have."

He took hold of both her wrists and hoisting as Pilar climbed heavily over the last boulder.

"Your binoculars," she said and lifted their strap over her head. "So it has come to El Sordo?"

"Yes."

"Poor El Sordo," she said in commiseration.

She was breathing heavily from the climb and she took hold of Robert Jordan's hand and gripped it tight in hers as she looked out over the country.

罗伯特·乔丹伸手按在普里米蒂伏的肩上。

"我们无能为力，"他说。"有办法的话，我会支援他们。"

"上面有条山路通那儿。我们可以带上两挺枪，骑马走那条路。就是下面那挺和你那挺。我们可以这样支援他们。"

"听。"罗伯特·乔丹说。

"我听到的就是这个，"普里米蒂伏说。

枪声一阵接一阵地传来。接着，他们听到自动步枪清脆的连发声中响起了手榴弹沉闷的爆炸声。

"他们失败了，"罗伯特·乔丹说。"雪停了，他们就完了。我们去的话，也要完了。我们现有的力量不能分散。"

比拉尔费力地攀上最后一块岩石，他握住了她的两只手腕，把她拉上来。

"你的望远镜，"她说着把望远镜上的带子从脖子上摘下来。"原来艾苏道遇上啦？"

"是啊。"

"可怜的艾苏道，"她同情地说。

她一路爬得气喘吁吁，抓住了罗伯特·乔丹的一只手，紧紧握在自己手里，眺望着山野的那边。

"Now for El Sordo. Can we do anything?" Pilar asked.

"Nothing."

"Poor," she said. "I was fond of El Sordo. You are sure, sure that he suffers disaster?"

"Yes. I have seen much cavalry."

"More than here?"

"Another full troop on their way up there."

"Listen to it," Pilar said. "Poor, poor El Sordo."

They listened to the firing.

"Primitivo wanted to go up there," Robert Jordan said.

"Are you crazy?" Pilar said to the flat-faced man. "What kind of lunacies are we producing here?"

"I wish to aid them."

"Another romantic. Do you not believe you will die quick enough here without useless voyages?" Pilar said.

"You must act like a man," she said to Primitivo. "A grown man. You with your gray hairs and all."

"Don't joke at me," Primitivo said sullenly. "If a man has a little heart and a little imagination—"

"He should learn to control them," Pilar said. "You will die soon enough with us. There is no need to seek that with strangers."

"现在来谈艾苏道的问题。我们能做点什么吗？"比拉尔问道。

"没办法。"

"真可怜，"她说。"我很喜欢艾苏道。你肯定，肯定他遭殃了吗？"

"是啊。我看到很多骑兵。"

"比这里的还多？"

"还有一整队在上山。"

"听枪声，"比拉尔说。"真可怜，可怜的艾苏道。"

他们倾听着枪声。

"普里米蒂伏要到那边去，"罗伯特·乔丹说。

"你疯了吗?"比拉尔朝那个扁脸汉子说。"我们这儿竟然会出这样的疯子？"

"我想支援他们。"

"又是个不切实际的人。你去了也没用，即使不去，待在这儿也快死了，你难道不信？"比拉尔说。

"你必须像个男子汉，"她对普里米蒂伏说。"成熟的男子汉。瞧你，一脸灰胡子什么的。"

"别拿我开玩笑，"普里米蒂伏阴沉地说。"如果一个人只要有点心肠和头脑的话……"

"他就该懂得克制自己，"比拉尔说，"不一会儿，你就要跟我们一起死啦。没有必要跟外人一起去找死啦。"

战地钟声 For Whom the Bell Tolls

与此同时，艾苏道在小山顶上作战，除了这座山之外没有别的选择。他极目远望，看到了这座山，就选中了它，策马朝它跑来，背上背着沉重的自动步枪，马儿吃力地爬着坡，身子在他胯下颠簸，一袋手榴弹在他身体的一侧晃荡着，一袋自动步枪的弹药盘碰撞着他身体的另一侧。华金和伊格纳西奥不时停一会儿，开几枪，停一会儿，开几枪，好让他有时间找个有利的地形把枪架上。

给他们惹祸的积雪还没完全融化。他的马被打中了，它呼哧呼哧地喘着气，缓慢而蹒跚地爬上通向山顶的最后一段路，伤口鲜血直流，洒在雪地上。艾苏道拉着马笼头，肩上搭着马缰绳，使劲拉着马一起向山上爬。枪弹噼啪地射在岩石上，他肩上挎着两袋沉重的弹药，拼命爬山，接着他挑了个合适的地方，抓住马鬃，利索、熟练而深情地冲马儿开了一枪。于是马脑袋向前一冲，马身栽倒，填补了两块岩石之间的缺口。

Meanwhile, El Sordo was making his fight on a hilltop. But he had had no choice except this hill and he had picked it as far away as he could see it and galloped for it, the automatic rifle heavy on his back, the horse laboring, barrel heaving between his thighs, the sack of grenades swinging against one side, the sack of automatic rifle pans banging against the other, and Joaquín and Ignacio halting and firing, halting and firing to give him time to get the gun in place.

There had still been snow then, the snow that had ruined them, and when his horse was hit so that he wheezed in a slow, jerking, climbing stagger up the last part of the crest, splattering the snow with a bright, pulsing jet, El Sordo had hauled him along by the bridle, the reins over his shoulder as he climbed. He climbed as hard as he could with the bullets spatting on the rocks, with the two sacks heavy on his shoulders, and then, holding the horse by the mane, had shot him quickly, expertly, and tenderly just where he had needed him, so that the horse pitched, head forward down to plug a gap between two rocks.

El Sordo had gotten the gun to firing over the horse's back and he fired two pans, the gun clattering, the empty shells pitching into the snow, the smell of burnt hair from the burnt hide where the hot muzzle rested, him firing at what came up to the hill, forcing them to scatter for cover, while all the time there was a chill in his back from not knowing what was behind him. Once the last of the five men had reached the hilltop the chill went out of his back and he had saved the pans he had left until he would need them.

There were two more horses dead along the slope and three more were dead here on the hilltop. He had only succeeded in stealing three horses last night and one had bolted when they tried to mount him bareback in the corral at the camp when the first shooting had started.

Of the five men who had reached the hilltop three were wounded. El Sordo was wounded in the calf of his leg and in two places in his left arm. He was very thirsty, his wounds had stiffened, and one of the wounds in his left arm was very painful. He grinned somewhere inside the pain in his head and inside the nausea that came whenever he moved his arm and looked around at what there was left of his band.

艾苏道把枪架在马背上射击，发射了两盘子弹。枪身格格作响，空弹壳迸入雪地里，搁在马身上的灼热的枪筒烫焦了马皮，散发出马鬃的焦煳味。他对冲上山来的敌人射击，迫使他们分散开去找掩护，同时总觉得背上发冷，不知道背后会发生什么情况。等他们五个人中的最后一个到达山顶，他才不觉得背上发冷。他保留了剩下的那几盘子弹，以备不时之需。

山坡上还有两匹死马，这儿山顶上也有三匹。昨晚他只仅仅偷到了三匹马。当他们跟敌人交上火，在营地的马栏里来不及备鞍就想跨上马去时，其中有一匹溜掉了。

到达山顶的五人中有三个负了伤。艾苏道腿肚子上受了伤，左臂上有两处伤。他感到非常口渴，伤口麻木变硬，左臂上有个伤口很痛。每当他挪动那条胳膊，扭头望望周围剩下的弟兄时，就感到头痛恶心，他就咧嘴苦笑着。

The five men were spread out like the points of a five-pointed star. They had dug with their knees and hands and made mounds in front of their heads and shoulders with the dirt and piles of stones. Using this cover, they were linking the individual mounds up with stones and dirt. Joaquín, who was eighteen years old, had a steel helmet that he dug with and he passed dirt in it.

He had gotten this helmet at the blowing up of the train. It had a bullet hole through it and every one had always joked at him for keeping it. But he had hammered the jagged edges of the bullet hole smooth and driven a wooden plug into it and then cut the plug off and smoothed it even with the metal inside the helmet.

When the shooting started he had clapped this helmet on his head so hard it banged his head as though he had been hit with a casserole and, in the last lung-aching, leg-dead, mouth-dry, bullet-spatting, bullet-cracking, bullet-singing run up the final slope of the hill after his horse was killed, the helmet had seemed to weigh a great amount and to ring his bursting forehead with an iron band. But he had kept it. Now he dug with it in a steady, almost machinelike desperation. He had not yet been hit.

他们五个人分散开像五角星的五个角。他们用双手双膝挖掘，用泥土和石块在头和肩膀前面筑起了土墩。有了这些土墩当掩护，他们用石块和泥土把各个土墩联起来。十八岁的华金有个钢盔，用它来挖掘和传送泥土。

他这只头盔是在炸火车时搞到的。头盔上有个子弹窟窿，大家常常取笑他保存这头盔。但他敲平了窟窿边的豁口，在里面堵了个木塞，然后把木塞头削掉，磨得和钢盔内壁一般平。

枪声刚刚响起时，他猛地把钢盔扣在头上，哐啷一声，好像头上给菜锅砸了一下。他的马被打死后，他肺部剧痛，两腿沉重，嘴里干渴，在子弹纷飞、枪声大作中冲上山坡最后一段路时，那顶头盔仿佛变得非常重，像一道铁箍一样箍住了他快要炸裂的前额。但是他没有丢掉它。他现在像台机器似的用它不停地拼命挖土。他还没中弹。

El Sordo looked very carefully around the withers of the dead horse and there was a quick hammering of firing from behind a boulder well down the slope and he heard the bullets from the submachine gun thud into the horse. He crawled along behind the horse and looked out of the angle between the horse's hindquarters and the rock. There were three bodies on the slope just below him where they had fallen when the fascists had rushed the crest under cover of the automatic rifle and submachine gunfire and he and the others had broken down the attack by throwing and rolling down hand grenades.

There were other bodies that he could not see on the other sides of the hillcrest. There was no ground by which attackers could approach the summit and El Sordo knew that as long as his ammunition and grenades held out and he had as many as four men they could not get them out of there unless they brought up a trench mortar. He did not know whether they had sent to La Granja for a trench mortar. Perhaps they had not, because surely, soon, the planes would come. It had been four hours since the observation plane had flown over them.

艾苏道从死马的肩部边万分小心地朝外望了一眼，山坡下方一块大岩石后面立刻射来一梭子弹，他听到手提机枪子弹射进马身上的噗噗声。他在马尸后面匍匐爬去，从马臀部和一块岩石之间的缺口朝外望去。就在他下面的山坡上有三具法西斯分子尸体，他们在自动步枪和手提机枪的火力掩护下向山顶冲锋时倒下的；他当时和其他人把手榴弹扔下去或从山坡上滚下去，粉碎了这次进攻。

山顶的另一边还有些尸体，他没法看到。敌人没有可以借以冲上山顶的掩护地方，而艾苏道知道，他们还有四个人，只要弹药和手榴弹够用，敌人就没法把他们从这里赶走，除非拉来迫击炮。他不知道他们是否已派人到拉格兰哈去拉迫击炮。也许没去，飞机当然就快来了。侦察机从他们头上飞过已有四个小时了。

这座山真像梅毒下疳，艾苏道寻思着，我们就是上面的恶脓。但是他们愚蠢地进攻时被我们杀死了不少。他们怎么会以为这样就可以打垮我们呢？他们有了这样新式的武器，忘乎所以，昏了头啦。他们猫着腰冲上山的时候，他扔了个手榴弹，一蹦一跳地滚下山坡，把带头强攻的年轻军官炸死了。他在一片黄色的闪光和灰色的尘雾中看到这个军官身子朝前一冲，栽倒在他这时躺着的地方，就像一大堆破烂的旧衣服，这是他们进攻所达到的最远的地方。艾苏道望望这具尸体，然后望着山坡下方的其他尸体。

“比拉尔是头号婊子，”下巴抵在泥里的那人说，“这婊子知道我们在这儿要完蛋了。”

“她帮不上忙，”艾苏道说。那人这句话是在他正常的耳朵一边说的，他不用回头就听到了。“她能有什么办法？他们布满了整个山坡。她怎样攻击他们呢？他们有150人。”

This hill is truly like a chancre, El Sordo thought, and we are the very pus of it. But we killed many when they made that stupidity. How could they think that they would take us thus? They have such modern armament that they lose all their sense with overconfidence. He had killed the young officer who had led the assault with a grenade that had gone bouncing and rolling down the slope as they came up it, running, bent half over. In the yellow flash and gray roar of smoke he had seen the officer dive forward to where he lay now like a heavy, broken bundle of old clothing marking the farthest point that the assault had reached. El Sordo looked at this body and then, down the hill, at the others.

“Who is a whore of whores is Pilar,” the man with his chin in the dirt said. “That whore knows we are dying here.”

“She could do no good,” El Sordo said. The man had spoken on the side of his good ear and he had heard him without turning his head. “What could she do? They are spread around a hillside. How would she come on them? There are a hundred and fifty of them.”

"But if we hold out until dark," Joaquín said to El Sordo.

"And if Christmas comes on Easter," the man with his chin on the ground said.

"That they should aid us now," another man said. "That all the cruts of Russian sucking swindlers should aid us now."

"Save your cartridges and do not talk so much or you will be very thirsty," El Sordo said. "There is no water on this hill."

"Take this," the man said and rolling on his side he pulled a wineskin that he wore slung from his shoulder over his head and handed it to El Sordo. "Wash your mouth out, old one. You must have much thirst with your wounds."

"Let all take it," El Sordo said.

"Then I will have some first," the owner said and squirted a long stream into his mouth before he handed the leather bottle around.

"El Sordo, when think you the planes will come?" the man with his chin in the dirt asked.

"Any time," said El Sordo. "They should have come before."

"Do you think these sons of the great whore will attack again?"

"Only if the planes do not come."

"God knows they've enough planes with what we saw yesterday."

"Too many," El Sordo said.

“不过，要是我们能撑到天黑的话，”华金对艾苏道说。

“要是圣诞节成了复活节的话，” 下巴抵在泥里的人说。

“他们现在就该来帮助我们，” 另一个说。“那伙肮脏的俄国骗子手现在都该来帮助我们。”

“要节省子弹，话别太多，要不然会很口渴，”艾苏道说。“这儿山上没水。”

“喝这个吧，”那人说着，侧过身子从头上褪下挎在肩上的皮酒袋，递给艾苏道。“漱漱口，老伙计。你受了伤，一定很口渴。”

“大家喝，”艾苏道说。

“我先喝点，”酒袋主人说着，向自己嘴里挤了一长道酒，这才把它递给大家。

“艾苏道，你看飞机什么时候来？”下巴抵在泥里的人问。

“随时都会来，”艾苏道说。“他们早该来了。”

“你认为这些混蛋会再进攻吗？”

“只要飞机不来。”

“我的上帝，拿我们昨天看到的来说，他们的飞机是够多的。”

“太多啦，”艾苏道说。

El Sordo lay now on his good side and looked up at the sky. He was lying on a heap of empty cartridge hulls but his head was protected by the rock and his body lay in the lee of the horse.

Just then some one shouted from down the slope.

"Listen, bandits!" the voice came from behind the rocks where the closest automatic rifle was placed. "Surrender now before the planes blow you to pieces."

"What is it he says?" El Sordo asked.

Joaquín told him. El Sordo rolled to one side and pulled himself up so that he was crouched behind the gun again.

"Maybe the planes aren't coming," he said. "Don't answer them and do not fire. Maybe we can get them to attack again."

"If we should insult them a little?" Joaquín asked.

"No," El Sordo said. "Give me your big pistol. Who has a big pistol?"

"Here."

"Give it to me." Crouched on his knees he took the big 9 mm. Star and fired one shot into the ground beside the dead horse, waited, then fired again four times at irregular intervals. Then he waited while he counted sixty and then fired a final shot directly into the body of the dead horse.

艾苏道把没受伤的一侧身子贴在地面上，抬头望着天空。他躺在一堆空弹壳上，但他的头有岩石遮掩着，身体伏卧在马尸背后。

正在这时，山坡下有人喊话了。

"听着，土匪！"声音来自岩石后面，那儿架着离他们最近的自动步枪。"飞机要来把你们炸得粉身碎骨，还是现在就投降吧。"

"他说什么？"艾苏道问。

华金告诉了他。艾苏道侧身一滚，抬起上半身，这样又蹲伏在机枪后面了。

"飞机也许不会就来，"他说。"别回话，别开枪。说不定我们可以引他们再来进攻。"

"我们骂他们几声怎么样？"华金问。

"不行，"艾苏道说。"把你的大手枪给我。谁有大手枪？"

"这儿。"

"把枪给我。"他双膝跪着，拿着一支9毫米口径的星牌大手枪，朝马尸旁边的地上打了一枪，等了一会儿，又断断续续地打了四枪。接着，他等着数到六十，然后对准马尸体上打了最后一枪。

El Sordo grinned and handed back the pistol.

"Reload it," he whispered, "and that every one should keep his mouth shut and no one shoot."

"Bandit!" the voice shouted from behind the rocks.

No one spoke on the hill.

"Bandit! Surrender now before we blow you to little pieces."

"They're biting," El Sordo whispered happily.

As he watched, a man showed his head over the top of the rocks. There was no shot from the hilltop and the head went down again. El Sordo waited, watching, but nothing more happened. He turned his head and looked at the others who were all watching down their sectors of the slope. As he looked at them the others shook their heads.

"Let no one move," he whispered.

"Sons of the great whore," the voice came now from behind the rocks again.

"Red swine."

El Sordo grinned. He could just hear the bellowed insults by turning his good ear. This is better than the aspirin, he thought. How many will we get? Can they be that foolish?

The voice had stopped again and for three minutes they heard nothing and saw no movement.

艾苏道露齿笑笑，交还手枪。

"再上子弹，"他低声说，"大家都别说话，谁也不许开枪。"

"土匪！"岩石后有人大声喊着。

山上没人说话。

"土匪！还是现在投降吧，我们就要把你们炸得粉身碎骨啦。"

"他们要上钩啦，"艾苏道高兴地低声说。

他正望着，有人从岩石堆后面探出头来了。山顶上没人射击，那脑袋又缩回去了。艾苏道等待着，张望着，却再没出现什么动静。他转过头，看到其他的人都在观察各自前面的山坡。他望着他们，他们都摇摇头。

"谁也不许动，"他低声说。

"婊子养的，"岩石后又传来了骂声。

"共匪。"

艾苏道露齿笑着。他侧过那只正常的耳朵，才能听清这大声臭骂。他想，这比阿司匹林有效啊。我们能打死几个呢？他们能那样愚蠢吗？

骂声又停了，他们有三分钟没听到任何声音，也没见到什么动静。

战地钟声 For Whom the Bell Tolls

Then the sniper behind the boulder a hundred yards down the slope exposed himself and fired. The bullet hit a rock and ricocheted with a sharp whine. Then El Sordo saw a man, bent double, run from the shelter of the rocks where the automatic rifle was across the open ground to the big boulder behind which the sniper was hidden. He almost dove behind the boulder.

El Sordo looked around. They signaled to him that there was no movement on the other slopes. El Sordo grinned happily and shook his head. This is ten times better than the aspirin, he thought, and he waited, as happy as only a hunter can be happy.

Below on the slope the man who had run from the pile of stones to the shelter of the boulder was speaking to the sniper.

"Do you believe it?"

"I don't know," the sniper said.

"It would be logical," the man, who was the officer in command, said. "They are surrounded. They have nothing to expect but to die."

The sniper said nothing.

"What do you think?" the officer asked.

"Nothing," the sniper said.

山坡上100码开外的一块岩石后面埋伏着的人伸出头来，开了一枪。子弹打在一块岩石上，随着一声尖厉的呼啸弹了开去。艾苏道看到有人猫腰从架着自动步枪的岩石后面跑出来，穿过空地，朝躲在一块大岩石后的狙击手跑过去。他几乎是纵身一跳扑到大岩石后边去的。

艾苏道朝四周望着。他们对他打手势，表示其他山坡上没有动静。艾苏道高兴地咧嘴笑，而且摇摇头。他想，这可比阿司匹林强上十倍。他等着，这股高兴劲儿只有猎人才会有。

山坡下从岩石堆后奔到大岩石后的那个人正在对狙击手讲话。

“你相信吗？”

“不知道，”狙击手说。

“这是合乎情理的，”这个担任指挥官的人说，“他们被包围了，没了指望，只有死路一条。”

狙击手什么也没说。

“你怎么想的？”指挥官问。

“看不出来，”狙击手说。

The officer looked at his wristwatch. It was ten minutes to three o'clock.

"The planes should have come an hour ago," he said. Just then another officer flopped in behind the boulder. The sniper moved over to make room for him.

"You, Paco," Captain Mora said. "How does it seem to you?"

Lieutenant Berrendo was breathing heavily from his sprint up and across the hillside from the automatic rifle position.

"For me it is a trick," he said.

"But if it is not? What a ridicule we make waiting here and laying siege to dead men."

"We have done something worse than ridiculous already," Lieutenant Berrendo said. "Look at that slope."

He looked up the slope to where the dead were scattered close to the top. From where he looked the line of the hilltop showed the scattered rocks, the belly, projecting legs, shod hooves jutting out, of El Sordo's horse, and the fresh dirt thrown up by the digging.

"What about the mortars?" asked Lieutenant Berrendo.

"They should be here in an hour. If not before."

"Then wait for them. There has been enough stupidity already."

指挥官看看手表：差十分三点。

"一个钟头以前，飞机就该来了，"他说。正在这时，另一个军官猛冲到大岩石后面。狙击手挪过身子，给他让点地方。

"你，帕科，"莫拉上尉说，"你看是怎么回事？"

贝仑多中尉刚从山坡上架自动步枪的位置猛冲过来，正在喘着粗气。

"我看这是个诡计，"他说。

"要是不是呢？我们在这儿苦等，包围着几个死人，太荒唐了。"

"我们干的事岂止可笑，"贝仑多中尉说，"瞧这山坡。"

他抬头望山坡，那里尸体一直遍布到山顶。从他那儿望去，看得见山顶上一片凌乱的山石、艾苏道的死马的肚子、伸出的马腿、撅出的马蹄以及新翻起的泥土。

"迫击炮怎么搞的？"贝仑多中尉问。

"再过一小时该来啦。那是说最多一小时。"

"那就等迫击炮吧。蠢事已经干得够多啦。"

"Bandit!" Captain Mora shouted suddenly, getting to his feet and putting his head well up above the boulder so that the crest of the hill looked much closer as he stood upright. "Red swine! Cowards!"

Lieutenant Berrendo looked at the sniper and shook his head. The sniper looked away but his lips tightened.

Captain Mora stood there, his head all clear of the rock and with his hand on his pistol butt. He cursed and vilified the hilltop. Nothing happened. Then he stepped clear of the boulder and stood there looking up the hill.

"Fire, cowards, if you are alive," he shouted. "Fire on one who has no fear of any Red that ever came out of the belly of the great whore."

This last was quite a long sentence to shout and the officer's face was red and congested as he finished.

Captain Mora had a red face and a black, British-looking moustache and there was something wrong about his eyes. They were dark and the lashes were dark, too. As you looked at them they seemed to focus slowly.

Then "Reds, cowards!" he shouted and commenced cursing again.

"土匪！"莫拉上尉突然站起身来大喊，脑袋暴露在大岩石上面。他这样站直了身体，山顶显得近多了。"共匪！怕死鬼！"

贝仑多中尉望望狙击手，摇摇头。狙击手转过头去，但抿紧了嘴唇。

莫拉上尉站在那儿，一手按在手枪把上，脑袋完全暴露在岩石上方。他朝山顶恶骂、诅咒，那里什么也没有发生。接着他干脆从岩石后面走出来，站在那儿抬头望着山顶。

"没死的话，开枪吧，怕死鬼，"他大声叫喊。"开枪打我这个不怕婊子生的共匪的人吧。"

最后这句话很长，等他喊完了，脸涨得通红。

莫拉上尉长着一张红脸膛，留着两撇黑色的英国式小胡子，眼睛有点毛病。这双眼睛是黑色的，睫毛也是黑色的。你如果仔细看他的眼睛，会发现它们似乎不会立刻就把注意力集中在你身上。

"共匪，怕死鬼！"他接着大喊，又开始咒骂。

Captain Mora stood absolutely clear now and, sighting carefully, fired his pistol at the only target that the hilltop presented: the dead horse that had belonged to El Sordo. The bullet threw up a puff of dirt fifteen yards below the horse. The captain fired again. The bullet hit a rock and sung off.

The captain stood there looking at the hilltop. Lieutenant Berrendo was looking at the body of the other lieutenant just below the summit. The sniper was looking at the ground under his eyes. Then he looked up at the captain.

"There is no one alive up there," the captain said. "You," he said to the sniper, "go up there and see."

The sniper looked down. He said nothing.

"Don't you hear me?" the captain shouted at him.

"Yes, my captain," the sniper said, not looking at him.

"Then get up and go." The captain still had his pistol out. "Do you hear me?"

"Yes, my captain."

"Why don't you go, then?"

"I don't want to, my captain."

"You don't want to?" The captain pushed the pistol against the small of the man's back. "You don't want to?"

"I am afraid, my captain," the soldier said with dignity.

莫拉上尉完全没有掩护，站着用手枪仔细瞄准，朝山顶上的唯一目标，艾苏道的死马，开了一枪。子弹打在死马下面 15 码的地方，溅起了一股泥土。上尉又开了一枪。子弹射在山石上，嗖的一声弹开去。

上尉站在那里望着山顶。贝仑多中尉望着离山顶不远的另一个中尉的尸体。狙击手看着眼前的地面，然后抬头望望上尉。

“上面没有活人了，”上尉说。“你，”他对狙击手说，“到上面去看看。”

狙击手垂下了头，一声不吭。

“你没听到我的话吗？”上尉对他大喝一声。

“不是，上尉，”狙击手说，并不朝他看。

“那么站起来，走。”上尉仍握着手枪。“你听到我的话吗？”

“是，上尉。”

“那为什么不去？”

“我不想去，上尉。”

“你不想去？”上尉用手枪抵住了他的后腰。“你不想去？”

“我怕，上尉，”士兵理直气壮地说。

Lieutenant Berrendo, watching the captain's face and his odd eyes, thought he was going to shoot the man then.

"Captain Mora," he said.

"Lieutenant Berrendo?"

"It is possible the soldier is right."

"That he is right to say he is afraid? That he is right to say he does not want to obey an order?"

"No. That he is right that it is a trick."

"They are all dead," the captain said. "Don't you hear me say they are all dead?"

"You mean our comrades on the slope?"

"Shoot," he shouted, standing on the gray granite boulder and waved both his arms. "Shoot me! Kill me!"

On the hilltop El Sordo lay behind the dead horse and grinned.

El Sordo, his chest shaking, barely peeped past the horse's crupper and saw the captain on top of the boulder waving his arms. Another officer stood by the boulder. The sniper was standing at the other side. El Sordo kept his eye where it was and shook his head happily.

"Shoot me," he said softly to himself. "Kill me!" Then his shoulders shook again. The laughing hurt his arm and each time he laughed his head felt as though it would burst. But the laughter shook him again like a spasm.

贝仑多中尉望着上尉的脸和异样的眼睛，以为他要将这个士兵就地正法。

"莫拉上尉，"他说。

"贝仑多中尉？"

"也许这个士兵是对的。"

"他说害怕，是对的？他说不想服从命令，也是对的？"

"不对。他说这是诡计，没错。"

"他们全都死了，"上尉说。"你没听到我说他们全都死了吗？"

"你是指躺在山坡上的我们的同志？"

"开枪呀，"他站在灰色的花岗岩石上挥舞着两臂大喊。"开枪打我吧！杀死我吧！"

山顶上，伏在死马后面的艾苏道咧嘴笑了。

艾苏道笑得胸口直颤，从马屁股旁偷偷张望，看到上尉站在大岩石上挥舞着双臂，另一个军官站在岩石旁边。狙击手站在另一边。艾苏道目不转睛地盯着这目标，高兴地晃着头。

"开枪打我吧，"他低声自语。"杀死我吧！"他的肩膀又颤动起来。他一笑胳膊就痛，脑袋也像要炸裂似的，但是他又笑起来像浑身痉挛似的。

The captain, standing in the open beside the boulder, commenced to shout filth at the hilltop. There is no language so filthy as Spanish. There are words for all the vile words in English and there are other words and expressions that are used only in countries where blasphemy keeps pace with the austerity of religion.

Now the captain stopped shouting and turned to Lieutenant Berrendo. His eyes looked stranger than ever.

"Paco," he said, happily, "you and I will go up there."

"Not me."

"What?" The captain had his pistol out again.

I hate these pistol brandishers, Berrendo was thinking. They cannot give an order without jerking a gun out. They probably pull out their pistols when they go to the toilet and order the move they will make.

"I will go if you order me to. But under protest," Lieutenant Berrendo told the captain.

"Then I will go alone," the captain said. "The smell of cowardice is too strong here."

Holding his pistol in his right hand, he strode steadily up the slope. Berrendo and the sniper watched him. He was making no attempt to take any cover and he was looking straight ahead of him at the rocks, the dead horse, and the fresh-dug dirt of the hilltop.

上尉站在大岩石旁，毫无遮蔽，开始朝山顶谩骂。没有语言比西班牙语更龌龊。英语里有的脏话它都有，另外还有一些词语只在亵渎神灵和敬重神灵并驾齐驱的国家里使用。

上尉这时不喊了，转身朝着贝仑多中尉。他的眼神显得更加古怪。

“帕科，”他高兴地说，“你和我一起上山吧。”

“我不。”

“什么？”上尉又拔出手枪。

贝仑多在想，我讨厌这种挥舞手枪的家伙。他们不拔手枪就下不了命令。也许他们上厕所也要拔出手枪才能使上劲。

“如果你下命令，我可以去，但我不愿意，”贝仑多中尉对上尉说。

“我一个人去，”上尉说，“这儿怕死鬼的臭味太浓了。”

他右手握着枪，稳稳当当地大步走上山坡。贝仑多和狙击手望着他。他无意找掩护，笔直望着他面前山顶上的岩石、马尸和一堆新挖出的泥土。

El Sordo lay behind the horse at the corner of the rock, watching the captain come striding up the hill.

Only one, he thought. We get only one. But from his manner of speaking he is a big prey. Look at him walking. Look what an animal. Look at him stride forward. This one is for me. This one I take with me on the trip. This one coming now makes the same voyage I do. Come on, Comrade Voyager. Come striding. Come right along. Come along to meet it. Come on. Keep on walking. Don't slow up. Come right along. Come as you are coming. Don't stop and look at those. That's right. Don't even look down. Keep on coming with your eyes forward. Look, he has a moustache. What do you think of that? He runs to a moustache, the Comrade Voyager. He is a captain. Look at his sleeves. I said he was a big prey. He has the face of an English.

He squeezed the trigger of the automatic rifle gently and it pounded back three times against his shoulder with the slippery jolt the recoil of a tripoded automatic weapon gives.

艾苏道伏在马尸后面岩石的一角，注视着上尉大步爬上山来。

他想，只有一个。我们只赚到一个。但从他的口气听来，他是个大猎物。瞧他走路的样子，瞧这畜生，瞧他大步向前地走来了，这家伙归我了，我带这家伙上路啦。现在过来的这个人跟我是同路。来吧，同路人同志，迈开大步，径直过来吧，过来领教领教。来啊，一直走啊，别放慢脚步，笔直过来吧，就像这样走来吧。别停下来看那些死人啦。这就对了。别往脚下看啊。眼睛向前看，继续走啊。瞧，他留着小胡子。你觉得这小胡子怎么样？他爱留小胡子，这位同路人同志。他是个上尉，瞧他的袖章。我说过他是个大猎物嘛。他的脸像英国人。

他轻轻扣动自动步枪的扳机，这种自动武器射击时的后坐力使三脚架朝后滑动，枪托在他肩头连撞了三下。

上尉脸朝下倒在山坡上。他的左臂压在身下。握手枪的右臂伸出在脑袋前方。山坡下又一齐向山顶开枪了。

贝仑多中尉伏在大岩石后面，心想，现在非得在火力掩护下冲过开阔地带啦。他听到山顶传来的艾苏道低沉而嘶哑的声音。

“强盗！”声音传来，“强盗！开枪打我吧！杀死我吧！”

艾苏道伏在山顶上自动步枪后面，笑得胸部发痛，笑得自以为脑袋要裂开了。

“强盗，”他又愉快地喊着，“杀死我吧，强盗！”然后他愉快地摇着头。他想，我们同路的旅伴可真不少啊。

他打算等这军官离开大岩石掩护的时候，用自动步枪干掉他。他迟早不得不离开那里。艾苏道知道他躲在那里没法指挥，他认为时机很好，能把他干掉。

正在这时，山上的其他人第一次听到飞机的声音。

The captain lay on his face on the hillside. His left arm was under him. His right arm that had held the pistol was stretched forward of his head. From all down the slope they were firing on the hillcrest again.

Crouched behind the boulder, thinking that now he would have to sprint across that open space under fire, Lieutenant Berrendo heard the deep hoarse voice of El Sordo from the hilltop.

“Bandit!” the voice came. “Bandit! Shoot me! Kill me!”

On the top of the hill El Sordo lay behind the automatic rifle laughing so that his chest ached, so that he thought the top of his head would burst.

“Bandit,” he shouted again happily. “Kill me, bandit!” Then he shook his head happily. We have lots of company for the Voyage, he thought.

He was going to try for the other officer with the automatic rifle when he would leave the shelter of the boulder. Sooner or later he would have to leave it. El Sordo knew that he could never command from there and he thought he had a very good chance to get him.

Just then the others on the hill heard the first sound of the coming of the planes.

艾苏道没有听到飞机声。他正用自动步枪朝大岩石下坡的那一边瞄准。他想，等我看到他的时候，他肯定在奔跑，如果不留神，会打不中。他跑这段路时，我可以朝他后背射击。我应当让机枪随着他转动，打他前面。或者让他逃，然后朝他射击，打他前面。我要在那块岩石边上收拾他，对准他前面打枪。接着他觉得自己的肩被碰了一下，扭头看到华金灰白而惊恐的脸。他朝小伙子指点的方向一看，见到三架飞机正在飞来。

正在这时，贝仑多中尉突然从大岩石后面猛冲出来，低着头，撒开两腿，冲下山坡，奔到岩石堆后架着自动步枪的地方。

艾苏道在注视飞机，根本没有看到他溜了。

“帮我把枪抽出来，”他对华金说，小伙子就把架在马尸和岩石间的自动步枪拖出来。

飞机正在不慌不忙地飞来。它们排成梯队飞行，形体和声音越来越大。

El Sordo did not hear them. He was covering the down-slope edge of the boulder with his automatic rifle and he was thinking: when I see him he will be running already and I will miss him if I am not careful. I could shoot behind him all across that stretch. I should swing the gun with him and ahead of him. Or let him start and then get on him and ahead of him. I will try to pick him up there at the edge of the rock and swing just ahead of him. Then he felt a touch on his shoulder and he turned and saw the gray, fear-drained face of Joaquín and he looked where the boy was pointing and saw the three planes coming.

At this moment Lieutenant Berrendo broke from behind the boulder and, with his head bent and his legs plunging, ran down and across the slope to the shelter of the rocks where the automatic rifle was placed.

Watching the planes, El Sordo never saw him go.

"Help me to pull this out," he said to Joaquín and the boy dragged the automatic rifle clear from between the horse and the rock.

The planes were coming on steadily. They were in echelon and each second they grew larger and their noise was greater.

"Lie on your backs to fire at them," El Sordo said. "Fire ahead of them as they come."

He lay back and sighted with the automatic rifle as the planes came on steadily.

Through the hammering of the gun, there was the whistle of the air splitting apart and then in the red black roar the earth rolled under his knees and then waved up to hit him in the face and then dirt and bits of rock were falling all over. The whistle came again and the earth rolled under him with the roar. Then it came again and the earth lurched under his belly and one side of the hilltop rose into the air and then fell slowly over them where they lay.

The planes came back three times and bombed the hilltop but no one on the hilltop knew it. Then the planes machine-gunned the hilltop and went away. As they dove on the hill for the last time with their machine guns hammering, the first plane pulled up and made wing-over and then each plane did the same and they moved from echelon to V-formation and went away into the sky in the direction of Segovia.

"朝天卧倒，射击飞机，"艾苏道说。"等它们飞来，朝它们前面射击。"

他仰卧着，用自动步枪瞄着笔直地飞来的飞机。

在嗒嗒的枪声中，一声呼啸声划破长空，接着轰的一声，眼前一片又红又黑的景象，他膝下的土地震动起来，掀起泥土，打在他的脸上，泥土和碎石块劈头盖脸地落下来。呼啸声又响了，随着一声轰响，他身下的土地又震动起来。接着又是一声轰响，他肚子下面的土地突然坠落，山顶的一边腾空升起，接着泥土砂石渐渐落下来，砸在他们的身上。

飞机又飞回来了三次，轰炸山顶，但是山顶上的人谁也不知道了。飞机用机枪扫射山顶后飞走了。当这些飞机最后一次向山顶俯冲、用机枪嗒嗒地扫射时，第一架飞机拉起机头，横转飞过去，跟着每架飞机依样行事，队形就由梯形变为V形，朝塞哥维亚方向飞去。

After the planes went away Robert Jordan and Primitivo heard the firing start and his heart seemed to start again with it. A cloud of smoke drifted over the last ridge that he could see in the high country and the planes were three steadily receding specks in the sky.

They've probably bombed hell out of their own cavalry and never touched El Sordo and Company, Robert Jordan said to himself. The damned planes scare you to death but they don't kill you.

"The combat goes on," Primitivo said, listening to the heavy firing. He had winced at each bomb thud and now he licked his dry lips.

"Why not?" Robert Jordan said. "Those things never kill anybody."

Then the firing stopped absolutely and he did not hear another shot.

When the firing first stopped it did not affect him. Then as the quiet kept on a hollow feeling came in his chest. Then he heard the grenades burst and for a moment his heart rose. Then everything was quiet again and the quiet kept on and he knew that it was over.

战地钟声 *For Whom the Bell Tolls*

飞机离开以后，罗伯特·乔丹和普里米蒂伏听到枪声开始响了，他的心似乎又随着枪响而剧烈地跳动着。他能望到一片烟雾飘过高地上他能看见的最远的山脊，飞机在空中变成了三个固定的越来越小的斑点。

“说不定他们的狂轰滥炸炸了自己的骑兵，根本没炸到艾苏道一伙，”罗伯特·乔丹自言自语。“那些该死的飞机吓得你要死，却不一定把你炸死。”

“还在打哪，”普里米蒂伏听着猛烈的枪声说。炸弹每次爆炸声都使他战栗，他这时舔着干燥的嘴唇。

“为什么不打？”罗伯特·乔丹说，“那些玩意儿根本杀不了谁。”

接着枪声完全停了，他再也听不到射击声。

枪声刚刚停时，他倒不觉得怎么样。然而持续的寂静却使他心里感到空落落的。他接着听到手榴弹的爆炸声，心里顿时振奋起来。接着又是鸦雀无声，就此一片寂静，他知道，战斗结束了。

Pablo was responsible for hiding the horse of the dead horseman. Hiding in the pine forest, he saw the cavalry of their enemy. He counted the dead and the wounded and he recognized El Sordo's automatic rifle. He did not know what the poncho-wrapped bundle was which flapped against the led horse's flanks as the stirrup leathers swung but when, on his way home, he came in the dark onto the hill where El Sordo had fought, he knew at once what the long poncho roll contained. In the dark he could not tell who had been up on the hill. But he counted those headless corpses that lay there and then made off across the hills for his own camp.

Walking alone in the dark, with a fear like a freezing of his heart from the feeling the holes of the bomb craters had given him, from them and from what he had found on the hill, he put all thought of the next day out of his mind. He simply walked as fast as he could to bring the news.

When he came back to the camp, they didn't come back yet. The idea struck him that he would die like El Sordo. He rushed to Robert's sacks, cut them open, took out the exploders quickly and hid them in a dark corner.

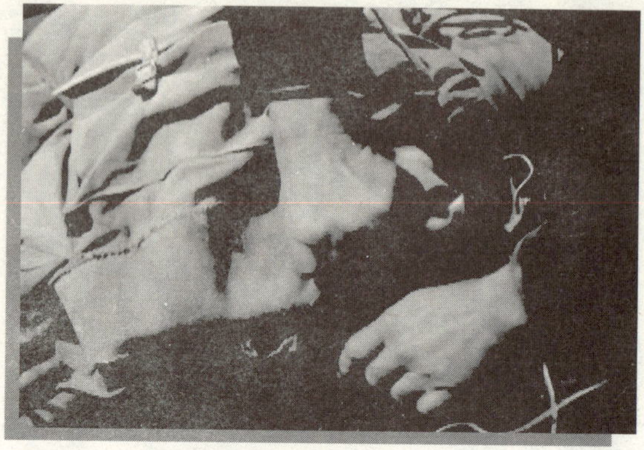

巴勃罗负责藏死去的骑手的马，躲在松林里看到了敌人的骑兵。他数着死者和伤员的人数，认出了艾苏道的自动步枪。那只用披风包成的包裹，随着马镫皮带的晃动，碰撞着带头的马的两侧，他不知道这里面是什么东西，可是等他在回营地的路上摸黑走上了艾苏道战斗过的山头，他立刻明白了这一长卷东西里面包的是什么了。他在黑暗中分辨不出山上躺着的人是谁。但是他把这些无头尸体数了一下，就越过山岭回自己的营地去了。

他这时独自在黑暗中走着，那些弹坑使他震惊，那些弹坑以及他在小山上发现的情况使他心里凉了半截，心里一点也不考虑转天的事情了。他只顾加快脚步回去通知大家。

当他回到营地时，他们还没有回来。一个念头突然袭上他的心头，他将要像艾苏道一样死去。他冲到罗伯特的背包前，用刀割开背包，迅速拿出引爆装置，藏到了一个黑暗的角落里。

Pablo drank sullenly and stared straight at the table. His eyes were focused on the wine bowl but he was not seeing it. Robert Jordan, Pilar and Maria came back and stared at him. Pablo told them what he had seen and what he had heard.

Anselmo was arranged to watch the road during the attack. Robert Jordan looked up as Anselmo came in.

"I come from above," Anselmo said to Robert Jordan.

"Pablo has told us," Robert Jordan said.

"There were five dead on the hill and they had taken the heads," Anselmo said. "I was there in the dark."

Robert Jordan nodded. Pablo sat there looking at the wine bowl and saying nothing. There was no expression on his face and his small pig-eyes were looking at the wine bowl as though he had never seen one before.

"Sit down," Robert Jordan said to Anselmo.

The old man sat down at the table on one of the hide-covered stools and Robert Jordan reached under the table and brought up the pinch-bottle of whiskey. It was about half-full. Robert Jordan reached down the table for a cup and poured a drink of whiskey into it and shoved it along the table to Anselmo.

"Drink that, old one," he said.

巴勃罗阴郁地喝着酒，直勾勾地瞪着桌子。他的眼光集中在酒缸上，但是视而不见。罗伯特·乔丹、比拉尔和玛丽亚回来后，都盯着他看。巴勃罗把他的所见所闻都告诉了他们。

安塞尔莫在激战时被派出去守望公路。他进来时，罗伯特·乔丹抬头望了他一眼。

"我从山上来，"安塞尔莫对罗伯特·乔丹说。

"巴勃罗告诉我们了，"罗伯特·乔丹说。

"山上有五个死人，敌人把脑袋都砍掉了，"安塞尔莫说。"我摸黑到那儿去过。"

罗伯特·乔丹点点头。巴勃罗坐在那儿望着酒缸，沉默不语。他脸上毫无表情，那双贪婪的小眼睛盯着酒缸，仿佛他从没见过酒缸似的。

"坐下吧，"罗伯特·乔丹对安塞尔莫说。

老人在桌边一只蒙着皮革的凳子上坐下来，罗伯特·乔丹伸手到桌子下面取出一瓶威士忌。瓶里大约有半瓶酒。罗伯特·乔丹伸手在桌上拿了一只杯子，斟了些威士忌，把它放在桌上，推向安塞尔莫。

"喝点吧，老头子，"他说。

"What passed on the road?" Robert Jordan asked.

"There was much movement," Anselmo said. "I have it all noted down as you showed me. I have one watching for me and noting now. Later I will go for her report."

"Did you see anti-tank guns? Those on rubber tires with the long barrels?"

"Yes," Anselmo said. "There were four camions which passed on the road. In each of them there was such a gun with pine branches spread across the barrels. In the trucks rode six men with each gun."

"Four guns, you say?" Robert Jordan asked him.

"Four," Anselmo said. He did not look at his papers.

"Tell me what else went up the road."

While Robert Jordan noted Anselmo told him everything he had seen move past him on the road. Anselmo told it from the beginning and in order with the wonderful memory of those who cannot read or write, and twice, while he was talking, Pablo reached out for more wine from the bowl.

"There was also the cavalry which entered La Granja from the high country where El Sordo fought," Anselmo said.

"公路上有什么动静？"罗伯特·乔丹问。

"情况不少，"安塞尔莫说。"我照你的吩咐，都记下来了。我找了一个人替我守望、做记录。过一会儿我去向她要情报。"

"你见到反坦克炮吗？有橡皮轮胎和长炮筒的家伙？"

"见到了，"安塞尔莫说。"路上开过四辆军用卡车。每辆上装有一门这种炮，上面的炮筒被松枝遮盖着，卡车上每门炮有六个人守着。"

"你说有四门炮？"罗伯特·乔丹问他。

"四门，"安塞尔莫说。他没看记录。

"跟我谈谈路上还有什么情况。"

安塞尔莫把他所看到的公路上的调动情况全都告诉罗伯特·乔丹，罗伯特·乔丹作着记录。安塞尔莫以既不识字又不会写字的人所擅长的惊人的记忆力从开头说起，讲得很有条理。他讲的时候，巴勃罗两次伸手从缸里舀酒。

"还有一队到拉格兰哈去的骑兵，他们是从艾苏道作战的高地上来的，"安塞尔莫说。

"Who beside you has been through the lines to the side of the Republic?"

"Andrés."

"How long would it take you to get to Navacerrada from here?" Robert Jordan asked Andrés.

"Carrying no pack and taking his precautions, in three hours with luck. We came by a longer, safer route because of the material."

"You can surely make it?"

"There is no such thing as surely."

"Not for you either?"

"No."

That decides that, Robert Jordan thought to himself. If he had said that he could make it surely, surely I would have sent him. But I don't have another choice.

"I will write a dispatch and send it by you," Robert Jordan said. "I will explain to you where you can find the General. You will be at the Mayor of the Division."

"But is that not a place?"

"Certainly it is a place," Robert Jordan explained patiently. "But it is a place the General will have selected. It is where he will make his headquarters for the battle. It will probably be a cave or dugout, a refuge, and wires will run to it."

Robert Jordan commenced writing in his notebook.

"除你之外，谁还越过火线到共和国那边去过？"

"安德烈斯。"

"你从这儿到纳瓦塞拉达去，要多长时间？"罗伯特·乔丹问安德烈斯。

"不背包裹，小心留神，运气好的话，要3个小时。要带着情报，我们会挑一条较长但较安全的路线。"

"你准能到达目的地吗？"

"哪有什么说得准的事情！"

"你也没准？"

"是啊。"

罗伯特·乔丹心想，就这样决定吧，如果他说准能到达目的地，我当然会派他去，但没有选择余地了。

"我写份急件，你送过去，"罗伯特·乔丹说，"我来跟你讲到什么地方去找将军。他在师参谋部。"

"师参谋部可是个地方？"

"当然是个地方，"罗伯特·乔丹耐心地解释，"不过这是将军自己挑选的地方。他把作战司令部设在那儿。很可能是个山洞，或者地下掩体，有电话线通到那儿。"

罗伯特·乔丹开始在他的笔记本上写着。

Concentrating on his report to Golz, trying to put it in the fewest words and still make it absolutely convincing, trying to put it so the attack would be cancelled, absolutely, yet convince them he wasn't trying to have it called off because of any fears he might have about the danger of his own mission, but wished only to put them in possession of all the facts, Robert Jordan tore the page and wrote it carefully.

I probably should send two copies, he thought. But if I do we will not have enough people to blow it if I have to blow it. What do I know about why this attack is made? Maybe it is only a holding attack. Maybe they want to draw those troops from somewhere else. Perhaps they make it to draw those planes from the North. Maybe that is what it is about. Perhaps it is not expected to succeed. What do I know about it? This is my report to Golz. I do not blow the bridge until the attack starts. My orders are clear and if the attack is called off I blow nothing. But I've got to keep enough people here for the bare minimum necessary to carry the orders out.

罗伯特·乔丹正在集中注意力给戈尔兹写报告，力求简洁，而且要力透纸背，说服对方完全取消这次进攻，但又要使他们相信，他之所以主张取消这次进攻，并非出于害怕执行他自己的使命时可能遇到危险，而只是希望他们了解所有的情况。他撕下这页纸，认真地写着。

他想，也许我应该分送两份。然而既要这样做，又要炸桥的话，人手就不够了。关于发动这次进攻的原因，我知道些什么呢？也许这只是一次牵制性攻势，也许他们是想吸引其他地方的军队，也许他们这样干是为了吸引北方的飞机，也许是为了这个吧。他们也许并不指望这次进攻获得成功。我知道些什么呢？这是我写给戈尔兹的报告。我要等到进攻开始才炸桥，我接到的命令是清楚无误的。要是取消这次进攻，我就什么也不炸。但是我必须在这儿保持万一执行命令所需要的人手。

Pablo looked from the wine bowl to Anselmo's face as he drank and then he looked back at the wine bowl.

"Listen, English," Pablo said, still looking at the wine bowl.

"I am writing," Robert Jordan said without looking up.

"Listen, English," Pablo spoke directly to the wine bowl. "There is no need to be disheartened in this. Without El Sordo we have plenty of people to take the posts and blow your bridge."

"Good," Robert Jordan said without stopping writing.

"Plenty," Pablo said. "I have admired your judgment much today, English," Pablo told the wine bowl. "I think you have many ideas. You are smarter than I am. I have confidence in you."

Robert Jordan didn't hear what Pablo said.

"English," Pablo said.

"What did you say?" he asked Pablo.

"That I have confidence, English." Pablo was still addressing the wine bowl.

Man, I wish I had, Robert Jordan thought. He went on writing. I wish the attack could be cancelled, because the enemy is well-prepared. If the attack has to be carried out, we will probably fail.

安塞尔莫喝酒的时候，巴勃罗的目光从酒缸上移到他脸上，接着又回过头来望着酒缸。

"听着，英国人，"巴勃罗说，仍然盯着那只酒缸。

"我在写哪，"罗伯特·乔丹说，没有抬头。

"听着，英国人，"巴勃罗直接对着酒缸说，"这件事你不用灰心丧气。没有了艾苏道，我们还有很多人，能攻下哨所，炸掉你的桥。"

"好，"罗伯特·乔丹一边说，一边不停地写。

"很多人，"巴勃罗说。"今天我很佩服你的果断，英国人，"巴勃罗对着酒缸说，"我看你很有主意。你比我聪明。我信得过你。"

巴勃罗的话，他一句也没听见。

"英国人，"巴勃罗说。

"你说什么？"他问巴勃罗。

"我有信心了，英国人，"巴勃罗仍然对着酒缸说。

伙计啊，罗伯特·乔丹想，但愿我有信心啊。他继续写着。但愿能够取消这次进攻，敌人已经准备好了。如果还要进攻的话，我们恐怕会失败的。

Robert Jordan folded his letter and said to Andrés, "You must ask for the General and for the Mayor of the Division. You must give this to the General or to the Chief of his Mayor or to another whose name I have written. One of them will surely be there even if the others are out inspecting the preparations for the attack. Do you understand now?"

"Yes."

Robert Jordan showed him the small, round, wooden-backed rubber stamp with the seal of the SIM and the round, tin-covered inking pad no bigger than a fifty-cent piece he carried in his pocket. "That seal they will honor. You must go quickly but first you must understand."

"This of staffs and divisions is a mystery to me. Always have I gone to such things as definite places such as a house."

"With this General," Robert Jordan said, "it will be some place very close to the lines. It will be underground to protect from the planes. You will find it easily by asking, if you know what to ask for. You will only need to show what I have written. You must get there quickly."

罗伯特·乔丹折好了信对安德烈斯说："你得去打听一下将军和师参谋部的所在地。你得把这份情报交给将军或者参谋长，或者另外一个人，我已经把这人的名字写在上面了。即使他们外出视察进攻的准备工作，也肯定有一个会留守在那里。你现在明白了吗？"

"明白了。"

罗伯特·乔丹从口袋里掏出一个圆形的木柄小橡皮图章给他看，上面有 SIM 三个字母，还有一个和五角硬币差不多大小的铁壳圆形小印台。"这个公章会引起他们的重视。你得马上走，但先要弄明白。"

"参谋部啦，师啦，这些名堂，我是莫名其妙的。我去的地方总是像房子之类有确切的地点的。"

"这个将军的指挥所，"罗伯特·乔丹说，"该在靠火线很近的某处。为了防飞机轰炸，可能会设在地下。你知道了要打听什么，一问就能找到。你只要拿出我写的东西就行了。你得赶快到那儿去。"

So now everything had been done that there was to do that night. All orders had been given. Every one knew exactly what he was to do in the morning. Either it would come now with the coming of the daylight or it would not come. I believe that it will come, Robert Jordan told himself, walking back down from the upper post where he had gone to speak to Primitivo.

Golz makes the attack but he has not the power to cancel it. Permission to cancel it will have to come from Madrid. The chances are they won't be able to wake anybody up there and if they do wake up they will be too sleepy to think. I should have gotten word to Golz sooner of the preparations they have made to meet the attack, but how could I send word about something until it happened? They did not move up that stuff until just at dark.

He found everybody out of the mouth of the cave and asked Pilar, "What passes with you?"

"Pablo is gone," the big woman said to him.

"When?" he asked.

"It must be an hour."

"And?"

"What should we do?" other people asked.

"Do what we should do without him."

那天晚上该做的事情这时都落实了。命令全部下达了。人人都知道了自己早晨要执行的确切任务，无论天亮时发动进攻与否。罗伯特·乔丹到上面的岗哨跟普里米蒂伏说话之后，在回来的路上对自己说：我相信会发动的。

戈尔兹部署了这次进攻，但他没有权力撤销。要撤销必须得到马德里的批准。他们很可能没法叫醒那儿的人，即使叫得醒，那些人也会昏昏欲睡，不会认真考虑。我应该把敌人为了对付进攻所作的准备的情况提早报告给戈尔兹，但是事情还没有发生，我怎能事先就打报告呢？天一黑敌人才调动那些武器。

他发现大家都站在洞外，就问比拉尔："你们怎么啦？"

"巴勃罗溜掉啦，"这大个子妇人对他说。

"什么时候？"他问。

"准有一小时了。"

"那又怎样？"

"我们怎么办？"其他人问。

"做我们该做的事，不管他。"

Robert Jordan and Maria stayed out of the cave. "You taught me a lot, beautiful girl," he said in English.

"What did you say?"

"I have learned much from you."

"It is you who are educated."

Educated, he thought. I have the very smallest beginnings of an education. The very small beginnings. If I die on this day it is a waste because I know a few things now. I wonder if you only learn them now because you are over-sensitized because of the shortness of the time? Anselmo is my oldest friend. Agustín, with his vile mouth, is my brother, and I never had a brother. Maria is my true love and my wife. I never had a true love. I never had a wife. She is also my sister, and I never had a sister, and my daughter, and I never will have a daughter. I hate to leave a thing that is so good.

"I find life very interesting," he said to Maria. She was sitting beside him on the robe, her hands clasped around her ankles. It was night still and here was no promise of morning except that as he looked up through the pines he saw how low the stars had swung.

战地钟声 *For Whom the Bell Tolls*

罗伯特·乔丹和玛丽亚待在洞外。“你教了我很多东西，漂亮姑娘，”他用英语说。

“你在说什么？”

“我从你那儿学到很多东西。”

“你才是受过教育的人。”

受过教育，他想，我受的教育才仅仅是开了个头。要是我们今天死了，那就可惜了，我现在才懂得了一些事理。我难以肯定，是不是因为时间短促，现在你才会变得过于敏感，才学到了一些知识。安塞尔莫是我最熟悉的朋友。满嘴脏话的奥古斯丁是我的兄弟，而我从没有过兄弟。玛丽亚是我真正的爱人，我的妻子。我从没有过真正的爱人，没有过妻子。她也是我的妹妹，而我从没有过妹妹，她还是我的女儿，而我永远不会有女儿啦。我真不愿意和这样的好事说再见。

“我发现生活挺有意思的，”他对玛丽亚说。她坐在他身边的睡袋上，双手抱着脚踝。这时仍是黑夜，还没有天亮的意思，不过他抬头穿过松林望去，看见星星悬挂得很低。

"Robert," Maria said.

"Yes, beautiful girl."

"In this of today we will be together, will we not?"

"After the start, yes."

"Not at the start?"

"No. You will be with the horses."

"I cannot be with you?"

"No. I have work that only I can do and I would worry about you."

"But you will come fast when it is done?"

"Very fast," he said and grinned in the dark.

"Listen. Pilar told me something—"

"Say it."

"No. It is better not to. "

"What was it you were going to say?"

"I do not wish to say it."

"Perhaps it would be better to say it if it could be important."

"You think it is important?"

"Yes."

"But how can you know when you do not know what it is?"

"From your manner."

"I will not keep it from you then. Pilar told me that we would all die tomorrow and that you know it as well as she does and that you give it no importance. She said this not in criticism but in admiration."

"She said that? She is a manure-mouthed superstitious bitch," he said.

“罗伯特，”玛丽亚说。

“嗯，漂亮姑娘。”

“今天行动起来，我们可以在一起，对吗？”

“完成行动以后，可以在一起。”

“从一开始的时候不行吗？”

“不行。你得照看马匹。”

“我不能和你在一起吗？”

“是的。我的工作只有我能干，你在身边我要操心的。”

“你完成后很快就回来吗？”

“很快，”他说，在黑暗中咧嘴笑了。

“听着，比拉尔跟我讲过一件事。”

“说吧。”

“还是不说的好。”

“你刚才想说的是什么事？”

“我不想说了。”

“是要紧事，也许还是说的好。”

“你认为要紧？”

“对。”

“你还不知道是什么事，怎么知道要紧呢？”

“从你的态度看得出来。”

“那我就不瞒你了。比拉尔曾对我说，我们明天都要死了，还说你跟她一样清楚，可是你不把它当一回事。她说这话不是批评，而是钦佩你。”

“她这样说的吗？她这个胡说八道又迷信的婊子，”他说。

"Pilar wants me to tell you the truth. Even if she doesn't tell me to do it, I'll tell you." Maria continued.

"I don't want to listen."

"I must tell it to you. They took us to the barbershop which was across the square from the city hall. I saw my face in the mirror of the barbershop and the faces of those who were holding me and the faces of three others who were leaning over me and I knew none of their faces but in the glass I saw myself and them, but they saw only me. And it was as though one were in the dentist's chair and there were many dentists and they were all insane. My own face I could hardly recognize because my grief had changed it but I looked at it and knew that it was me. But my grief was so great that I had no fear nor any feeling but my grief. At that time I wore my hair in two braids and as I watched in the mirror one of them lifted one of the braids and pulled on it so it hurt me suddenly through my grief."

"比拉尔让我告诉你我的遭遇，就是她不让我说，我也想告诉你，"玛丽亚继续说。

"可我不想听。"

"可我一定要说。他们带着我们穿过广场，在镇公所对面的理发店门口停下了。我在理发店的镜子里看到了自己的脸，看到了那些抓住我的人的脸，看到了另外三个俯在我身上的人的脸，这些脸，我一个也不认得，但是在镜子里我看到了自己和他们，而他们只看到了我。那就像一个人坐在牙科诊所的椅子上，有很多牙科医生围着他，他们都发了疯。我几乎没法认出自己的脸了，因为我伤心得脸都变形了，但我望着它，知道那是自己的脸。然而我伤心得已不感到害怕，也没其他感觉了，只是伤心。当时我梳着两条辫子，我从镜子里见到有个人抓住了一条辫子猛拉，这使我在悲伤中，突然间疼痛难忍。"

Maria continued, "And then he cut it off close to my head with a razor. And I saw myself with one braid and a slash where the other had been. Then he cut off the other braid but without pulling on it and the razor made a small cut on my ear and I saw blood come from it. Can you feel the scar with your finger?"

"Yes. But would it be better not to talk of this?"

"This is nothing. I will not talk of that which is bad. So he had cut both braids close to my head with a razor and the others laughed and I did not even feel the cut on my ear and then he stood in front of me and struck me across the face with the braids while the other two held me and he said, 'This is how we make Red nuns. This will show you how to unite with your proletarian brothers. Bride of the Red Christ!' And he struck me again and again across the face with the braids which had been mine and then he put the two of them in my mouth and tied them tight around my neck, knotting them in the back to make a gag and the two holding me laughed."

玛丽亚接着说:"他用剃刀齐着发根把整条辫子割了下来。我看到自己只剩了一条辫子和另一条辫子的残根。他没有再拉拽,就把另一条辫子也割了,剃刀划破了我的耳朵,我看到流血了。你用指头能摸到伤疤吗?"

"能。不过还是别谈这事了,好吗?"

"没什么。我不谈那件惨绝人寰的事。他就这样用剃刀把我的辫子齐着发根割了下来,其他人哈哈大笑。我简直感觉不到耳朵上的伤口的痛。他站在我面前,用辫子抽打我的脸,而其他两个人抓住了我。他说,'这就是我们制造赤色尼姑的方法。这就叫你明白,怎样和你的无产阶级兄弟们打成一片。红色基督的新娘子!'他用辫子一遍又一遍地抽打着我的脸,然后用辫子勒住我的嘴,紧紧扎住我的脖子,在后面打了个结,这样塞住了我的嘴。两个按住我的人哈哈大笑。"

Maria almost cried, "And all of them who saw it laughed and when I saw them laugh in the mirror I commenced to cry because until then I had been too frozen in myself from the shooting to be able to cry. Then the one who had gagged me ran a clippers all over my head; first from the forehead all the way to the back of the neck and then across the top and then all over my head and close behind my ears and they held me so I could see into the glass of the barber's mirror all the time that they did this and I could not believe it as I saw it done and I cried but I could not look away from the horror that my face made with the mouth open and the braids tied in it and my head coming naked under the clippers. And when the one with the clippers was finished he took a bottle of iodine from the shelf of the barber and with the glass wand that is in the iodine bottle he touched me on the ear where it had been cut and the small pain of that came through my grief and through my horror."

玛丽亚几乎快哭了,"看到的人都哈哈大笑。我在镜子里看到他们笑的样子,我哭起来了,直到那时为止,枪杀使我麻木得哭不出来。那个堵我嘴的人用理发推子在我头上到处乱推,先从前额开始,一直推到后脖子根,然后在头顶上横推过去,满头都推到了,耳朵后面的地方都没漏掉。他们抓住我不让我动,所以我在理发店的镜子里看到给我剃光头的全部经过。剃完头,我真不敢相信,我不停地哭,但我没法不看我自己脸上的那副恐怖模样:张着嘴、勒着辫子,推子经过的地方,头发全光了。拿推子的人剃完了头,从理发店的架子上拿了瓶碘酒,用碘酒瓶里的玻璃棒擦我耳朵上的伤口,在我的伤心和惊恐之中,添上了零星的痛苦。"

"I saw all of this as it happened in the mirror and I no longer cried for my heart was frozen in me for my father and my mother and what happened to me now was nothing and I knew it. Then he put down the iodine bottle and picked up the clippers and said, 'Next,' and they took me out of the barbershop holding me tight by each arm and I stumbled over the barber lying there still in the doorway on his back with his gray face up, and we nearly collided with Concepción Gracla, my best friend, that two of them were bringing in and when she saw me she did not recognize me, and then she recognized me, and she screamed, and I could hear her screaming all the time they were shoving me across the square, and into the doorway, and up the stairs of the city hall and into the office of my father where they laid me onto the couch. And it was there that the bad things were done."

"My rabbit," Robert Jordan said and held her as close and as gently as he could. But he was as full of hate as any man could be.

"我在镜子里望着他们的一举一动，不再哭泣，我父亲和母亲的遭遇已使我伤心至极，我自己这时的遭遇已无足轻重了。这我心里明白。他放下碘酒瓶，拿着推子说，'下一个。'于是他们紧紧抓着我两条胳膊，把我从理发店里拖了出去。理发师还是仰天躺在门口，脸色灰白，我在他身上绊了一跤，当时有两个人正把我最好的朋友孔塞普西昂·格拉西亚拖进去，我和她几乎撞在一起。她当时看见了我却不认得我了，后来才认出是我，就尖叫起来。他们推推搡搡地把我带进广场对面镇公所的大门，一直上楼到我父亲的办公室，把我按倒在长沙发上。这一路上，我始终听到她的尖叫声。他们就是在那儿干下伤天害理的事来的。"

"我的兔子，"罗伯特·乔丹说，尽量温柔地紧搂着她。可是他满腔仇恨。

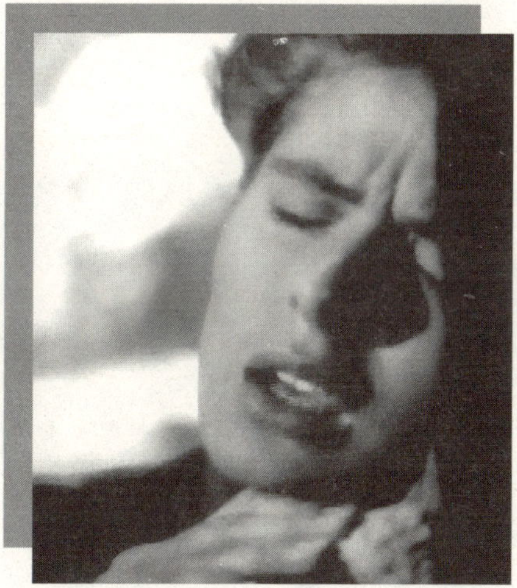

"But I know not how. Where things were done to me I fought until I could not see. I fought until—until—until one sat upon my head—and I bit him—and then they tied my mouth and held my arms behind my head—and others did things to me."

"Do not talk more about it. Do not tell me any more for I cannot bear my hatred now."

She was stiff and cold in his arms and she said, "No. I will never talk more of it. But they are bad people and I would like to kill some of them with you if I could. But I have told you this only for your pride if I am to be your wife. So you would understand."

"I am glad you told me," he said. "For tomorrow, with luck, we will kill plenty."

"But will we kill Falangists? It was they who did it."

"They do not fight," he said gloomily. "They kill at the rear. It is not them we fight in battle."

"But can we not kill them in some way? I would like to kill some very much."

"I have killed them," he said. "And we will kill them again. At the trains we have killed them."

"可我不知道他们要拿我怎样。当初他们糟蹋我的时候，我拼命挣扎，直到我什么都看不见。我挣扎到……到……到有个人坐在我头上……我就咬他……后来他们用绳子勒住我的嘴，把我两手反捆在脑后，别人就糟蹋我。"

"别再说了。别再跟我说了，现在仇恨使我已受不了啦。"

她在他怀里变得僵硬、冰冷。她说，"不说了，我再也不谈这事了。可他们是坏人，如果可能的话，我要跟你一起杀他们几个才解恨。不过我刚才告诉你那些，只是为了你的自尊心，因为我要做你的妻子了，应该让你知道。"

"很高兴你告诉了我，"他说，"明天走运的话，我们可以杀很多人。"

"我们要杀长枪党吗？坏事是他们干的。"

"他们不打仗，"他阴郁地说。"他们在后方杀人。和我们交锋的不是他们。"

"难道我们没办法杀他们吗？我真想杀几个这种人。"

"这种人我杀过，"他说。"今后我们还要杀。炸火车的时候我们杀过。"

"I would like to go for a train with you," Maria said. "The time of the train that Pilar brought me back from I was somewhat crazy. Did she tell you how I was?"

"Yes. Do not talk of it."

"I was dead in my head with numbness and all I could do was cry. But there is another thing that I must tell you. This I must. Then perhaps you will not marry me. But, Robert, if you should not wish to marry me, can we not, then, just be always together?"

"I will marry you."

"No. I had forgotten this. Perhaps you should not. It is possible that I can never bear you either a son or a daughter for Pilar says that if I could it would have happened to me with the things which were done. I must tell you that. Oh, I do not know why I had forgotten that."

"It is of no importance, rabbit," he said. "First it may not be true. That is for a doctor to say. Then I would not wish to bring either a son or a daughter into this world as this world is. And also you take all the love I have to give."

"我想和你一起去炸一次火车,"玛丽亚说,"那次炸火车后,比拉尔把我带走时,我有点疯疯癫癫了。她跟你讲过我那时的情形吗?"

"讲过。别谈这事了。"

"我当时头脑昏昏沉沉,只会哭。可是我还有一件事要告诉你。我非说不可。说了你也许不会娶我了。可是,罗伯特,要是你不愿意娶我,我们还能不能在一起呢?"

"我会娶你。"

"不。这件事我忘了。也许你不应该娶我。我可能永远不会给你生儿育女了,因为比拉尔说,要是会生育,他们糟蹋我之后我就会生了。我必须告诉你这件事。唉,我怎么会把这件事忘了。"

"这并不重要,兔子,"他说。"首先,情况可能还不是这样,这得由医生来断定。其次,我不希望把儿女带到这样混乱的世界上来。此外,我要把我的爱全部给你。"

After they talked, they bade good night. Maria couldn't fall asleep, so she came for Jordan, who was sleeping out of the cave.

"I love you, rabbit," he said to the girl.

"I was saying that you must not worry about your work because I will not bother you nor interfere. If there is anything I can do you will tell me."

"There's nothing," he said. "It is really very simple."

"I will learn from Pilar what I should do to take care of a man well and those things I will do," Maria said. "Then, as I learn, I will discover things for myself and other things you can tell me."

"There is nothing to do."

"Man, there is nothing! Your sleeping robe, this morning, should have been shaken and aired and hung somewhere in the sun. Then, before the dew comes, it should be taken into shelter."

"Go on, rabbit."

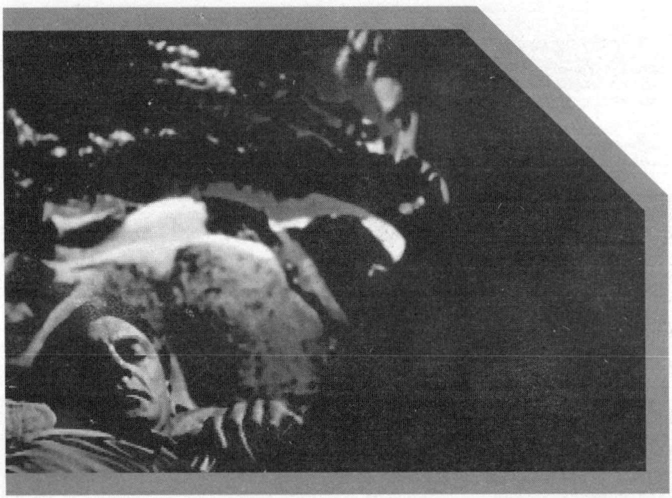

"Your socks should be washed and dried. I would see you had two pairs."

"What else?"

"If you would show me I would clean and oil your pistol."

"Sure. I'll show you."

"If you will teach me to shoot it either one of us could shoot the other and himself, or herself, if one were wounded and it were necessary to avoid capture."

说了这些话，他们就互道晚安，去睡觉了。玛丽亚睡不着，她来找罗伯特·乔丹，他正躺在洞外睡觉。

"我爱你，兔子，"他对姑娘说。

"我说，你千万别担心你的工作，我不会来麻烦你，也不会来妨碍你。有什么事我可以出力的，你对我说好了。"

"什么事也没有，"他说，"其实事情很简单。"

"我要问比拉尔，该做什么才能照顾好男人，然后我就去做那些事情，"玛丽亚说，"这样，我一边学，一边也会自己发现一些事情，另外有些事情呢，你也可以对我说。"

"什么事也不要你做。"

"你啊，什么事也没有！你的睡袋今天早晨就该拍一拍，挂在有太阳光的地方晒一晒，然后在降露水前收起来。"

"说下去，兔子。"

"你的袜子得洗、得晒。我要让你有两双。"

"还有呢？"

"你要是肯教我，我就给你擦枪、上油。"

"当然啦。我一定教你。"

"如果你教我开枪，万一我或你受了伤，为了不被俘虏，有必要时你可以枪杀我，我也可以枪杀你，或者自杀。"

"Very interesting," Robert Jordan said. "Do you have many ideas like that?"

"Not many," Maria said. "But it is a good one. Pilar gave me this and showed me how to use it," she opened the breast pocket of her shirt and took out a cut-down leather holder such as pocket combs are carried in and, removing a wide rubber band that closed both ends, took out a single-edged razor blade. "I keep this always," she explained. "Pilar says you must make the cut here just below the ear and draw it toward here." She showed him with her finger. "She says there is a big artery there and that drawing the blade from there you cannot miss it. Also, she says there is no pain and you must simply press firmly below the ear and draw it downward. She says it is nothing and that they cannot stop it if it is done."

"That's right," said Robert Jordan. "That's the carotid artery."

"But I would rather have you shoot me," Maria said. "Promise if there is ever any need that you will shoot me."

"Sure," Robert Jordan said. "I promise."

"真有趣儿,"罗伯特·乔丹说。"你有很多这样的主意吗? "

"不太多,"玛丽亚说。"不过这是个好主意。比拉尔把这个给了我，还教我怎么用," 她解开衬衫前胸的口袋,掏出一只放梳子的短小的皮套子,解开扎住两端的宽橡皮筋，抽出一张单面刮胡子刀片。"我一直带着这个,"她解释说。"比拉尔说,该搁在耳朵下面,朝这里一划。"她用手指比划给他看。"她说这里有根大动脉,用刀片朝这儿一划,绝对不会划错。她还说,不会有痛苦,只要在耳朵下面按紧,用刀片向下划。她说,这是轻而易举的,只要划成了,他们就拿你没办法了。"

"她说得不错,"罗伯特·乔丹说,"那是颈动脉。"

"可是我宁愿你枪杀我,"玛丽亚说。"答应吧,如有必要你一定要枪杀我。"

"行,"罗伯特·乔丹说,"我答应。"

"But there are other things I can do for you," Maria told him, sitting close beside him, now, very serious and womanly.

"Besides shoot me?"

"Yes. I can roll cigarettes for you when you have no more of those with tubes. Pilar has taught me to roll them very well, tight and neat and not spilling."

"Excellent," said Robert Jordan. "Do you lick them yourself?"

"Yes," the girl said, "and when you are wounded I will care for you and dress your wound and wash you and feed you—"

"Maybe I won't be wounded," Robert Jordan said.

"Then when you are sick I will care for you and make you soups and clean you and do all for you. And i will read to you."

"Maybe I won't get sick."

"Then I will bring you coffee in the morning when you wake—"

"Maybe I don't like coffee," Robert Jordan told her.

"No, but you do," the girl said happily. "This morning you took two cups."

"不过，我还可以替你做其他的事，"玛丽亚对他说，紧挨在他身边坐着，十分严肃，显出一副女性的娇态。

"除了枪杀我之外还能干别的事吗？"

"有。等你吸完了那些带嘴的烟卷，我可以给你卷烟。比拉尔教过我怎么把烟卷得好好的，又紧又齐，不会绽开。"

"棒极了，"罗伯特·乔丹说。"是你自己舔湿卷烟纸的吗？"

"是呀，"姑娘说。"等你受了伤，我来看护你，给你包扎伤口，给你擦身，给你喂饭……"

"要是我没受伤呢？"罗伯特·乔丹说。

"等你得了病，我来照顾你，给你做汤，把你弄得干干净净，事事伺候你，还读书给你听。"

"要是我没病呢？"

"你早晨醒来，我会给你端来咖啡。"

"要是我不爱喝咖啡呢？"罗伯特·乔丹对她说。

"不，你爱喝，"姑娘快乐地说，"你今天早晨就喝了两杯。"

"Suppose I get tired of coffee and there's no need to shoot me and I'm neither wounded nor sick and I give up smoking and have only one pair of socks and hang up my robe myself. What then, rabbit?" he patted her on the back. "What then?"

"Then," said Maria, "I will borrow the scissors of Pilar and cut your hair."

"I don't like to have my hair cut."

"Neither do I," said Maria. "And I like your hair as it is. So. If there is nothing to do for you, I will sit by you and watch you and in the nights we will sleep together."

Pilar hurried out of the mouth of the cave for Robert and looked very solemnly. "What's up?" Robert Jordan asked.

"Pablo has taken something of yours," the woman said miserably.

"So. What?"

"I do not know," she told him. "Come and see."

In the dark they walked over to the entrance of the cave, ducked under the blanket and went in. Robert Jordan followed her in the dead-ashes, bad-air and sleeping-men smell of the cave, shining his electric torch so that he would not step on any of those who were sleeping on the floor.

"如果我喝腻了咖啡，没有必要枪杀我，我既不受伤，也不得病，戒了烟，只有一双袜子，自己晒睡袋，那怎么办，兔子？"他拍拍她的背，"那怎么办？"

"那么，"玛丽亚说，"我要向比拉尔借把剪刀，给你理发。"

"我不爱理发。"

"我也不喜欢，"玛丽亚说。"我喜欢你现在的发型。那么，要是没事为你做，我就坐在你身边，看着你，晚上，我们可以一起睡觉。"

比拉尔从山洞里匆匆走出来找罗伯特，她表情非常严肃。"怎么啦？"罗伯特·乔丹问。

"巴勃罗拿了你的一些东西，"妇人悲伤地说。

"原来这样。拿了些什么？"

"不知道，"她对他说。"过来看看吧。"

他们在黑暗中走到洞口，撩起挂毯，钻进洞里。山洞里满是熄灭了的炉灰，污浊的空气和熟睡人们鼻息的气味，罗伯特·乔丹跟随着比拉尔走进去，打开手电，以免踩着睡在地上的人。

The two sacks were at the head of Pilar's bed which was screened off with a hanging blanket from the rest of the cave. The bed smelt stale and sweat-dried and sickly-sweet the way an Indian's bed does as Robert Jordan knelt on it and shone the torch on the two sacks. There was a long slit from top to bottom in each one. Holding the torch in his left hand, Robert Jordan felt in the first sack with his right hand. This was the one that he carried his robe in and it should not be very full. It was not very full. There was some wire in it still but the square wooden box of the exploder was gone. So was the cigar box with the carefully wrapped and packed detonators. So was the screw-top tin with the fuse and the caps.

Robert Jordan felt in the other sack. It was still full of explosive. There might be one packet missing.

He stood up and turned to the woman. There is a hollow empty feeling that a man can have when he is waked too early in the morning that is almost like the feeling of disaster and he had this multiplied a thousand times.

两个背包放在比拉尔的床头，床前挂着一条毯子，和山洞的其余部分隔开。罗伯特·乔丹跪在床上，手电光照在两个背包上，闻到一股印第安人床上发出的隔夜的、令人作呕的干掉的汗味。每个背包上从上到下有一条长长的裂缝。罗伯特·乔丹左手拿着手电，伸出右手在第一个背包里摸索。这个背包是装睡袋的，本来就不满，现在仍旧不满。一些电线还在里面，但是装引爆器的方木盒却不见了。被拿走的还有装仔细包扎好的雷管的雪茄烟盒，还有放导火线和火帽的带有螺旋盖的铁罐。

罗伯特·乔丹在另一个背包里摸索。里面仍装满了炸药。也许少了一包。

他站起身来，转身向着妇人。人在早上被叫醒得太早，会有一种仿佛大难临头般的空虚感，他现在的感觉比这要大一千倍。

Robert Jordan put his hand on the woman's shoulder. "It is nothing, Pilar," he told her. "What is gone is of small importance. We shall improvise something that will do as well."

"Was it part of your mechanism for the exploding?"

"Yes. But there are other ways to do the exploding. Tell me, did Pablo not have caps and fuse? Surely they would have equipped him with those?"

"He has taken them," she said miserably. "I looked at once for them. They are gone, too."

He squatted by the pannier. He reached into the pannier and picked out four grenades. Three were the oval bomb type, serrated, heavy iron with a spring level held down in position by a cotter pin with pulling rig attached.

"Have they always exploded?" Robert Jordan held the gray painted grenade in his hand, trying the bend of the cotter pin with his thumbnail.

"Always," Pilar said. "There was not a dud in any of that lot we used."

"And how quickly?"

"In the distance one can throw it. Quickly. Quickly enough."

罗伯特·乔丹一手放在妇人的肩上。"没有什么，比拉尔，"他对她说，"丢掉的东西不太重要。我们找些东西替代也行。"

"其中有你的爆破设备？"

"有。不过还有别的引爆办法。告诉我，巴勃罗自己没有雷管和导火线吗？以前人家给他炸药时肯定配备这种东西吗？"

"他拿走了，"她悲伤地说。"我刚才马上就找过。也都不见了。"

他挨着背篓，蹲在地上。他伸手到背篓里拿了四颗手榴弹，有三颗是椭圆形的、有棋盘格凹纹的手雷，厚实的铁壳上端有一根用开尾销扣住的弹簧杆和拉环。

"准能爆炸吗？"罗伯特·乔丹一手握着漆成灰色的手榴弹，用大拇指的指甲试了一下开尾销的弯管。

"准能，"比拉尔说。"我们用过的那一批中间没有一颗哑的。"

"爆炸得有多快？"

"扔得到多远，就在那里爆炸。快。够快的。"

"And these?"

He held up a tin-shaped bomb, with a tape wrapping around a wire loop.

"They are a garbage," Pilar told him. "They blow. Yes. But it is all flash and no fragments."

"But do they always blow?"

"Always," Pilar said. "There is no always either with our munitions or theirs."

He looked up from where he was squatted by the table and saw Maria and she smiled at him. He grinned back with the front of his face and selected four more grenades and put them in his pockets. I could unscrew the detonators and just use them, he thought. But I don't think the fragmentation will have any bad effect. It will come instantaneously with the explosion of the charge and it won't disperse it. At least, I don't think it will. I'm sure it won't. Have a little confidence, he told himself. Show yourself a little confidence now.

He grinned at Maria again but the grin was still no deeper than the skin that felt tight over his cheekbones and his mouth.

"那么这些呢？"

他举起一颗汤罐头形的手雷，拉环用一条带子绑着。

"这些是废物，"比拉尔对他说。"会炸。不错。但是只有火，没有弹片。"

"可是准能炸吗？"

"哪有准能的事，"比拉尔说，"我们的军火也好，他们的军火也好，没有百分之百的。"

他蹲在桌边，抬头望去，看见了玛丽亚，她在对他微笑。他也朝她露齿笑笑，但皮笑肉不笑。他又挑了四颗手榴弹，放进衣袋。我扭松手榴弹中的雷管，就拿它来引爆，他想。但我想弹壳爆裂不会引起什么不良的后果，弹壳一旦爆裂，立刻就能引爆炸药包，不会使炸药包分散，至少我认为不会分散，我肯定不会分散。他对自己说，要有点信心，现在显出一点信心来吧。

他又露齿对玛丽亚笑笑，但这一笑仅仅绷紧了颧骨和嘴边的皮肤，仍是皮笑肉不笑。

"One other thing, English," Pilar said as softly as her harsh whisper could be soft. "In that thing of the hand—"

"What thing of the hand?" he said angrily.

"No, listen. Do not be angry, little boy. In regard to that thing of the hand. That is all gypsy nonsense that I make to give myself an importance. There is no such thing."

"Leave it alone," he said coldly.

"Listen, English—" Pilar began. Robert Jordan looked toward her and as he did he saw her mouth open and the unbelieving look come on her face and he swung toward the cave mouth reaching for his pistol. There, holding the blanket aside with one hand, the short automatic rifle muzzle with its flash-cone jutting above his shoulder, was Pablo standing short, wide, bristly-faced, his small red-rimmed eyes looking toward no one in particular.

"Hello, English," he said. "I have three from the bands of Elias and Alejandro with their horses."

"And the exploder and the detonators?"

"I threw them down the gorge into the river," Pablo said still looking at no one. "But I have thought of a way to detonate using a grenade."

"So have I."

"还有一件事，英国人，"比拉尔用粗哑的嗓音尽量温柔地小声说。"至于手的事……"

"什么手的事？"他恼怒地说。

"不，听着。别生气，小兄弟。至于手相的事情，全是吉卜赛人的胡扯，是我有意抬高自己的身价罢了。没有这种事。"

"别谈这个了，"他冷冷地说。

"听着，英国人……"比拉尔开始说。罗伯特·乔丹朝她望去，只见她张开了嘴，脸上露出一副诧异的神色。他一边伸手拔手枪，一边飞快地转身对着洞口。洞口站着一个人，这人一手撩开毯子，短自动步枪的锥形枪口在肩胛上面露出来；他又矮又宽，满脸胡子，眼睑发红，一双小眼睛茫茫然地不知望着谁。正是巴勃罗。

"喂，英国人，"他说，"我把埃利亚斯和亚历杭德罗队里的三个兄弟和他们的马带来了。"

"引爆器和雷管在哪？"

"我扔到峡谷下面的河里去了，"巴勃罗说，还是茫茫然地不知望着谁。"不过我想出一个用手榴弹引爆的办法。"

"我也想到了。"

"What passes with you?" Pilar asked.

"Nothing. I had a moment of weakness. I went away but I am come back." He turned to Robert Jordan and said. "At bottom I am not a coward."

"Three was all I could get from Elias and Alejandro," Pablo said. "I have ridden since I left here. Nine of you could never have done it. Never. I knew that last night when the English explained it. Never. There are seven men and a corporal at the lower post. Suppose there is an alarm or that they fight?"

"I am glad to see you," Robert Jordan said. He walked over to him.

"So I rode for the others to make it possible for it to be successful. I have brought the best that I could get. I have left them at the top so I could speak to you, first. They think I am the leader."

"You are," Pilar said. "If you wish." Pablo looked at her and said nothing. Then he said simply and quietly, "I have thought much since the thing of El Sordo. I believe if we must finish we must finish together. But you, English. I hate you for bringing this to us."

"你是怎么回事？"比拉尔问。

"没什么。我一时软弱。我逃跑了，可我现在回来了。"他转身对罗伯特·乔丹说，"其实我不是胆小鬼。"

"从埃利亚斯和亚历杭德罗那儿我只能搞到三个人，"巴勃罗说。"我离开了这儿，一直骑着马跑。你们九个人是绝对应付不了的。绝对不行。英国人昨晚讲的时候我就明白，绝对不行。下面的哨所里有七个士兵和一个班长。要是有警报器，或者他们拼命抵抗呢？"

"见到你我很高兴，"罗伯特·乔丹说。他走到他身边。

"所以我骑马去找人，想能够把这次袭击搞成功。我把能找到的最棒的人带来了。我把他们留在山头上，好让我先来跟你谈谈。他们以为我是队长哪。"

"你愿意的话，"比拉尔说，"你是队长。"巴勃罗望着她，一句话也没有。他直截了当地悄声说，"艾苏道出事以后，我想了很多。我看哪，如果我们不得不送死的话，就一起完蛋吧。可是你啊，英国人，我恨你给我们带来厄运。"

"Well, you are welcome," Pilar said to him. "I did not think you couldst be the ruin you appeared to be."

"Having done such a thing there is a loneliness that cannot be borne," Pablo said to her quietly.

Pablo went on explaining to Pilar as though the others were not there. "I do not like to be alone. See? Yesterday all day alone working for the good of all I was not lonely. But last night."

"Your predecessor the famous Judas Iscariot hanged himself," Pilar said.

"Don't talk to me that way, woman," Pablo said. "Have you not seen? I am back. Don't talk of Judas nor nothing of that. I am back."

"How are these people you brought?" Pilar asked him. "Have brought anything worth bringing?"

"Good men," Pablo said. He took a chance and looked at Pilar squarely, then looked away.

"Good ones and stupids. Ready to die and all. According to your taste. The way you like them."

Pablo looked Pilar in the eyes again and this time he did not look away. He kept on looking at her squarely with his small, red-rimmed pig eyes.

"好，欢迎你，"比拉尔对他说。"我想你还不至于堕落到那种地步。"

"这次出走了，叫人感到孤单得受不了，"巴勃罗悄悄地对她说。

巴勃罗继续向比拉尔解释，好像其他人都不存在。"我不喜欢孤孤单单的。明白吗?昨天一整天我独自一人为大家的利益做事，不觉得孤单。可是昨天晚上哪……"

"加略人犹大，你那臭名昭著的老祖宗，最后是上吊自尽的，"比拉尔说。

"别这样跟我说话，太太，"巴勃罗说。"你没看见吗?我回来了。别讲叛徒犹大什么的了。我回来了。"

"你带来的是些什么人?"比拉尔问他。"带来的人可顶用?"

"都是好汉，"巴勃罗说。他趁机正眼看了她一下，然后望着别处。

"好汉和傻子。准备送死就是了。符合你的品味。你喜欢的就是这种人。"

巴勃罗又朝她的眼睛望着，这次不向别的地方看了。他那双眼睑通红的像猪眼一样的小眼睛直盯着她。

战地钟声 *For Whom the Bell Tolls*

In the dark they came up the hill through the timber to the narrow pass at the top. They were all loaded heavily and they climbed slowly. The horses had loads too, packed over the saddles.

"These I have brought think this is to be successful because I have brought them," Pablo said. "Do not say anything to disillusion them."

"Good," Robert Jordan said. "But let us make it successful."

"They have three horses, see?" Pablo said cautiously.

"Good," said Robert Jordan. "We will keep all the horses together."

"With those three I will deal with the lower post as well as El Sordo would have," Pablo said.

We went over this all ten minutes ago, Robert Jordan thought. I wonder why this now—

"There is a possibility of making it to Gredos," Pablo said. "Truly, I have thought much of it."

I believe you've had another flash in the last few minutes, Robert Jordan said to himself. But you're not going to convince me that I am invited. Do not ask me to believe too much.

他们摸黑穿过树林爬上山坡，来到山顶一条狭窄的山口。他们全都背着沉重的装备，缓慢地爬山。马鞍上也驮着东西。

"我带来的人以为这回事情准能干成，因为是我把他们带来的，"巴勃罗说。"别说叫他们泄气的话。"

"好，"罗伯特·乔丹说，"我们来把事情干成吧。"

"他们有三匹马，明白吗？"巴勃罗谨慎地说。

"好，"罗伯特·乔丹说，"我们把所有的马都集中在一起。"

"我带这三个人去对付下面的哨所，就像艾苏道会干的那样，"巴勃罗说。

罗伯特·乔丹想，十分钟之前我们已经全都讨论过了。不知道为什么现在……

"我们是有可能转移到格雷多斯山区去的，"巴勃罗说。"说实话，这问题我动了不少脑筋。"

罗伯特·乔丹对自己说，我看你脑子里在这最后几分钟内又闪出什么念头，但是你别打算让我相信你欢迎我一起去，别指望我给你太多的信任。

Robert Jordan went over to Pilar. "Listen, woman," he said softly.

"What now?" she whispered huskily, swinging a cinch hook clear from under the horse's belly.

"You understand that there is to be no attack on the post until you hear the falling of the bombs?"

"How many times do you have to tell me?" Pilar said. "You are getting like an old woman, English."

"Only to check," Robert Jordan said. "And after the destruction of the post you fall back onto the bridge and cover the road from above and my left flank."

"Do understand all?" Robert Jordan asked.

"Why not?" Pablo said. "Destroy the post. Cut the wire. Fall back on the bridge. Cover the bridge until you blow."

"And nothing to start until the commencement of the bombardment."

"Thus it is."

"Well then, much luck." Pablo grunted. Then he said, "You will cover us well with the machine gun and with your small machine gun when we come back, eh, English?"

"Off the top of the basket," Robert Jordan said.

After that, according to Robert's plan, the two groups prepared for the attack, waiting for the daylight.

罗伯特·乔丹向比拉尔走去。“听着,大娘,”他低声说。

“现在怎么啦? ”她哑着嗓子小声说，把马腹下的肚带钩解了下来。

“你要听到手榴弹的爆炸声才能袭击哨所,明白吗? ”

“你得跟我说多少回啊? ”比拉尔说。“英国人,你变得像个老太婆啦。”

“不过是想核实一下,”罗伯特·乔丹说,“端掉了哨所,你得回过头来向桥靠拢,从上面和我的左翼用火力封锁公路。”

“大家都明白了? ”罗伯特·乔丹问。

“怎么不明白? ”巴勃罗说。“端掉哨所。切断电线。回过头来向桥靠拢。封锁桥面,等你炸桥。”

“轰炸开始之前不许有任何行动。”

“就这样。”

“那就行了。祝你好运。”巴勃罗咕噜了一声,他接着说,“我们回头赶来的时候,你会用机枪和你的小机枪好好掩护我们,英国人,对吗? ”

“全力以赴,”罗伯特·乔丹说。

之后,他们两组人按罗伯特安排的那样去准备进攻,等待天亮。

Robert Jordan said to himself, you can do nothing now to protect her except to keep her out of it, and that you are doing. There are evidently going to be plenty of horses if you can believe the signs. The best thing you can do for her is to do the job well and fast and get out, and thinking of her will only handicap you in this. So do not think of her ever.

Having thought this out, he waited until Maria came up walking with Pilar and the horses.

"Hi, beautiful girl," he said to her in the dark, "How are you?"

"I am well, Robert," she said.

"Don't worry about anything," he said to her and shifting the gun to his left hand he put a hand on her shoulder.

"I do not," she said.

"It is all very well organized," he told her.

"I would rather be with you."

"No. The horses are where you are most useful."

"Good," she said. "There I will be."

Just then one of the horses whinnied and from the open place below the opening through the rocks a horse answered, the neigh rising into a shrill sharply broken quaver.

罗伯特·乔丹对自己说，你现在要保护玛丽亚，除了别让她卷进战斗以外，别无他法，而你现在正在这样做。如果种种迹象靠得住的话，显然会有很多马匹。你为她所能做的最好的事情，就是赶快把桥炸掉，撤离此地，而惦念着她只会妨碍你炸桥。所以别再想她了。

得出了这个结论，他等着玛丽亚跟比拉尔牵着马走过来。

"喂，漂亮姑娘，"他在黑暗中对她说，"你好吗？"

"很好，罗伯特，"她说。

"什么也别担心，"他对她说。他把机枪移到左手里，伸出右手放在她肩上。

"我不担心，"她说。

"一切都安排得很好，"他告诉她。

"我宁愿跟你在一起。"

"不。最需要你干的事是看住马。"

"好吧，"她说。"我去。"

正在这时，有匹马嘶叫起来，下面空地上有匹马回应着，声音穿过岩石的缺口传来，响得像一阵尖厉的断断续续的震颤声。

"Good-by, beautiful girl," Robert Jordan said. "I will see you soon."

He had an unreal feeling about all of this now as though he had said it all before or as though it were a train that were going, especially as though it were a train and he was standing on the platform of a railway station.

"Good-by, Robert," she said. "Take much care."

"Of course," he said. He bent his head to kiss her and his pack rolled forward against the back of his head so that his forehead bumped hers hard. As this happened he knew this had happened before too.

"Don't cry," he said, awkward not only from the load.

"I do not," she said. "But come back quickly."

"Do not worry when you hear the firing. There is bound to be much firing."

"No. Only come back quickly."

"Good-bye, beautiful girl," he said awkwardly.

"Good-bye, Robert."

"Good-bye, beautiful girl," he said. "Good-by, rabbit."

"Good-bye, my Robert." she said and he went over to where Anselmo was standing and said, "Let's go."

"再见，漂亮姑娘，"罗伯特·乔丹说，"我不久就要和你再见的。"

他对这一切产生了一种虚幻的感觉，好像他以前说过这些话，又好像有一列火车正要开出，尤其像真有一列火车，而他正站在站台上。

"罗伯特，再见，"她说，"多保重。"

"当然，"他说。他低下头去亲吻她，背上的包向前一滚，撞在他后脑勺上，因而他俩的前额重重地碰了一下。碰撞的时候，他想起这情形以前也发生过。

"别哭，"他别扭地说，倒不仅仅是因为背着东西。

"我不哭，"她说。"可你快回来啊。"

"听到枪声别担心。今天必然会枪声大作。"

"不担心。只要你快些回来。"

"再见，漂亮姑娘，"他别扭地说。

"再见，罗伯特。"

"再见，漂亮姑娘，"他说，"再见，兔子。"

"再见，我的罗伯特，"她说。他走到安塞尔莫站着的地方，说，"咱们走吧。"

Walking carefully, downhill, Anselmo in the lead, Robert Jordan placed his feet carefully so that he would not slip. He put his left hand out again and touched the rough bark of a tree trunk, then as he braced himself his hand feeling a smooth place, the base of the palm of his hand coming away sticky from the resinous sap where a blaze had been cut, they dropped down the steep wooded hillside to the point above the bridge where Robert Jordan and Anselmo had watched the first day.

Now Anselmo was halted by a pine tree in the dark and he took Robert Jordan's wrist and whispered, so low Jordan could hardly hear him, "Look. There is the fire in his brazier."

It was a point of light below where Robert Jordan knew the bridge joined the road.

"Here is where we watched," Anselmo said.

They put the packs down behind the base of the pine trunks and he followed Anselmo over to the level place where there was a clump of seedling pines.

Robert Jordan lay on the pine-needle floor of the forest and listened to the first stirring in the branches of the pines of the wind that would come with daylight. Anselmo found another place to ambush himself.

他们小心地爬下山去，安塞尔莫领头，罗伯特·乔丹小心地一步步踩着，免得摔跤。他伸出左手，摸到一根粗糙的树干，挺起身子，手上摸到一块光溜溜的树皮割开的地方，就把手缩回去，手心下部沾着黏糊的树脂。他们从树木丛生的陡坡上一路爬下来，来到桥上方的一个地方，那里就是罗伯特·乔丹和安塞尔莫第一天侦察的地方。

黑暗中，安塞尔莫被一棵松树挡住了去路，他握着罗伯特·乔丹的手腕，小声地说："瞧，那家伙的火盆里有火。"声音低得罗伯特·乔丹几乎听不到。

这一点火光所在的地方，罗伯特·乔丹知道，就是下面公路与桥梁的连接处。

"这里就是我们上次侦察的地方，"安塞尔莫说。

他们把背包放在几棵松树的树根背后，他跟着安塞尔莫向一块长着一簇小松树的平地走去。

罗伯特·乔丹伏在树林的里铺满松针的地上，倾听着随黎明而来的晨风吹拂树枝的沙沙声。安塞尔莫另找了个地方埋伏起来。

战地钟声 *For Whom the Bell Tolls*

罗伯特·乔丹把手提机枪的子弹夹抽出来，前后推动枪机。黑暗中，他把枪头转过来，拉开枪机，嘴唇凑在枪口上，往枪筒里吹了口气，舌头触及枪筒边，尝到了滑腻的金属味和油味。他把枪搭在一条胳膊的小臂上，枪口朝上，免得松针和其他东西掉到里面去。他用大拇指把所有的子弹从子弹夹中退出来，放在一块摊在面前的手帕上，然后在黑暗中摸着每颗子弹，在手指间拨弄一下，再把子弹一颗颗地推回子弹夹里去。这时，他手里的子弹夹又变得沉甸甸的，他把子弹夹再推进手提机枪里，咔嗒一声上好了。他匍匐在一棵松树后面，机枪横架在他左胳膊的小臂上，注视着下面的那点火光。他有时见不到这火光，他知道这是因为岗亭里的哨兵走到了火盆的前面。他就伏在那儿等着天亮。

Robert Jordan took the clip out of the submachine gun and worked the lock back and forth. Then he turned the gun, with the lock open and in the dark he put the muzzle to his lips and blew through the barrel, the metal tasting greasy and oily as his tongue touched the edge of the bore. He laid the gun across his forearm, the action up so that no pine needles or rubbish could get in it, and shucked all the cartridges out of the clip with his thumb and onto a handkerchief he had spread in front of him. Then, feeling each cartridge in the dark and turning it in his fingers, he pressed and slid them one at a time back into the clip. Now the clip was heavy again in his hand and he slid it back into the submachine gun and felt it click home. He lay on his belly behind the pine trunk, the gun across his left forearm and watched the point of light below him. Sometimes he could not see it and then he knew that the man in the sentry box had moved in front of the brazier. He lay there and waited for daylight.

Robert Jordan lay behind the trunk of a pine tree on the slope of the hill above the road and the bridge and watched it become daylight. He loved this hour of the day always and now he watched it; feeling it bright within him, as though he were a part of the slow lightening that comes before the rising of the sun; when solid things darken and space lightens and the lights that have shone in the night go yellow and then fade as the day comes.

The pine trunks below him were hard and clear now, their trunks solid and brown and the road was shiny with a wisp of mist over it. The dew had wet him and the forest floor was soft and he felt the give of the brown, dropped pine needles under his elbows. Below he saw, through the light mist that rose from the streambed, the steel of the bridge, straight and rigid across the gap, with the wooden sentry boxes at each end. But as he looked the structure of the bridge was still spidery and fine in the mist that hung over the stream.

罗伯特·乔丹在公路和桥上方的山坡上，伏在一棵松树后面，看着天色渐渐亮起来。他总是喜欢一天中的这个时刻，如今仔细看着天色，觉得心里也亮堂起来，仿佛自己就是太阳升起前天色逐渐变亮的光明的一部分；那时候，随着太阳升起，有形的实体色泽加深，空间变得明朗，在夜里照耀的灯光变成黄色，接着消失。

他下面的一棵棵松树这时显得明确而清晰，树干坚实，呈黄褐色，公路上蒙着一层泛着白光的薄雾。露水打在他身上湿漉漉的，树林里地面柔软，他感到落在地上的褐色松针在胳膊肘的压力下往下陷。他透过河床上升起的轻雾，看到下面那座笔直而坚挺的钢铁桥梁架在峡谷上，两端各有一座木制岗亭。但在他看来，笼罩在河上的薄雾使那座桥的钢架结构显得像静止的蜘蛛网般细巧。

战地钟声 *For Whom the Bell Tolls*

Robert Jordan lay there and watched the road and tried not to think at all. A squirrel chittered from a pine tree below him and he watched the squirrel come down the tree trunk, stopping on his way down to turn his head and look toward where the man was watching. He saw the squirrel's eyes, small and bright, and watched his tail jerk in excitement.

Then the squirrel crossed to another tree, moving on the ground in long, small-pawed, tail-exaggerated bounds. On the tree trunk he looked back at Robert Jordan, and then pulled himself around the trunk and out of sight. Then Robert Jordan heard the squirrel chitter from a high branch of the pine tree and he watched him there, spread flat along the branch, his tail jerking.

He looked down through the pines to the sentry box again. He would like to have had the squirrel with him in his pocket. He would like to have had anything that he could touch. He rubbed his elbows against the pine needles but it was not the same. He thought, nobody knows how lonely you can be when you do this. That I blow it well and that she gets out all right. He was waiting for the beginning of the attack quietly.

罗伯特·乔丹伏在那里望着公路，什么也不想考虑。一只松鼠在他下面一棵松树上吱吱地叫，他看着它顺树干往下爬，半路上停了一下，扭头张望注视它的人。他看到松鼠的眼睛又小又亮，注意到它的尾巴兴奋地抖动着。

松鼠用小爪子和巨大的尾巴在地上跳远似的蹦跳着，跳上了另一棵树。它在树干上回头望望罗伯特·乔丹，接着在树干上绕了一圈，就消失了。罗伯特·乔丹接着听到松鼠在松树的一根高枝上吱吱地叫，他望着它平伏在树枝上，抖动着尾巴。

他透过松林又向下面的岗亭望去。他很想捉住这只松鼠藏在衣袋里。他很想有样东西可以触摸一下。他用胳膊肘蹭蹭松针，但那是不一样的。他想，没有人知道在干这种事时你有多孤独，希望我能顺利完成炸桥，希望她顺利脱身。他静静地等待着进攻的开始。

Meanwhile, Andrés took the message for General Golz to cancel this ridiculous attack.

The fascists held the crests of the hills here. Then there was a valley that no one held except for a fascist post in a farmhouse with its outbuildings and its barn that they had fortified. Andrés, on his way to Golz with the message from Robert Jordan, made a wide circle around this post in the dark. He knew where there was a trip wire laid that fired a set-gun and he located it in the dark, stepped over it, and started along the small stream bordered with poplars whose leaves were moving with the night wind.

There was no continual defensive line and could easily have passed this position in the dark and made his way farther into the government territory before running into some one who would challenge him. But it seemed safer and simpler to get it over here.

Andrés had challenged at the government position. That was, he had lain down where the ground fell sharply away below the triple belt of wire and shouted up at the rock and earth parapet.

"Hello!" he had shouted. "Hello, militiaman!"

与此同时，安德烈斯去给戈尔兹将军送信设法取消这次荒唐的进攻。

法西斯分子占领着这里的这些山头。在山谷里有一家带外屋和牲口棚的农舍，法西斯分子把它建成工事，当做哨所，此外没有设防。安德烈斯带着罗伯特·乔丹的信件去找戈尔兹，在黑夜中兜了个大圈子，绕过这个哨所。他知道什么地方安有绊索，踩上就会牵动上了膛的枪扳机。他在黑夜中辨认出来，跨了过去，沿着一条岸边栽有白杨树的小河走着，树叶随着夜风摆动。

这里没有延绵不断的防线，在撞见质问他口令的人之前，他本可以轻易地在黑夜里绕过这个据点，在有人查问口令前，深入政府军的地区。但是，通过这一关卡看来更安全、更简单。

安德烈斯在政府军阵地前喊了口令。也就是说，他伏在三重铁丝网下陡峭地斜坡上，抬头朝着石块和土坯垒成的矮墙大声呼喊。

"你们好，"他大声喊道。"你们好，民兵们！"

战地钟声 *For Whom the Bell Tolls*

Andrés heard a bolt snick as it was pulled back. Then, from farther down the parapet, a rifle fired. There was a crashing crack and a downward stab of yellow in the dark. Andrés had flattened at the click, the top of his head hard against the ground.

"Don't shoot, Comrades," Andrés shouted. "Don't shoot! I want to come in."

"How many are you?" some one called from behind the parapet.

"One. Me. Alone."

"Who are you?"

"Andrés. From the band of Pablo. With a message."

"Have you your rifle and equipment?"

"Yes, man."

"We can take in none without rifle and equipment," the voice said. "Nor in larger groups than three."

"I am alone," Andrés shouted. "It is important. Let me come in."

He could hear them talking behind the parapet but not what they were saying. Then the voice shouted again, "How many are you?"

"One. Me. Alone. For the love of God."

Then the voice came, "Listen, fascist."

"I am not a fascist," Andrés shouted. "I am a guerilla from the band of Pablo. I come with a message for the General Staff."

安德烈斯听到枪栓往后扳的咔嗒声。在矮墙后更远一点的地方,有人放了一枪。枪声砰地一响,黑暗中嗖地闪了一道向下的黄光。安德烈斯听到了枪栓声,立刻卧倒,头顶紧紧地抵在地面上。

"别开枪,同志们,"安德烈斯喊道。"别开枪!我要过去。"

"你们几个人?"矮墙后有人喊着。

"一个。我。只有一个。"

"你是谁?"

"安德烈斯。巴勃罗队里的人。带着封信件。"

"你带着步枪和弹药?"

"带着,老兄。"

"我们不放带步枪和弹药的人进来,"那声音说。"三个人以上也不准进来。"

"我是一个人,"安德烈斯喊道。"有要紧事情。让我过去吧。"

他能听到他们在矮墙后面说话,但听不清说些什么。接着那声音又喊道:"你们是几个人?"

"一个。我。只有一个。看在上帝的分上。"

接着那声音说:"听着,法西斯。"

"我不是法西斯,"安德烈斯喊道。"我是巴勃罗队里的游击队员。我给总参谋部带来封信。"

"He's crazy," Andrés heard some one say. "Toss a bomb at him."

"Listen," Andrés said. "I am alone. I am completely by myself. Don't be in the midst of the holy mysteries, and I am alone. Let me come in."

"He speaks like a Christian," he heard some one say and laugh.

Then some one else said, "The best thing is to toss a bomb down on him."

"No," Andrés shouted. "That would be a great mistake. This is important. Let me come in."

It was for this reason that he had never enjoyed trips back and forth between the lines. Sometimes it was better than others. But it was never good.

"You are alone?" the voice called down again.

"How many times must I tell you? I AM ALONE."

"Then if you should be alone stand up and hold your rifle over your head."

Andrés stood up and put the carbine above his head, holding it in one hand.

"Now come through the wire. We have you covered with the machine gun," the voice called.

"Before we loose the machine gun on you," another shouted.

"You're not very amiable," Andrés said.

He was working his way through the wire.

"他是个疯子，"安德烈斯听到有人在说，"给他扔个手雷。"

"听着，"安德烈斯说，"只有我一个。就我一个。别疑神疑鬼啦，我就是一个人。让我过去吧。"

"他说话像个基督徒，"他听到有人笑着说。

接着另外有人说，"最好还是给他扔个手雷。"

"别，"安德烈斯喊道。"那就大错特错了。有要紧事情。放我过去吧。"

就为了这种原因，他一直不喜欢出入火线。有时盘问得宽些，但总是不愉快的。

"只有你一个人？"那声音又朝下面喊道。

"我得跟你说多少回啊？只有我一个人。"

"你要是一个人，那么站起来，把枪举过头。"

安德烈斯站起来，单手握着卡宾枪，举过了头。

"现在从铁丝网里钻进来。我们用机枪对着你，"那声音喊道。

"别等我们用机关枪向你扫射，"另一个喊着。

"你们可真不友善！"安德烈斯说。

他就费力地钻着铁丝网。

"I command here," a man said. "Let me see your papers."

He took them into a dugout and looked at them with the light of a candle. There was the little square of folded silk with the colors of the Republic and the seal of the SIM in the center. There was the safe conduct pass giving his name, age, height, birthplace and mission that Robert Jordan had written out on a sheet from his notebook and sealed with the SIM rubber stamp and there were the four folded sheets of the dispatch to Golz which were tied around with a cord and sealed with wax and the impression of the metal SIM seal that was set in the top end of the wooden handle of the rubber stamp.

"I have orders to deliver that dispatch to the General commanding the Thirty-Fifth Division, which makes an attack at daylight in these hills and it is already late at night and I must go. But I must go now to Navacerrada and go on from there. Will you send me to your commander who will give me transport to go on from there?" Andrés said.

"I take you to the Commander."

"这里我指挥,"有一个人说。"给我看你的证件。"他把证件拿进掩体,借着烛光看。那是一小块折成方形的印着共和国国旗的绸子,中央盖着军事情报部的公章。还有一张是罗伯特·乔丹用笔记本上的纸写的,上面写有他的姓名、年龄、身高、出生地点和任务的安全通行证,上面盖着军事情报部橡皮图章。还有一份给戈尔兹的急件,一共四张折好的纸,用一根绳子扎好,用蜡封好,上面盖上在军事情报部橡皮图章木柄顶端的金属章。

"我受命给指挥三十五师的将军送一份急件,他们天亮时要在这一带山里发动进攻,现在已经是深夜了,我得走啦。可我必须马上到纳瓦塞拉达去,到了那里还要上路。带我到你们的指挥官那儿去吧,让他派车把我送去,好吗?"安德烈斯说。

"我带你去见指挥官。"

Andrés had fòllowed this company commander to battalion headquarters where the battalion commander, who was named Gomez and who had been a barber before the movement, was filled with enthusiasm on hearing the account of his mission. He had decided to take him there himself in order to expedite things by motorcycle. They turned into the little smashed-roofed mountain-resort town where brigade headquarters was and Gomez had braked the motorcycle like a dirt-track racer and leaned it against the wall of the house where a sleepy sentry came to attention as Gomez pushed by him into the big room where the walls were covered with maps and a very sleepy officer with a green eyeshade sat at a desk with a reading lamp and two telephones.

This officer looked up at Gomez and said, "What doest you here? Have you never heard of the telephone?"

"I must see the Lieutenant-Colonel," Gomez said.

"He is asleep," the officer said. "I could see the lights of that bicycle of yours for a mile coming down the road. Dose wish to bring on a shelling?"

"Call the Lieutenant-Colonel, I say."

"Go obscenity yourself."

Gomez took his heavy 9 mm. Star pistol out of its holster and shoved it against the officer's shoulder.

安德烈斯跟随连长来到他所属的营部，营长听了他的使命后热情满怀。这位名叫戈麦斯的营长在革命前是个理发师。他决定亲自驾驶摩托车带他到那儿去赶快完成这件事。他们拐进一个被炸坏屋顶的山区疗养院，旅部就设在那里。戈麦斯像个赛车运动员一样刹住了摩托车，把车子停靠在屋子的墙边，门口有个睡眼惺忪的门卫对他行了一个立正。戈麦斯把他推开，走进一个大房间，房里四壁挂满了地图，有个昏昏欲睡的军官戴着一顶绿色的护目眼罩坐在写字台旁，上面摆着一盏台灯和两架电话机。

这位军官抬头望望戈麦斯说，“你到这儿来有什么事？你从没听说过有电话这东西吗？”

“我必须见中校，”戈麦斯说。

“他在睡觉，”军官说。“在1英里外我就看见你亮着车灯在路上开来。你想把炮弹招来吗？”

“叫醒中校，我说。”

“滚你的。”

戈麦斯从枪套里拔出沉重的9毫米口径的星牌手枪，猛地抵在军官肩上。

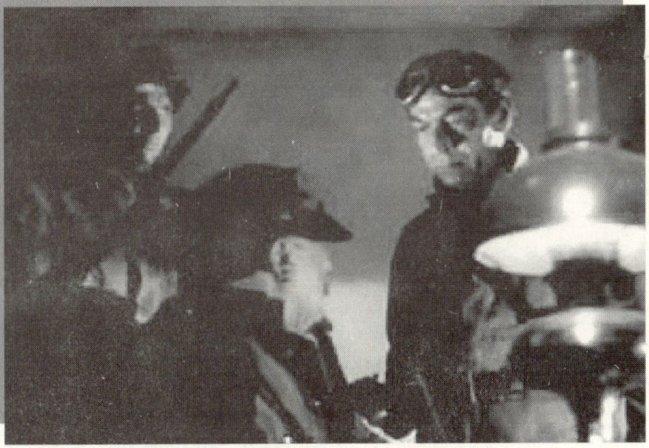

“叫醒他，你这个法西斯杂种，”戈麦斯说。“叫醒他，否则我宰了你。”

“冷静点，”军官说。

安德烈斯在台灯光中见到戈麦斯恨得脸都变了形，但是他所说的只是“叫醒他”。

“勤务兵，”军官用轻蔑的声音喊道。

一名士兵进来了，敬个礼，又出去了。

过了一会儿，穿着睡衣裤的米兰达中校来到屋里，戈麦斯马上立正敬礼。

“戈麦斯，什么风把你吹来了？”中校问。

戈麦斯给他看安德烈斯的证件和急件。中校对通行证快速地看了一眼，就望着安德烈斯，点了点头，微微一笑，然后如饥似渴地看急件，最后把通行证和急件一起交还给安德烈斯。

“戈麦斯，你还是用摩托车把他送去吧。”中校说。“给他们开一张到戈尔兹将军参谋部去的可靠的通行证，我来签字，”他对戴着绿色赛璐珞护眼罩的军官说，“用打字机打，佩贝。这是他的详细情况，”他示意安德烈斯把通行证拿出来，“盖上两个章。”

“你们现在必须马上就走，”他对戈麦斯和安德烈斯说。“开车当心。”

“Rouse him, you fascist bastard,” Gomez said. “Rouse him or I'll kill you.”

“Calm yourself,” the officer said.

Andrés saw Gomez's face draw with hate in the light of the reading lamp. But all he said was, “Rouse him.”

“Orderly,” the officer called in a contemptuous voice.

A soldier came to the door and saluted and went out.

After a while, as the Lieutenant-Colonel Miranda came into the room in his pajamas, Gomez drew himself stiff and saluted.

“What brings you, Gomez?” the Lieutenant-Colonel asked.

Gomez showed him Andrés's papers and the dispatch. The Lieutenant-Colonel looked at the safe conduct quickly, looked at Andrés, nodded and smiled, and then looked at the dispatch hungrily, and then handed both the safe-conduct and dispatch back to Andrés.

“You had better take him, Gomez, on the motor,” the Lieutenant-Colonel said. “Write them a very strong safe conduct to the Mayor of General Golz for me to sign,” he said to the officer in the green celluloid eyeshade. “Write it on the machine, Pepe. Here are the details,” he motioned for Andrés to hand over his safe-conduct, “and put on two seals.”

“You must go now quickly,” he said to Gomez and Andrés. “Be careful with the motor.”

Andrés, holding tight onto the seat where Gomez was forking the motor, bent his head against the wind as the motorcycle moved, noisily exploding, into the light-split darkness of the country road that opened ahead sharp with the high black of the poplars beside it, dimmed and yellow-soft now as the road dipped into the fog along a stream bed, sharpening hard again as the road rose and, ahead of them at the crossroads, the headlight showed the gray bulk of the empty trucks coming down from the mountains.

Where they came onto the main highroad to Navacerrada on which the trucks were rolling back from the mountain there was a control. But when Gomez showed the sentry at the control his safe conduct from the Lieutenant-Colonel Miranda the sentry put the light from a flashlight on it, showed it to the other sentry with him, then handed it back and saluted.

"Continue," he said. "But without lights."

Then ahead all the trucks were stopped and riding on, working his way ahead past ambulances, staff cars, an armored car, another, and a third, all halted, they found another control where there had been a smash-up.

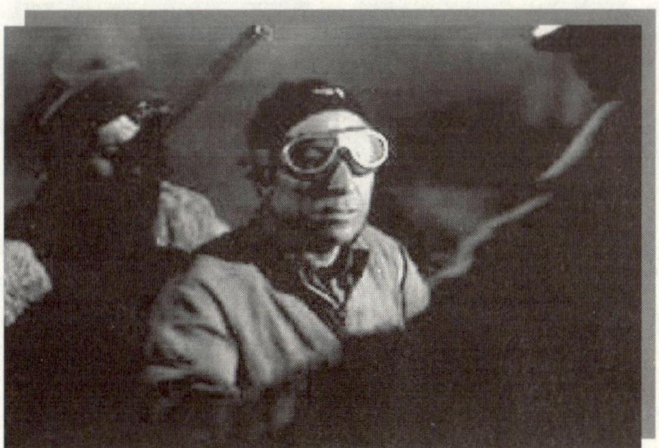

戈麦斯叉开双臂驾着摩托车，安德烈斯紧抓了座位，低头迎着风，摩托车噗噗地行驶在乡间大路上，车灯劈开了黑夜，前方的路面在路边两排黑黑的高大的白杨树中显得格外清晰，沿着大路下坡闯入小河河床边升起的薄雾里显得模糊而昏黄，等到路面上升时，又显得越来越分明了，他们前面出现了交叉路，车灯照亮了从山上开下来的一行灰暗的空卡车。

他们来到通向纳瓦塞拉达的公路干线，公路上有不少卡车从山区开回来。他们遇到一个关卡。戈麦斯向关卡哨兵出示米兰达中校签发的通行证，哨兵就用手电照着通行证，给和他在一起的另一个哨兵过目后，交还了证件，行了个礼。

"往前走，"他说。"可不准开灯。"

接着，前面所有的车辆都停下了，他们钻空子继续朝前驶，越过了几辆救护车、几辆参谋部用车和一辆装甲车，接着是第二辆，第三辆，都停在那里。他们发现前面又是一个关卡，那里发生了车祸。

Andrés and Gomez were on the motorcycle on the road again and it was getting light. Now Andrés, holding again to the back of the seat ahead of him as the motorcycle climbed turn after switchback turn in a faint gray mist that lay over the top of the pass, felt the motorcycle speed under him, then skid and stop and they were standing by the motorcycle on a long, down-slope of road and in the woods, on their left, were tanks covered with pine branches. There were troops here all through the woods. Andrés saw men carrying the long poles of stretchers over their shoulders. Three staff cars were off the road to the right, in under the trees, with branches laid against their sides and other pine branches over their tops.

Inside the dugout Duval, General Golz's chief of staff, holding the opened dispatch from Robert Jordan in his left hand, glancing at his wrist watch on the same hand, reading the dispatch for the fourth time, each time feeling the sweat come out from under his armpit and run down his flank, said into the telephone, "Get me position Segovia, then. He's left? Get me position Avila."

He kept on with the phone. It wasn't any good. He had talked to both brigades. He called the observation post and General Golz was not there.

安德烈斯和戈麦斯又驾摩托车驶上了公路，天开始变亮了。安德烈斯又抓住了面前的座位后部，摩托车在笼罩着山口最高处的灰色薄雾中弯弯曲曲地驶上山去，他感到所乘的摩托车在加快速度，接着车子慢下来，停住了。他们在一段漫长的下坡路上跳下车来，站在车旁。左边树林里有些盖着松枝的坦克。这一带树林里到处是部队。安德烈斯看到有的扛着抬杆很长的担架。公路右边几棵树底下停着三辆参谋部的汽车，车身两边覆盖着树枝，车顶上盖着松枝。

在防空洞里，戈尔兹将军的参谋长杜瓦尔左手拿着展开的罗伯特·乔丹送来的急件，望望同一只手上的手表，第四次读这份急件，每次都觉得腋下渗出汗水，从两肋往下淌。他对着电话筒说，“给我接塞哥维亚阵地。他走了吗？给我接阿维拉阵地。”

他不停地打电话。他给两个旅都打了电话。一点用处也没有。他给观察哨打电话，可戈尔兹将军不在那儿。

"Get me planes one," Duval said, suddenly taking all responsibility. He would take responsibility for holding it up. It was better to hold it up. You could not send them to a surprise attack against an enemy that was waiting for it. You couldn't do it. It was just murder. You couldn't. You mustn't.

"Cancel the call to planes one," he told the signaler. "Get me the Sixty-Ninth Brigade observation post."

He was still calling there when he heard the first sound of the planes.

It was just then he got through to the observation post.

"Yes," Golz said quietly.

He was sitting leaning back against the sandbag, his feet against a rock, a cigarette hung from his lower lip and he was looking up and over his shoulder while he was talking. He was seeing the expanding wedges of threes, silver and thundering in the sky that were coming over the far shoulder of the mountain where the first sun was striking. He watched them come shining and beautiful in the sun. He saw the twin circles of light where the sun shone on the propellers as they came.

"给我接第一机队,"杜瓦尔说,突然决定负起全部责任。他要负起责任,停止这次进攻。还是停止的好。敌人已经做好了准备,你不能让他们去来次突然袭击。你不能这样干。这简直是谋杀。不能。千万不能。

"别接第一机队了,"他对接线员说。"给我接第六十九旅观察哨。"

他还在那里打电话,这时听到了第一阵飞机声。

而刚好在这时,他接通了观察哨。

"是的,"戈尔兹冷静地说。

他正背靠在沙袋上坐着,两脚抵在一块石头上,下嘴唇上叼着一支烟,他一边接电话,一边侧着头仰望。他打量着那越来越大的三三编队的楔形机群,在天空中银光闪闪,狂叫怒吼,从远处阳光初照的山肩上空飞过来。他望着飞来的飞机,在阳光中明亮而美丽。他看到飞机飞来时阳光照射在螺旋桨上形成的两个光轮。

"Yes," Golz said into the telephone and it was Duval on the wire. "We are finished. Right. As before. Right. A big pity. Right. It's a shame it came too late."

His eyes, watching the planes coming, were very proud. He saw the red wing markings now and he watched their steady, stately roaring advance.

This was how it could be. These were our planes. They had come, crated on ships, from the Black Sea through the Straits of Marmora, through the Dardanelles, through the Mediterranean and to here, unloaded lovingly at Alicante, assembled ably, tested and found perfect and now flown in lovely hammering precision, the V's tight and pure as they came now high and silver in the morning sun to blast those ridges across there and blow them roaring high so that we can go through.

Golz knew that once they had passed overhead and on, the bombs would fall, looking like porpoises in the air as they tumbled. And then the ridge tops would spout and roar in jumping clouds and disappear in one great blowing cloud.

"是的，"戈尔兹对着话筒说，打电话来的是杜瓦尔。"我们完蛋了。对。跟以往一样。对。太遗憾了。对。情报到得太迟了，真不像话。"

他望着飞来的飞机，眼神非常自豪。他这时看清了机翼上的红色标志，他看着它们平稳地堂皇地隆隆地向前飞着。

事情就是这样发生的。这是我们的飞机。它们由船只从黑海穿过马尔马拉海，穿过达达尼尔海峡，穿过地中海，运到这儿，小心翼翼地在阿利坎特卸下，精确地装配，试飞成功，证明性能良好。它们这时编成紧凑而清楚的V字队，正在悦耳的有规律的震荡声中，高高地银光闪闪地在晨曦中飞来轰炸对面的山脊，炸得它山崩地裂，让我们能够通过。

戈尔兹知道，一旦飞机在上空飞过去了，炸弹就会像翻腾的海豚那样从空中投下来。山脊会轰隆隆地迸裂，尘土飞扬，消失在一大片爆炸的烟雾中。

As Robert Jordan heard the bombs, the first thumping noise of them, before the echo of them came back in thunder from the mountain; he drew in a long breath and lifted the submachine gun from where it lay. His arm felt stiff from its weight and his fingers were heavy with reluctance.

The man in the sentry box stood up when he heard the bombs. Robert Jordan saw him reach for his rifle and step forward out of the box listening. He stood in the road with the sun shining on him. The helmet was on the side of his head and the sun was on his unshaved face as he looked up into the sky toward where the planes were bombing.

There was no mist on the road now and Robert Jordan saw the man, clearly and sharply, standing there on the road looking up at the sky. The sun shone bright on him through the trees.

Robert Jordan felt his own breath tight now as though a strand of wire bound his chest and, steadying his elbows, feeling the corrugations of the forward grip against his fingers, he put the oblong of the foresight, settled now in the notch of the rear, onto the center of the man's chest and squeezed the trigger gently.

罗伯特·乔丹一听到炸弹的第一阵砰砰的爆炸声，不等山间响起隆隆的回声，就深深地吸了口气，拿起手提机枪。他的手臂由于枪身的重压已经僵硬了，手指麻木得不大灵便了。

岗亭里的哨兵听到炸弹爆炸声就站起身来。罗伯特·乔丹看到他伸手去拿步枪，从岗亭里走出来倾听。他站在公路上，阳光照在他身上。他头上歪戴着钢盔，他抬头朝天空中飞机正在投弹的方向望去，阳光正好照射在他没刮过胡子的脸上。

公路上没雾，罗伯特·乔丹清楚而鲜明地看到哨兵站在公路上仰望着天空。阳光透过树丛照亮了他。

罗伯特·乔丹这时觉得自己呼吸急促，仿佛有一圈铁丝勒住了他的胸部。他稳住了胳膊肘，觉得有槽纹的枪把紧抵着自己的手指，他把落入表尺缺口内的长方形准星对准哨兵的胸膛中央，轻轻地扣动扳机。

Robert Jordan felt the quick, liquid, spastic lurching of the gun against his shoulder and on the road the man, looking surprised and hurt, slid forward on his knees and his forehead doubled to the road. His rifle fell by him and lay there with one of the man's fingers twisted through the trigger guard, his wrist bent forward. The rifle lay, bayonet forward on the road. He looked away from the man lying with his head doubled under on the road to the bridge, and the sentry box at the other end.

He could not see the other sentry and he looked down the slope to the right where he knew Anselmo was hidden. Then he heard Anselmo shoot, the shot smashing an echo back from the gorge. Then he heard him shoot again.

With that second shot came the cracking boom of grenades from around the corner below the bridge. Then there was the noise of grenades from well up the road to the left. Then he heard rifle firing up the road and from below came the noise of Pablo's cavalry automatic rifle spat-spat-spat-spatting into the noise of grenades.

罗伯特·乔丹感到枪托迅速、规则、痉挛地撞在自己的肩头上，公路上那个哨兵显得吃惊而痛苦，双膝一软，向前倒下，前额磕在路面上。他的步枪掉在他身旁，一个手指还钩在扳机护圈里，手腕向前弯曲着。他的步枪掉在公路上，枪上的刺刀指向公路前方。他的目光从这弓着头躺在公路上的哨兵，转向桥和它另一端的岗亭。

他看不到另一个哨兵，就顺着右下方的山坡望去，他知道安塞尔莫埋伏在那里。接着他听到安塞尔莫开枪了，枪声从河谷里传来回声。接着他听到安塞尔莫又开了一枪。

随着第二声枪响，桥下的拐角处传来咣咣的手榴弹爆炸声。紧接着这边公路左方远处传来手榴弹爆炸声。接着他听到这边公路上的步枪声，从下边公路上传来巴勃罗的骑兵用的自动步枪的嗒嗒声，和手榴弹声混杂在一起。

Robert Jordan saw Anselmo scrambling down the steep cut to the far end of the bridge and he slung the submachine gun over his shoulder and picked up the two heavy packs from behind the pine trunks and with one in each hand, the packs pulling his arms so that he felt the tendons would pull out of his shoulders, he ran lurching down the steep slope to the road. As he ran he observed the changing situation.

Just then he saw Anselmo shoot at the far end of the bridge, the noise of the shot clanging in the steel girders. He passed the sentry where he lay and ran onto the bridge, the packs swinging.

The old man came running toward him, holding his carbine in one hand. "There's nothing wrong," he shouted. "I had to finish him."

Robert Jordan, kneeling, opening the packs in the center of the bridge taking out his material, saw that tears were running down Anselmo's cheeks through the gray beard stubble.

"I killed one too," he said to Anselmo and jerked his head toward where the sentry lay hunched over in the road at the end of the bridge.

罗伯特·乔丹看到安塞尔莫顺着陡峭的山路爬下来，朝着桥的另一端冲来，他把手提机枪挎在肩上，提起松树后面的两个沉重的背包，一手提一个。背包重得使他觉得肩膀上的肌腱都要被抽出来了。他踌跚地冲下陡峭的山坡，来到公路上。他一边奔跑，一边注意观察随时变化的情况。

正在这时，他看到安塞尔莫在桥的另一端开了一枪，枪声在钢梁之间回响。他越过躺在地上的哨兵，晃着背包奔上桥面。

老头儿一手提着卡宾枪，向他跑过来。"没有差错，"他喊着。"我不得不干掉他。"

罗伯特·乔丹跪在桥中央，打开背包，取出他的东西。他看到眼泪顺着安塞尔莫脸颊一直淌到花白的胡子茬上。

"我也杀了一个，"他对安塞尔莫说，朝倒在桥这头公路上的哨兵甩了下头。

Robert Jordan was climbing down into the framework of the bridge. The girders were cold and wet with dew under his hands and he climbed carefully, feeling the sun on his back, bracing himself in a bridge truss, hearing the noise of the tumbling water below him, hearing firing, too much firing, up the road at the upper post. He was sweating heavily now and it was cool under the bridge. He had a coil of wire around one arm and a pair of pliers hung by a thong from his wrist.

"Hand me down a package at a time, old one," he called up to Anselmo. The old man leaned far over the edge handing down the oblong blocks of explosive and Robert Jordan reached up for them, shoved them in where he wanted them, packed them close, braced them, "Wedges, old one! Give me wedges!" smelling the fresh shingle smell of the new whittled wedges as he tapped them in tight to hold the charge between the girders.

Now as he worked, placing, bracing, wedging, lashing tight with wire, thinking only of demolition, working fast and skillfully as a surgeon works.

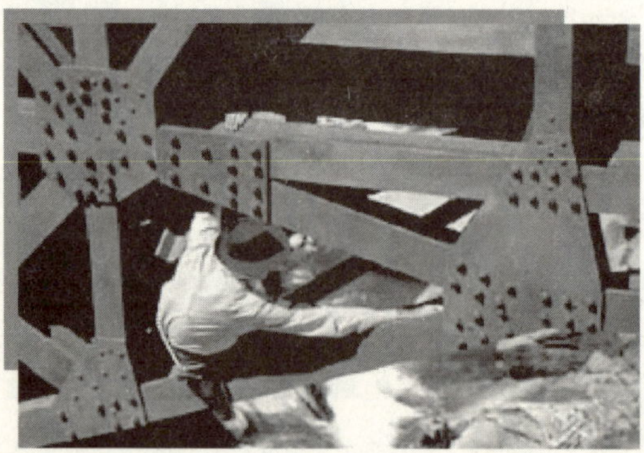

罗伯特·乔丹爬到桥面下的梁柱架中。他握住的有露水钢梁，又冷又湿。他小心翼翼地爬着，感到阳光照在背上。他在一根桥架上稳住了身子，听到下面哗啦啦的流水声，听到枪声，公路上段的哨所那边枪声响成一片。桥下阴凉，但他汗流浃背。他一条胳膊挽着一圈电线，手腕上缠着的皮带上挂着一把钳子。

"把炸药包一个一个往下递给我，老头子，"他向上面的安塞尔莫喊道。老头儿在桥边探出半个身子，把长方形的炸药包递下来，罗伯特·乔丹伸手接住，用力塞在桥梁下他要放的地方，一包包紧紧排好，牢牢固定好。"楔子，老头子！给我楔子！"他把一只只楔子轻轻敲紧，使炸药包牢固地嵌在钢梁之间，闻到了新削的木楔的清新木头香。

他忙着安放炸药，固定，加楔子，用铜丝绑紧，一心只想着炸桥，迅速而熟练地干着，仿佛在做外科手术。

They heard a rattle of firing from below on the road. Then there was the noise of a grenade. Then another, booming through the rushing noise the water made. Then it was quiet from that direction.

There was still firing up the road at the upper post. Too much firing, and Robert Jordan was lashing two grenades side by side on top of the braced blocks of explosive, winding wire over their corrugations so they would hold tight and firm and lashing it tight; twisting it with the pliers. He felt of the whole thing and then, to make it more solid, tapped in a wedge above the grenades that blocked the whole charge firmly in against the steel.

"The other side now, old one," he shouted up to Anselmo and climbed across through the trestle, like Tarzan in a rolled steel forest, he thought, and then coming out from under the dark, the stream tumbling below him, he looked up and saw Anselmo's face as he reached the packages of explosive down to him. A good face, he thought. Not crying now. That's all to the good.

这时他们听到下段公路上响起了一阵嗒嗒的枪声。接着是一枚手榴弹的爆炸声。接着又是一枚，在流水声中轰的一响。然后那个方向寂静无声了。

公路上段的哨所那边仍有枪声。枪声实在太密了。罗伯特·乔丹把两枚手榴弹并排扎在固定好的炸药包上，把铜丝绕在手榴弹上的凹纹里，这样它们可以绑得结结实实，最后用钳子把铜丝拧紧。他摸摸所有的炸药包，为了使它们更牢固，在手榴弹上面轻轻敲进一个楔子，使整个炸药包紧紧地抵在钢梁上。

"现在到另一边去，老头子，"他向桥面上的安塞尔莫喊道，就穿过桥架爬到另一边，心想，好像人猿泰山在钢铁般的林子里活动。他接着从桥下的阴影里探出身子，下面是滔滔流水，他伸手去接从上面递过来的炸药包，抬头看到了安塞尔莫的脸。他想，多善良的脸啊，现在没哭，这样真好。

And one side is done. This side now and we're done. This will drop it like what all. Nobody can keep you from blowing one side now. You're doing it just the way you should, Robert Jordan thought.

He leaned out and up into the sunlight and as he reached his hand up to take what Anselmo handed him, his head now above the noise of the falling water, the firing increased sharply up the road and then the noise of grenades again. Then more grenades.

"They rushed the sawmill then."

It's lucky I've got this stuff in blocks, he thought. Instead of sticks. What the hell. It's just neater. Although a lousy canvas sack full of jelly would be quicker. Two sacks. No. One of that would do. And if we just had detonators and the old exploder. Pablo threw my exploder in the river. That old box had been many places with me. In this river he threw it. He gave them hell there below just now. "Give me some more of that, old one." The old man nodded. "Almost through," Robert Jordan said. The old man nodded again.

罗伯特·乔丹想，桥的一边炸药已安放好了，现在把这一边搞好就完事了，这能把桥炸得粉碎，现在谁也阻挡不了你把桥的一边炸掉啦，你干得正如你应该干的那样。

他从桥下探身到阳光里，伸手去接安塞尔莫递给他的东西，他的头离下面的流水声远了一点，这时公路上段的枪声突然大作，接着又是手榴弹的爆炸声。又有更多的手榴弹的爆炸声。

"这样看来，他们在袭击锯木厂。"

他想，幸亏我的炸药是成块包扎，而不是条状的。那又怎么样？只不过整齐些罢了。然而满满一帆布袋的胶冻状炸药爆炸要快些。两袋，不，一袋就够了。如果有雷管和那旧的引爆器就好了。巴勃罗把引爆器扔到河里去了。那只旧盒子曾随我到过多少地方啊。他就扔在这条河里。他刚才在下面狠狠地打击敌人呢。"再给我一些，老头子，"老头子点点头。"差不多完了，"罗伯特·乔丹说。老头子又点点头。

Out from the cool dark under the bridge Robert Jordan leaned into the bright sun and shouted to Anselmo's bending face, "Give me the big coil of wire."

The old man handed it down. This coil of wire could pull the hand grenades.

Robert Jordan thought it was good to have the big coil of wire as he felt the cotter pins that held the rings that would release the levers on the hand grenades. He checked the grenades, lashed on their sides, had room for the levers to spring when the pins were pulled (the wire that lashed them ran through under the levers), then he attached a length of wire to one ring, wired it onto the main wire that ran to the ring of the outside grenade, paid off some slack from the coil and passed it around a steel brace and then handed the coil up to Anselmo.

"Hold it carefully," he said.

He climbed up onto the bridge, took the coil from the old man and walked back as fast as he could pay out wire toward where the sentry was slumped in the road, leaning over the side of the bridge and paying out wire from the coil as he walked.

罗伯特·乔丹从桥下阴凉的暗处探身到明亮的阳光中，冲着伸出头来的安塞尔莫叫道，"把那一大卷电线给我。"

老头儿把电线递了下来。这卷电线用来拉响手榴弹。

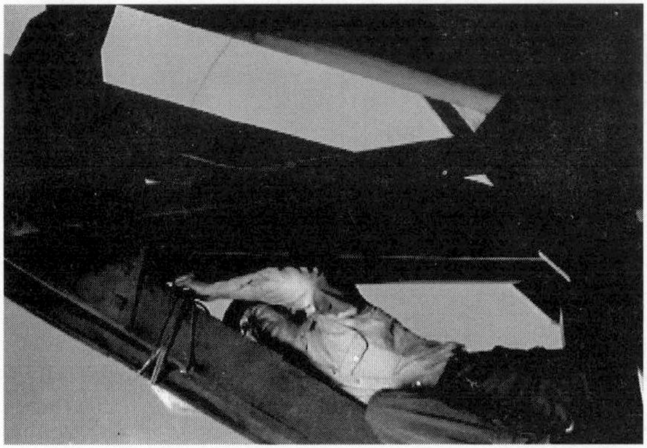

罗伯特·乔丹摸着手榴弹上能卡住使弹簧杆反弹出来的拉环的开尾销，这时他想，有了长段电线就行了。他仔细查看，绑在侧面的两颗手榴弹边上留有足够的空隙，这样在拉开尾销时弹簧杆能弹起来(绑手榴弹的铜丝是从弹簧杆下面绕过去的)；接着他把一段铜丝系在一只拉环上，把另一端系在通外侧的手榴弹的拉环的电线上，从大卷电线上放出一段，把这大卷绕过一根钢桥架，朝上递给安塞尔莫。

他说："小心拿着。"

他爬上桥面，从老头儿手里接过电线，身子探出在桥的一边，一边放线，一边尽快向那哨兵倒毙的地方倒退着走过去。

"Bring the sacks," Robert Jordan shouted to Anselmo as he walked backwards. As he passed he stooped down and picked up the submachine gun and slung it over his shoulder again.

Robert Jordan carried the wire clear past the end of the bridge, took a loop around the last stanchion and then ran along the road until he stopped beside a stone marker. He cut the wire and handed it to Anselmo.

"Hold this, old one," he said. "Now walk back with me to the bridge. Take up on it as you walk. No. I will."

At the bridge he pulled the wire back out through the hitch so it now ran clear and unfouled to the grenade rings and handed it, stretching alongside the bridge but running quite clear, to Anselmo.

"Take this back to that high stone," he said. "Hold it easily but firmly. Do not put any force on it. When you pull hard, hard, the bridge will blow. Comprehend?"

"Yes."

"Treat it softly but do not let it sag so it will foul. Keep it lightly firm but not pulling until you pull. Comprehend?"

"Yes."

"When you pull really pull. Do not jerk."

“把背包拿过来，”罗伯特·乔丹倒退着走，对安塞尔莫大声说。他俯身拾起手提机枪，重新挎在肩上。

罗伯特·乔丹放线走过桥头，在最后一根桥柱上绕了一圈，就径直奔到公路上一块石头路标旁停下来。他剪断电线，递给安塞尔莫。

“拿住了，老头子，”他说，“现在跟我回到桥上去。边走边把这段电线带上桥。不。还是我来吧。”

一到桥上，他把电线从桥柱上绕回来，它就一直沿着桥边直通到手榴弹的环上，没有勾住什么地方。他把电线的这一端递给安塞尔莫。

“拿着这个回到石头路标那儿去，”他说。“轻轻拿着，可是要抓紧。别使劲。只要用力一拉，桥就会爆炸。明白吗？”

“明白。”

“手里用力要小，可是别让电线下垂，免得勾住。轻轻拿稳了，不到时候别拉。明白吗？”

“明白。”

“要拉的时候，就使劲拉。别抖。”

At the same time, Pablo, the gypsy, and the three helpers first dealt with the lower post as well as El Sordo would have and then they cut the wire, fell back on the bridge, covered the bridge, and attacked the tanks that wanted to go through the bridge. Unfortunately, the gypsy exploded a tank and was shot to death.

Pilar and other people attacked the mill, fell back onto the bridge and covered the road from above. They annihilated the enemy successfully, but Fernando was wounded in the fight. He looked to be shot through the groin for he was holding himself there with both hands while two men held him on either side. His right leg was dragging, the side of the shoe scraping on the road as they walked him. Pilar was climbing the bank into the timber carrying three rifles.

Fernando lay back against the bank, dying. In front of him was one of the whitewashed stones that marked the edge of the road. His head was in the shadow but the sun shone on his plugged and bandaged wound and on his hands that were cupped over it. His legs and his feet were also in the sun. A fly crawled on his hands but the small tickling did not come through the pain.

与此同时，巴勃罗和吉卜赛人以及三个帮手首先对付下面的哨所，就像艾苏道会干的那样。然后他们切断电线，回过头来向桥靠拢，封锁桥面，去阻击要通过桥的坦克。不幸的是，吉卜赛人炸毁一辆坦克后，被敌人射杀牺牲了。

比拉尔带着其他人进攻锯木厂，回过头来向桥靠拢，从上面用火力封锁公路。他们成功地消灭了敌人，但是费尔南多在激战中受伤。他看上去像腹股沟被子弹击穿了，他双手按在上面，两个人一边一个架着他。他们扶着他走，他的右腿拖在地上，鞋帮在路面上刮着。比拉尔拿着三支步枪，正在爬上山坡，进入树林。

费尔南多仰靠在山坡上，快死了。他面前是一块刷成白色的标志公路边缘的界石。他的头在阴影中，阳光直射在塞了纱布、包扎好的伤口上，照在他捂住伤口的双手上。他的腿和脚也在阳光中。一只苍蝇在他双手上爬动，但是在剧痛中他不觉得这微微的瘙痒。

"Blow it if tanks come," Robert Jordan said. "But only if they come onto it. Blow it if armored cars come. If they come onto it. Anything else Pablo will stop."

Then he heard the tank coming down the road and he saw it over his shoulder just coming onto the long slope and he swung his wrist once around the wire and yelled to Anselmo, "Blow her!"

He dug his heels in and leaned back hard onto the tension of the wire with a turn of it around his wrist and the noise of the tank was coming behind and ahead there was the road with the dead sentry and the long bridge and the stretch of road below, still clear and then there was a cracking roar and the middle of the bridge rose up in the air like a wave breaking and he felt the blast from the explosion roll back against him as he dove on his face in the pebbly gully with his hands holding tight over his head.

His face was down against the pebbles as the bridge settled where it had risen and the familiar yellow smell of it rolled over him in acrid smoke and then it commenced to rain pieces of steel.

“坦克来了就炸桥，”罗伯特·乔丹说，“但要等它们开到桥上才炸。装甲车来了也炸，要等它们开到桥上。巴勃罗会阻止别的人马车辆过来。”

他接着听到公路上段开来一辆坦克，他回头看到它刚开上桥头长长的坡路。他把电线在手腕上挽了一圈，对安塞尔莫大喊一声：“炸桥！”

他站稳脚跟，身体使劲往后仰，猛拉绕在手腕上绷紧的电线，后面传来坦克的声音，前面是躺着那死哨兵的公路、长长的桥和对岸那段仍旧空荡荡的公路，接着轰隆一声巨响，桥的中段突然飞入空中，犹如浪花飞溅，他一下子扑倒在布满鹅卵石的小沟里，双手紧紧抱着头，感到爆炸的气浪从身后猛扑过来。

炸飞的桥身落了下来，落在原来的地方，一团带着熟悉的辛辣气味的黄色烟雾滚滚向他袭来，钢铁碎片开始如雨点般掉落下来，这时他的脸紧贴在鹅卵石地上。

After the steel stopped falling Robert Jordan was still alive and he raised his head and looked across the bridge. The center section of it was gone and fell into the valley below. There were jagged pieces of steel on the bridge with their bright, new torn edges and ends and these were all over the road.

Anselmo lay face down behind the white marking stone. Robert Jordan got to his feet, crossed the road, knelt by him and made sure that he was dead. He kicked a jagged piece of steel off the surface of the road. Then he swung the two rifles over his shoulder, holding them by the muzzles, and started up the slope into the timber. He did not look back nor did he even look across the bridge at the road.

The anger and the emptiness and the hate that had come with the let-down after the bridge, when he had looked up from where he had lain and crouching, seen Anselmo dead, were still all through him. In him, too, was despair from the sorrow that soldiers turn to hatred in order that they may continue to be soldiers. Now it was over he was lonely, detached and unelated and he hated every one he saw.

钢铁碎片都落下来后，罗伯特·乔丹还活着，他抬头望着对面的桥。桥的中段已炸掉了，掉入了山谷。桥面上散布着参差不齐的钢铁碎片，新炸裂的断口亮闪闪的，公路上遍地都是。

安塞尔莫扑倒在白色的石头路标后面。罗伯特·乔丹站起身来，穿过公路，在他身旁跪下，看出他确实已经死了。他一脚踢开路面上一块钢铁碎片。接着他把两支步枪挎在肩上，握住了枪筒登上山坡，进入树林。他没有回头看，甚至也没有向公路对面的桥望一望。

当他在卧倒的地方抬起头，看到安塞尔莫死了的时候，他心里充满了随着炸桥之后的放松而来的愤怒、空虚和憎恨，这时，这些感情仍然控制着他的全身。他心里还有一股由悲痛产生的失望情绪，士兵为了能继续心安理得地当士兵，往往把悲痛转化为憎恨。如今大功告成了，他感到寂寞、孤独而消沉，他憎恨所见到的每个人。

当他们兵分三路进攻时，玛丽亚负责照看马匹。她跟那几匹马一起待了好久，可是它们并不能使她感到安慰。她也不能使马感到安慰。她在树林里待着的地方望不到公路，也望不到桥。马匹原来圈在营地下面的树林里时，她常常喂点东西给那匹白脸栗色大种马，这使它很听话，这时枪声一响，她就用手臂搂着它的脖子。但她神经紧张，使这匹马也紧张起来。它听到了枪声和爆炸声，猛地把头一晃，张大了鼻孔。玛丽亚没法镇静下来，她来回走动着，轻轻拍着马匹，安抚它们，但反而使它们更加紧张、激动。

她试图设想正在进行的交火并不可怕，这只不过是巴勃罗和新来的那些人在下面，比拉尔和其他人在上面开枪，她用不着担心，也不必惊慌失措，而必须相信罗伯特。但是她做不到，于是桥上方和桥下方的枪声，像远方的暴风雨一样从远处山口传来的激战声，都可怕得使她几乎窒息。

When they attacked from three places, Maria was in charge of the horses. She had been with the horses for a long time, but they were no comfort to her. Nor was she any to them. From where she was in the forest she could not see the road nor could she see the bridge and when the firing started she put her arm around the neck of the big white-faced bay stallion that she had gentled and brought gifts to many times when the horses had been in the corral in the trees below the camp. But her nervousness made the big stallion nervous, too, and he jerked his head, his nostrils widening at the firing and the noise of the bombs. Maria could not keep still and she walked around patting and gentling the horses and making them all more nervous and agitated.

She tried to think of the firing not as just a terrible thing that was happening, but to realize that it was Pablo below with the new men, and Pilar with the others above, and that she must not worry nor get into a panic but must have confidence in Robert. But she could not do this and all the firing above and below the bridge and the distant sound of the battle that rolled down from the pass like the noise of a far-off storm was simply a horrible thing that almost kept her from breathing.

Then Maria commenced to pray for Robert quickly and automatically as she had done at school, saying the prayers as fast as she could and counting them on the fingers of her left hand, praying by tens of each of the two prayers she was repeating. Then the bridge blew and one horse snapped his halter when he rose and jerked his head at the cracking roar and he went off through the trees. Maria caught him finally and brought him back, shivering, trembling, his chest dark with sweat, the saddle down, and coming back through the trees she heard shooting below and she thought, I can not stand this longer. I cannot live not knowing any longer. I cannot breathe and my mouth is so dry. And I am afraid and I am no good and I frighten the horses and only caught this horse by hazard because he knocked the saddle down against a tree and caught himself kicking into the stirrups and now as I get the saddle up, Oh, God, I do not know. I cannot bear it. Oh please have him be all right, for all my heart and all of me are at the bridge.

接着玛丽亚迅速而不知不觉地为罗伯特祷告起来，就像她在学校里那样，尽量快地念祈祷文，用左手手指计着数，反复地把两段祈祷文默念了好几十遍。接着那座桥爆炸了，有匹马一听到这轰隆一声，就竖起身子，脑袋猛地一扭，啪的一声挣断了缰绳，跑进了树林。玛丽亚最后抓住了它，把它牵回来，它浑身发抖，胸脯被汗水弄得发了黑，马鞍耷拉着。她从树林里回来的时候，听到下面有枪声，就想，我再也受不了啦。我不知道真相，再也活不了啦。我喘不过气来，嘴里干得要命。我害怕，也没有办法，把马都吓坏了，这匹马在树上把马鞍撞了下来，马脚勾住了马镫，才侥幸地被我抓住了，现在要我把马鞍上好，啊，上帝啊，我不知道怎么办好。我受不了啦。我一心一意只求他平安无事，我的整个身心都扑在桥上。

Maria thought again, the Republic is one thing and we must win is another thing. But, Oh, Sweet Blessed Virgin, bring him back to me from the bridge and I will do anything you say ever. Because I am not here. There isn't any me. I am only with him. Take care of him for me and that will be me and then I will do the things for you and he will not mind. Nor will it be against the Republic. Oh, please forgive me for I am very confused. I am too confused now. But if you take care of him I will do whatever is right. I will do what he says and what you say. With the two of us I will do it. But this now not knowing I cannot endure.

Then, the horse tied again, she with the saddle up now, the blanket smoothed, hauling tight on the cinch she heard the big, deep voice from the timber below, "Maria! Maria! Your English is all right. Hear me? All right!"

Maria held the saddle with both hands and pressed her cropped head hard against it and cried. She heard the deep voice shouting again and she turned from the saddle and shouted, choking, "Yes! Thank you!"

玛丽亚又想，共和国是一码事，我们必须打胜仗是另一码事。但是，亲爱的圣母啊，只要您让他从桥上平安归来，我就听您差遣。我的心不在这儿。我根本不能独立存在。我的心只跟他在一起。求求您为了我保佑他，这样我才能活，今后我才能为您效劳，而他是不会在乎的。这样做也并不违反共和国。啊，请宽恕我，我心乱如麻。现在我的心太乱了，但是如果您保佑他，只要是正确的事我都干。你们俩怎么吩咐，我都照办。有了我们俩，我什么都能做。可现在不明真相，我受不了啦。

接着她拴好马匹，上好马鞍，铺平马毯，收紧肚带，这时她听到下面树林里传来洪亮的叫声："玛丽亚！玛丽亚！你的英国人平安无事。你听到了吗？平安无事！"

玛丽亚双手捧住马鞍，把短发紧贴在上面，哭了。她听到那洪亮的声音又响了一遍，就从马鞍上转过头来，哽咽着喊道："听到了！谢谢你！"

Robert Jordan ran up the hill through the pines. Agustín was close behind him and behind him Pablo was coming.

"Pilar!" Jordan shouted across the hill. "Come on, woman!"

The three of them were going as fast as they could up the steep slope. They could not run any more because the grade was too severe and Pablo, who had no load but the light cavalry submachine gun, had closed up with the other two.

"And your people?" Agustín said to Pablo out of his dry mouth.

"All dead," Pablo said. He was almost unable to breathe. Agustín turned his head and looked at him.

"We have plenty of horses now, English," Pablo panted.

"Good," Robert Jordan said. The murderous bastard, he thought. "What did you encounter?"

"Everything," Pablo said. He was breathing in lunges.

"What passed with Pilar?" He asked.

"She lost Fernando and one of the brothers—"

"Eladio," Agustín said.

"And you?" Pablo asked Robert Jordan.

"I lost Anselmo."

"There are lots of horses," Pablo said. "Even for the baggage." In fact, he shot those three men for their horses.

罗伯特·乔丹穿过松林向山上奔去。奥古斯丁紧跟在他后面，再后面跟着巴勃罗。

“比拉尔！”罗伯特·乔丹朝山坡那边叫喊。“过来，大娘！”

他们仨尽快地爬上陡峭的山坡。山坡太陡峭，他们没法奔跑。巴勃罗挎着一支骑兵用的手提机枪，没带其他东西，紧紧赶上了他们俩。

“你那一伙人呢？”奥古斯丁张开发干的嘴，问巴勃罗。

“全死了，”巴勃罗说。他几乎喘不过气来。奥古斯丁转过头来看着他。

“我们现在有不少马啦，英国人。”巴勃罗上气不接下气地说。

“好，”罗伯特·乔丹说着，心想，你这杀人成性的杂种。“你碰上了什么？”

“什么都碰上了，”巴勃罗说。他大口大口地喘着粗气。

“比拉尔那儿怎么样了？”他问道。

“她失去了费尔南多和两兄弟中的一个。”

“埃拉迪奥，”奥古斯丁说。

“你呢？”巴勃罗问罗伯特·乔丹。

“我失去了安塞尔莫。”

“马很多了，”巴勃罗说，“连驮行李也够了。”实际上，为了得到那三个人的马匹，他把他们都枪杀了。

Now they could see the horses tied to the trees, the sun coming down on them through the pine branches and they tossing their heads and kicking against the botflies and Robert Jordan saw Maria and the next thing he was holding her tight, tight, with the automatic rifle leaning against his side, the flash-cone pressing against his ribs and Maria saying, "You, Robert. Oh, you."

"Yes, rabbit. My good, good rabbit. Now we go."

"Are you here truly?"

"Yes. Yes. Truly. Oh, you!"

Then they were untying the halters and Robert Jordan had given the automatic rifle back to Agustín and slung his own submachine gun over his back, and he was putting bombs out of his pockets into the saddlebags, and he stuffed one empty pack inside the other and tied that one behind his saddle. Then Pilar came up, so breathless from the climb she could not talk, but only motioned.

Then Pablo stuffed three hobbles he had in his hand into a saddlebag, stood up and said, "How, woman?" and she only nodded, and then they were all mounting.

这时他们能看到拴在树干上的马匹，阳光透过松树的树枝投射在它们身上，它们摆着头，踢着腿，驱赶马蝇。罗伯特·乔丹看到了玛丽亚，就紧紧地、紧紧地拥抱着她，自动步枪移到了身子的一侧，锥形枪口抵着他的肋骨，听玛丽亚在说："你，罗伯特。哦，是你啊。"

"是我，兔子。我的乖兔子。我们马上走。"

"你真的在我身边吗？"

"是的，是的。真的。哦，你！"

接着他们解开马的缰绳。罗伯特·乔丹已经把自动步枪交还给奥古斯丁，把自己的手提机枪挎在背上，这时掏出衣袋里的手榴弹，装进鞍囊里。他把一只空背包塞进另一只里，一起绑在马鞍后面。比拉尔过来了，她爬坡累得气喘吁吁，说不出话来，只打手势。

巴勃罗把他手里的三根缚马脚的绳索塞在一只鞍囊里，直起腰来说："怎么样，太太？"她只点点头，于是大家就都上马了。

战地钟声 *For Whom the Bell Tolls*

Then Robert Jordan was looking through the thinning trees and he saw the oiled dark of the road below and beyond it the green slope of the hillside. We are above the culvert, he saw, and just below the height where the road drops down straight toward the bridge in that long sweep. We are around eight hundred yards above the bridge. That is not out of range for the Fiat in that little tank if they have come up to the bridge. Maria was scared to hold Robert's arm.

Just then Pablo dug both his spurs into the big bay and he plunged down the last pine-needled slope and cross the road in a pounding, sparking of shod hooves. The others came behind him and Robert Jordan saw them crossing the road and slamming on up the green slope and heard the machine gun hammer at the bridge. Then he heard a great noise coming. The boom was a sharp crack that widened in the cracking and on the hillside he saw a small fountain of earth rise with a plume of gray smoke. It came again, the swishing like the noise of a rocket and there was another up-pulsing of dirt and smoke farther up the hillside.

树木越来越稀疏了，罗伯特·乔丹穿过树木之间望去，见到下面黑色的柏油路和路对面绿茵茵的山坡。我们在涵洞上面，他看到，刚好在高地下面，公路笔直地通向桥头。我们的位置在桥的上方大约800码的地方。如果小坦克开到了桥头，那么我们仍旧在坦克菲亚特机枪射程之内。玛丽亚害怕得搂住了罗伯特的胳膊。

正在这时，巴勃罗一蹬脚，把两只马刺扎进大栗色马，一头冲下落满松针的山坡，冲过公路，马蹄铁砰砰直响，火星迸溅。其他的人跟在他后面，罗伯特·乔丹看到他们穿过公路，蹄声嗒嗒，爬上绿茵茵的山坡，听到桥那边响起了机枪射击声。然后他听到一声巨响，这声巨响是很清脆的爆裂声，引起了更大的回响，只见山坡上溅起一小股泥土，腾起一阵灰色烟雾。又一声巨响，像发射火箭的声音，山坡上又溅起了一股泥土和硝烟，比第一次还远。

Robert Jordan, as the last one, saw them all ahead in the edge of the timber watching him and he said, "Go on, horse!" and felt his big horse's chest surging with the steepening of the slope and saw the gray neck stretching and the gray ears ahead and he reached and patted the wet gray neck, and he looked back at the bridge and saw the bright flash from the heavy, squat, mud-colored tank there on the road and then he did not hear any whish but only a banging acrid smelling clang like a boiler being ripped apart and he was under the horse and the horse was kicking and he was trying to pull out from under the weight.

He could move all right. He could move toward the right. But his left leg stayed perfectly flat under the horse as he moved to the right. It was as though there was a new joint in it; not the hip joint but another one that went sideways like a hinge. Then he knew what it was all right and just then the horse kneed himself up and Robert Jordan's right leg, that had kicked the stirrup loose just as it should, slipped clear over the saddle and came down beside him. Maria came to check his wound.

作为最后一个，罗伯特·乔丹看到他们全在前面树林边注视着他，就说："快跑，马儿！"他感到马匹的胸脯由于山坡越来越陡峭而大起大伏，看到面前伸展着的灰脖子和一双灰耳朵，于是伸手拍拍马的汗水浸湿的灰脖子，然后回过头望着桥，看见公路上有辆笨重、低矮、土黄色的坦克发出一道闪光，接着听到的不是嗖嗖声，而是像锅炉炸裂般的带有辛辣火药味的砰的一声爆炸，他就被压在马身下面，马踢着腿儿，他竭力想从重压下脱身。

他还能动弹。他能向右边挪动。然而当他向右边挪动的时候，左腿仍然完全压在马身下，动弹不得。左腿上仿佛多长了一个关节，不是股关节，而是一个横向的铰链般的东西。他已确定是怎么回事了。这时马用膝盖抵着地面爬起身来，罗伯特·乔丹就把已及时踢掉马镫的右腿赶忙从马鞍上溜下来，搁在身边。玛丽亚过来查看他的伤势。

战地钟声 *For Whom the Bell Tolls*

Robert Jordan felt with his two hands of his thigh bone where the left leg lay flat against the ground and his hands both felt the sharp bone and where it pressed against the skin.

"Slit the trouser, will you?" he said to Pilar. Maria crouched by him and did not speak. The sun was on her hair and her face was twisted as a child's contorts before it cries. But she was not crying.

Pilar took her knife and slit his trouser leg down below the left-hand pocket. Robert Jordan spread the cloth with his hands and looked at the stretch of his thigh. Ten inches below the hip joint there was a pointed, purple swelling like a sharp-peaked little tent and as he touched it with his fingers he could feel the snapped-off thigh bone tight against the skin. His leg was lying at an odd angle. He looked up at Pilar. Her face had the same expression as Maria's.

"Beautiful girl," he said to Maria and took hold of her two hands. "Listen. We will not be retreating together—"

Then she started to cry.

"No, beautiful girl, don't," he said. "Listen. We will not retreat together now but I go always with you wherever you go."

罗伯特·乔丹用双手触摸平摊在地上的左腿，摸到了大腿骨头上锋利的骨折处和紧贴在上面的皮肉。

"割开裤腿，行吗？"他对比拉尔说。玛丽亚蹲在他身边，没有说话。阳光照在她头发上，她的脸抽搐得像小孩子要哭的模样，但她并没有哭。

比拉尔拿出刀子，在裤腿上从左侧裤袋下面一直划到底。罗伯特·乔丹双手揭开割开的裤腿，望着他那截大腿。在股关节下 10 英寸处，有一个突起的紫色肿块，像只尖顶的小帐篷。他用手指摸摸，能摸到折断的大腿骨紧紧地顶着皮肤。他的腿弯成一个古怪的角度。他抬头看着比拉尔，她脸上露出和玛丽亚一样的神情。

"漂亮姑娘，"他对玛丽亚说，握住她的双手，"听着，我们不能一起撤退了……"

她开始哭泣。

"不要，漂亮姑娘，别哭，"他说，"听着，我们现在不能一起撤退了，可是不管你走到哪里，我会永远跟你在一起。"

Maria said nothing and pushed her head against his cheek with her arms around him.

"Listen to this well, rabbit," he said. He knew there was a great hurry and he was sweating very much, but this had to be said and understood. "You will go now, rabbit. But I go with you. As long as there is one of us, there is both of us. Do you understand?"

"No, I stay with you," she shed tears on her cheek.

"No, rabbit. What I do now I do alone. I could not do it well with you. If you go then I go, too. Do you not see how it is? Whichever one there is, is both."

"I will stay with you."

"No, rabbit. Listen. That people cannot do together. Each one must do it alone. But if you go then I go with you. It is in that way that I go too. You will go now, I know. For you are good and kind. You will go now for us both."

"But it is easier if I stay with you," she said. "It is better for me."

"Yes. Therefore go for a favor. Do it for me since it is what you can do."

玛丽亚一句话也不说，双臂搂着他，头紧贴在他的脸颊上。

"好好听我说，兔子，"他说，他知道时间紧迫，他正在拼命出汗，然而这话必须说，要让她明白："你就要走了，兔子。然而我会和你在一起。只要我们俩有一个人活着，就有我们两个。明白吗？"

"不，我和你一起留下来，"她的眼泪顺着脸颊淌了下来。

"不，兔子。我现在要干的事只能我独自干。有你在身边，我没法干。可要是你走了，那么也就是我走了。你不明白这个道理吗？不管有我们中间哪一个，就有我们两个。"

"我要和你在一起。"

"不，兔子。听着，人们不能一起干。人人都得一个人干。可要是你走了，那么也就是我跟你走了，这样就等于我走了。你现在愿意离开了，我知道。你心地善良，你现在将为我们俩离开。"

"可是我留在你身边要好些，"她说，"我觉得这样好受些。"

"是的。所以你离开就是帮我的忙。为我离开吧，这是你能做到的。"

"Now I thank you for it. Now you are going well and fast and far and we both go in you. Now put your hand here. Now put your head down. Now do not think more. Now are you doing what you should. Now you are obeying. Not me but us both. The me in you. Now you go for us both. Truly. We both go in you now. This I have promised you. You are very good to go and very kind." Robert Jordan said.

She stood up slowly, crying, and with her head down. Then she dropped quickly beside him and then stood up again, slowly and tiredly, as he said, "Stand up, beautiful girl."

He turned his head, sweating, and looked down the slope, then back toward where the girl was in the saddle with Pilar by her and Pablo just behind.

She started to look around. "Don't look around," Robert Jordan said. "Go." And Pablo hit the horse across the crupper with a hobbling strap and it looked as though Maria tried to slip from the saddle but Pilar and Pablo were riding close up against her and Pilar was holding her and the three horses were going up the draw.

"Robert," Maria turned and shouted. "Let me stay!"

罗伯特·乔丹说："我现在为此感谢你。你好好地快走，走得远远的，就是我们俩一起走了。把你的手放在这里。低下你的头。现在别再想了。你要做你该做的事情。你听话啦。不是听我的，而是听我们俩的。你中有我。你现在离开是为了我们俩。真的。你离开就是我们俩一起离开。我向你保证。你愿意离开真好，你真善良。"

她低着头哭泣着，慢慢地站起身来。接着她突然扑倒在他身边，他说："站起来，漂亮姑娘，"她才缓慢地、疲乏地又站起来。

他冒着汗，转过头去俯视山坡，然后回头望着姑娘坐在马鞍上，比拉尔就在她身边，巴勃罗紧跟在后面。

她又要回过头来看。"别回头，"罗伯特·乔丹说，"走吧。"巴勃罗就用缚马腿的皮带抽了一下马屁股，玛丽亚似乎想从马鞍上溜下来，但比拉尔和巴勃罗紧挨着她骑着马，比拉尔抓住了她，三匹马跑出沟去。

"罗伯特，"玛丽亚转身叫喊。"让我留下！"

Agustín shot the wounded horse to death and he wheeled his horse and brought his right fist down as though he cursed again and rode up the draw.

Robert Jordan felt empty and drained and exhausted from all of it and from them going and his mouth tasted of bile. Now, finally and at last, there was no problem. However, all of it had been and however all of it would ever be now, for him, no longer was there any problem.

They were all gone now and he was alone with his back against a tree. He looked down across the green slope, seeing the dead horse, and on down the slope to the road with the timber-covered country behind it. Then he looked at the bridge and across the bridge and watched the activity on the bridge and the road. He could see the trucks now, all down the lower road. The gray of the trucks showed through the trees. Then he looked back up the road to where it came down over the hill. They will be coming soon now, he thought. I mustn't get faint and I'd better get down now. You better get fixed around some way where you will be useful instead of leaning against this tree like a tramp.

奥古斯丁开枪把受伤的马杀死，然后他掉转马头，右拳向下一挥，仿佛是一声诅咒，然后也跑出沟去。

因为这一切磨难，以及他们的离去，罗伯特·乔丹感到空虚、疲惫、筋疲力尽，而且嘴里发苦。现在，这一切终于结束了，没有任何问题了。现在不管以往的一切如何，不管未来的一切会怎样，对他来说，不会再有任何问题了。

如今他们都已经离开，他独自背靠着树干。他俯视着面前绿茵茵的山坡，看到死马，再顺着山坡一直望到下面的公路和路对面覆盖着树木的山野。接着他望着那座桥和桥对面的公路，注视着桥上和公路上的活动。他这时看到那些卡车全都开到了公路下段，灰色的车身在树林中显露出来。然后他回头望着从小山上直通下来的上段公路。他想，敌人马上就要来了。我千万不能晕过去，还是卧倒好些。你最好还是占一个能干点什么的位置，而不是像流浪汉一样在树上靠着。

Robert Jordan's luck held very good because he saw, just then, the cavalry ride out of the timber and cross the road. He watched them coming riding up the slope. He saw the trooper who stopped by the dead horse and shouted to the officer who rode over to him. He watched them both looking down at the gray horse. They recognized him of course. He and his rider had been missing since the early morning of the day before.

He rested easily as he could with his two elbows in the pine needles and the muzzle of the submachine gun facing to the enemy.

As the officer came trotting now on the trail of the horses of the band he would pass twenty yards below where Robert Jordan lay. At that distance there would be no problem. The officer was Lieutenant Berrendo.

Lieutenant Berrendo, watching the trail, came riding up, his thin face serious and grave. His submachine gun lay across his saddle in the crook of his left arm. Robert Jordan lay behind the tree, holding onto himself very carefully and delicately to keep his hands steady. He could feel his heart beating against the pine needle floor of the forest. He was awaiting the officer, riding up.

罗伯特·乔丹的运气仍然很好，此时，他看到骑兵队从树林里跑出来，跨过公路。他注视着他们在爬坡。他看到有个骑兵在死马跟前停下，对朝他骑来的军官呼喊。他看到他们两个低头察看那匹灰马。他们当然认得这匹马。自从昨天早晨以来，这匹马和它的主人就失踪了。

他把两只胳膊肘撑在松针地面上，尽可能卧得舒服些，手提机枪的枪口冲着敌人。

如果这名军官顺着游击队留下的马蹄印策马小跑而来，就要经过罗伯特·乔丹埋伏处下面 20 码的地方。隔着这段距离射击，不会有什么问题。这军官就是贝仑多中尉。

贝仑多中尉注视着马蹄印，策马跑过来，消瘦的脸严肃而庄重，他左臂弯里的手提机枪横搁在马鞍上。罗伯特·乔丹伏在树后面，小心谨慎地控制着自己，免得双手发抖。他感觉得到自己抵在树林里的松针地上的心脏怦怦地跳着。他等待着那个军官骑马过来。

For whom the bell tolls?

战地钟声究竟为谁敲响?

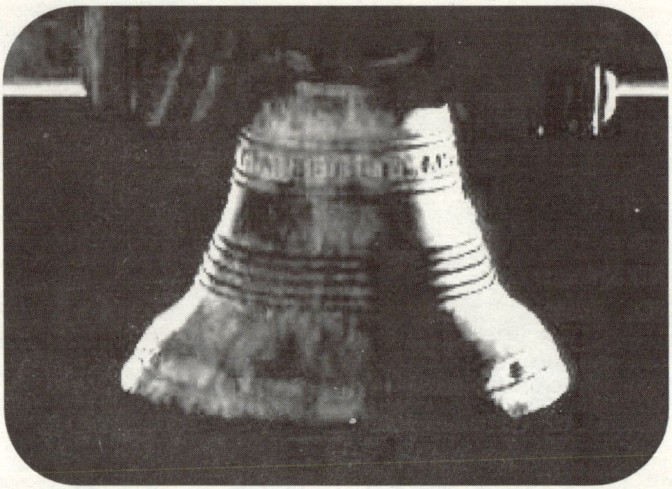